REBEL BOAST

BY MANLY WADE WELLMAN:

Find My Killer (*A Mystery Novel*)
Giant in Gray: A Biography of Wade Hampton of South Carolina
Dead and Gone: Classic Crimes of North Carolina

Books for Boys:

The Sleuth Patrol
The Mystery of Lost Valley
The Raiders of Beaver Lake
The Haunts of Drowning Creek
Wild Dogs of Drowning Creek
The Last Mammoth
Gray Riders: Jeb Stuart and His Men
Rebel Mail Runner
Flag on the Levee
To Unknown Lands
Young Squire Morgan

REBEL BOAST:

FIRST AT BETHEL—LAST AT APPOMATTOX

BY MANLY WADE WELLMAN

> *. . . Come from the four winds, O breath,*
> *and breathe upon these slain, that they may live.*
> —EZEKIEL 37:9

Illustrated with Photographs

HENRY HOLT AND COMPANY : New York

111 241

FIRST EDITION

LIBRARY OF CONGRESS CATALOG CARD NUMBER: 56–10520

89294–0116
PRINTED IN THE UNITED STATES OF AMERICA

For
the kith and kin, past and present,
of
Sim and Cary Whitaker,
Billy and Johnny Beavens,
and
George Whitaker Wills

"Dream of battled fields no more,
Days of danger, nights of waking . . ."

FOREWORD

Within recent years the memory of the Confederate South, passing from first hand to second, has become a memory of generals.

Robert E. Lee and Stonewall Jackson are clearest to our sight, the trim beard of silver-gray, the banner beard of shadowy brown. Not so plain are the lesser chiefs—Jeb Stuart with his saber and plume, bulky Longstreet, Pickett on Cemetery Ridge, terrible Forrest hewing down blue riders, Pemberton yielding up Vicksburg, Beauregard and Bragg and Joe Johnston and Wade Hampton and John B. Gordon and the rest. And all but lost in the smoky dimness are the lines of common soldiers, ragged and hungry and wolf-lean and wolf-deadly.

But they lived, too, those common soldiers. Such of them as survived the war fathered and grandfathered the men and women of today's South, and left to their children a tale, at once forlorn and wonderful, of how a war was bravely fought and bitterly lost. The most any simple veteran could say was that he had fought it through, to the death of hope. A scant handful blazoned themselves with the proud legend: "First at Bethel—Last at Appomattox."

Big Bethel on the Virginia Peninsula was not the true beginning of the Civil War, for that befell at Fort Sumter; but at Big Bethel the first hot blood was shed on both sides. And there were surrenders after Appomattox; but Appomattox made them inevitable, it was the assurance of the end of things. The very few who, at the last, could look back to the first, had bought their right to boast of it with the dearest currency, their wounds and their broken dreams.

A family group of five young men marched away to Big Bethel, and two lived to lay down their arms at Appomattox. Without meaning to, they made possible by a profuse and unconsciously eloquent mass of letters, diaries, and repeated oral traditions the survival of knowledge of what men they were, and how they fought and triumphed and lost. Here is the effort to set it down.

Many people assisted in many ways to make this book possible. The home letters of George Whitaker Wills, which first impelled me to seek out the entire story, were called to my attention by Dr. Bell Irvin Wiley of Emory College, Georgia. John R. Peacock of High Point, North Carolina, did much to establish primary direction and organization of research. The able and friendly staffs of the Southern Historical Collection, Chapel Hill, North Carolina; of the manuscript collection of the library of Duke University, Durham, North Carolina; of the State Department of Archives and History, Raleigh, North Carolina; and of the National Archives, Washington, D.C., guided me to a wealth of manuscript record. Mrs. William F. Dickens of Enfield, North Carolina, graciously arranged introductions, sought out and provided valuable source material, and gave sound advice on many aspects of the study. Miss Katie Riddick, Enfield's indefatigable local historian, clarified a number of baffling points and was particularly helpful in tracing family relationships and defining complex personalities. Dr. Andrew H. Horn, Librarian of the University of North Carolina, and his associate, Olan V. Cook, helped to find many authoritative works of history and reminiscence, and provided working quarters.

But particularly I am grateful for the generous, hospitable, and understanding help of the Wills-Whitaker-Beavens family connection. My warmest thanks go to Mrs. Stanley Whitaker of Centerville Plantation, Enfield; Miss Susie and Waldo Whitaker of Strawberry Hill, Enfield; R. M. Hunter of Arcola, North Carolina; Mrs. Lawrence Whitaker of Enfield; and the late Professor George Stockton Wills of Westminster, Maryland. These and others, in ways great and small but always important, succeeded in showing me the hearts of five brave Southern soldiers who do not deserve complete oblivion.

Here is as much of the truth about those five as is possible to discover, ninety-five years after they marched off to battle. I have not fictionized them. It would be both presumptuous and fatuous to put into their mouths words they did not say, or into their minds and hearts thoughts and emotions they did not know. The record they have left still speaks truly for them, word and thought and emotion.

Manly Wade Wellman

Chapel Hill, North Carolina
August 1, 1956

CONTENTS

Foreword 7

I THE SOUND OF THE DRUM 15

II ALL THE BOYS WELL IN CAMP 18

III UNTIL WE ARE PREPARED FOR IT 24

IV LESS FEAR IN EACH PASSING DAY 35

V THE GOD OF BATTLES IS ON OUR SIDE 45

VI SO IT IS WHEN ONE OF US DIES 59

VII WOUND UP IN LOVE AS BY A CLOAK 73

VIII I NEVER BEFORE KNEW WHAT SOLDIERING WAS 87

IX I BELONG TO GENERAL LEE'S ARMY 101

X OUR BRIGADE WAS IN IT GOOD 111

XI FOUGHT WELL AND WAS COMPLIMENTED 125

XII FALLEN IN LOVE ON SOMEBODY ELSE'S PLANTATION 138

XIII HARD, HARD TO BE A GOOD MAN 148

XIV STILL THE WILL IS HALF THE MAN 159

XV WASHINGTON WOULD HAVE BEEN IN OUR POSSESSION 169

XVI NEVER YET DID I SEE FELLOWS RUN AS THEY DID 179

XVII UPON THE VERGE OF TIME I STAND 189

XVIII I AM TIRED OF THIS FIGHTING 196

XIX TELL MOTHER, IF I FALL 206

XX LET US NOT MOURN AS THOSE WHO HAVE NO HOPE 216

XXI WE CAN STILL WEATHER THIS STORM 226

XXII BLOW, GABRIEL, BLOW 236

XXIII VALOR AND DEVOTION COULD ACCOMPLISH NOTHING 246

AFTERWORD 255

NOTES 257

BIBLIOGRAPHY 303

INDEX 307

REBEL BOAST

1

THE SOUND OF THE DRUM

They weren't at war yet. But they were going to be, they were bound to be, they had to be.

At little Enfield[1] in North Carolina, thirty-five miles south of the Virginia line and fifty miles west of Albermarle Sound, the spring of 1861 was richly gentle with blooms of peach and Judas tree and dogwood, with newly planted gardens and green lawns, with thickets in lettuce-tinted early leafage, with the stealthy first venturings of cotton sprigs on broad plantations round about. The taste of peace and isolation was in the sweet air, until from somewhere far off, at a fort called Sumter, outraged guns growled back and forth across harbor waters.

Suddenly war looked down with an unamiable relish on Enfield, and on Halifax County and North Carolina and all the tense world. War was coming, and men must fight in it. The proud militiamen of the Enfield Blues mustered for daily drill, under the flag sewn for them by the lovely hands of a noted belle, such a flag as was borne by those states already in the new-hatched Confederacy.[2] Seven stars shone on its blue field—South Carolina, Mississippi, Florida, Alabama, Georgia, Louisiana, Texas. Would North Carolina join the constellation?

Undoubtedly she would. Blistering were the terms in which her governor had rejected an appeal from Washington for two regiments to put down secession. "You can get no troops from North Carolina," he had telegraphed on April 15, and immediately he had called a convention to vote the state out of the Union. Without waiting to hear that convention's final decision, he had then ordered a camp of instruction to be established at Raleigh, and thirty thousand troops to be mustered.[3]

Eagerly the Blues looked for orders from the capital.[4] County Attorney Cary Whitaker[5] closed up his desk and donned the ostentatious gold epaulets of a junior second lieutenant. His serious, dark-bearded brother Sim,[6] at Strawberry Hill where Whitakers had lived ever since the Revolution, gave final work orders to his half-dozen slaves and reported as a private in the ranks. Eastward, in the village of Hamilton across the Edgecombe County line, ruddy-cheeked Billy Beavans[7] turned from the store counter where he clerked, smiled good-by all around to the girls who echoed his admiration, and headed for home to put on his uniform. Billy's eighteen-year-old brother Johnny,[8] at Centerville Plantation, and his schoolfellow and second cousin George Wills,[9] at Brinkleyville eighteen miles west, faced with young assurance the swift necessity of changing overnight from boys into soldiers. These, their kinsmen, and their friends rallied to the home-sewn banner.

None of them could understand or foresee the nature of the war to which they went. Ambushed in the future lay exhausting marches, hunger and rags and confusion and despair, sickness of body and heart and soul; the unexampled brightness of arterial blood fountaining the face or chest of a beloved comrade; the ear-bursting thunder of

massed artillery, the pebble-gourd rattle of musketry volleys, the flap of tattered flags, the stubborn, close-drawn,
enemy ranks opposite, the howling rush of the charge, the
murderous ecstasy of triumph, the pallid dismay of defeat.
For some of them these experiences would be crowned by
the supreme adventure of violent death.

On April 26, 1861—bright April, April of saucy
warmth beyond the April of the North—they marched
away, the Enfield Blues.[10]

Back they looked and harked toward a tuneful memory
of a happy, peaceful life. Every step carried them farther
away from the beloved familiarities of home cooking,
known fields and dooryards, the faces of parents, the laughter of girls at dancing parties. Billy Beavens, in from
Hamilton too late to join his company but eagerly making
ready to follow, took a pencil from his pocket and on a
blank page of his little diary achieved a sort of poetry:

> Sweet, very sweet was the sound of the violin
> When there was no warwhoop;
> But now the sad change is made,
> Instead of the violin we have the sound of the drum.[11]

II

ALL THE BOYS WELL IN CAMP

When the little funnel-stacked locomotive wheezed to a halt on Goldsboro's Center Street, the three soldiers climbed down from the car. Very quickly, one may be sure, people gathered to look in the bright afternoon of Saturday, April 27, 1861. Soldiers were no commonplace in Goldsboro. Not yet.

They were young, all three, and tall, and George Whitaker Wills was the youngest and tallest of them. Gaunt and towering—he was six feet one inch in his home-knit stockings—he lacked a month of his nineteenth birthday, and was by nature more reserved than his two comrades. His bright blue tunic and pantaloons fitted him like wax, and the shiny-visored forage cap was trig upon his abundant dark curls.[1] But he was nothing to look at, compared to Billy Beavans, who must have beamed back at the little boys and the big girls on Center Street.

"Smiling Billy," the ladies called the oldest Beavans boy back in Halifax County, and they vied for his compliments, his jokes, the tags of labored but gallant verse he contrived. As Billy strode with his companions across the packed dirt of the street from where the Wilmington and

Weldon tracks paralleled those of the Carolina Railroad, he cut a dashing figure in his uniform. He was five feet ten inches tall, graceful of figure, and he was twenty-one years old that spring. His cheeks were rosy, his nose was straight, his jaw strong but finely angled, his eyes ever so slightly aslant and bright, his hair dark.[2] This adventure, to Billy, beat counter-jumping at that store in Hamilton.

They were a day late to the muster of the Enfield Blues. Billy had had to wind up his job, and the other two had come by the stage from Brinkleyville to meet him and go as a trio to the camp of instruction at Raleigh and beyond that to the war that couldn't help but start any day now, any moment.[3]

The third soldier, Jesse Page,[4] was by seniority and by his respected civilian calling the party's unofficial head. He was a thirty-year-old Methodist minister, and lately he had taught at the Elba Female Academy at Brinkleyville. As tall as Billy, with a massive head and brilliant eyes, he knew Latin, Greek, and Hebrew, and he had a fine pulpit voice. In 1857 he had married George's pretty, studious sister, Miss Martha Eliza Wills. George was fond of him, though thirty was much older than eighteen, and George called his brother-in-law Mr. Page.

George liked Billy, too, and did not mind too much when Billy patronized him. After all, he and Billy were kinsmen—their mothers were first cousins, members of Enfield's numerous and respected Whitaker family[5]; and blood relationship, even at one or two removes, is especially important in the South. Billy's father, John Beavans, had taught George at the Whitaker's Chapel Academy, a good school for boys. Its students excelled in handwriting and spelling and grammar. John Beavans was a Virginian, from Portsmouth, and maybe that contributed to Billy's self-assurance, his aggressive gaiety that found outlet in song and verse and swift sociality.

George was more quiet than his cousin or his brother-in-law, and possibly more thoughtful than either. Just now, three hours from home on his way to war, he must have thought of his beloved parents, the Reverend Mr. William H. Wills and gentle Anna Maria Baker Whitaker Wills; of his sisters and brothers and the pleasant square mile of home farm, and the servants.

But someone had come from home with George, someone closer to him than brother-in-law or cousin. From the cars came a medium-sized, chocolate-brown man of twenty-five, laden with luggage. Washington Wills—"Wash," [6] they called him—had been assigned by the Reverend Mr. Wills to follow George to war. He was also known to Jesse Page and to Billy Beavans, who often had visited the Wills plantation. Wash could read and write, he could be trusted with important errands, he was both cheerful and resourceful. He was a skilled cook and valet.

The people of Goldsboro answered questions. No train to Raleigh on the Carolina line until tomorrow—not before noon, if then. Perforce, the party sought hotel accommodations. After that they strolled out, in the weather "pretty and fair," to look at the town.

They were not strangers in Goldsboro, only three hours by rail from Enfield; but it was worth seeing again.[7] In that country of scattered hamlets Goldsboro was a metropolis, with more than eight hundred inhabitants. There were three churches, too, and the local Baptists were going to build a fourth. Center Street was lined with brick structures, stores and offices and hotels, a courthouse, and a jail. Saloons also; Billy Beavans would take a toddy on occasion, though perhaps just now he deferred the pleasure to please his two more abstemious friends.[8] There were other diversions for young men with good manners and good humor. The prettier ladies on Goldsboro's board sidewalks undoubtedly reminded Billy of several he had admired at home. To these he had written verses, and one, perhaps, he had addressed more tenderly than the others:

> Though I may be far away
> Amidst trials, difficulties and dangers
> Yet I hope I may hear each day
> That you are free from troubles. . . .[9]

Billy may not have received all the admiring glances. George did not have Billy's handsomeness, but he was attractive. His tall, lean body had large bones, with a fair breadth to the sloping shoulders. His brows were well shaped, his nose long, his mouth full but firm, and his jaw resolute. His expression was habitually grave beyond his years. By habit he was neat and careful about his dress. His blue uniform fitted him smoothly.

But he was not one to flirt, like Smiling Billy. His thoughts were on a girl left behind him. Miss Fannie her name was, a spectacularly lovely blonde who attended Elba Academy with George's younger sisters.[10] Jesse Page, too, must be missing his young wife. And Wash had hated to leave Leah, his comely mulatto consort who as housekeeper in the Wills home lorded it over the other servants and sometimes over her white folks too.[11]

Wash had taken the luggage to the hotel. Apparently there was a great deal of it—soldiers staggered under their burdens of personal property in the spring of 1861. In Billy's luggage, for instance, were books, for he read much and with pleasure. He knew Daniel Defoe, Bernardin St. Pierre, Walter Scott, John Stuart Mill, Fox's *Book of Martyrs,* and, of course, the Bible—two copies of the Bible he possessed, and a Bible dictionary to boot. As for future reading, he particularly wanted William Tappan Thompson's *Major Jones' Courtship* and the works of Lord Byron.[12] Laughter and poetry were among Billy Beavans' chief literary reliances.

Back to the hotel after supper, the three went to bed early. Perhaps they did not sleep well. All had been away from home before, but not on their way to battlefields. Waking on Sunday morning, they attended services at the Methodist Church. If the idea was Jesse Page's, he did not have to argue strenuously to persuade his friends; George was the son and brother of ministers, and Billy, if not notably devout, was a churchgoer by family habit.[13] Afterward they took noon dinner and at one o'clock boarded a train for Raleigh.

At the depot in the state capital an officer directed them to the eastern suburbs. There the sixteen acres of state fair grounds[14] had been turned into a military post, named Camp Ellis for the governor who, though dangerously ill, moved surely and arbitrarily to put North Carolina into the Confederacy and the coming war.

Noise beat up from Camp Ellis as George and his friends approached. Inside the substantial board fence were gathered hundreds, thousands of men in varied uniforms, militia companies from everywhere. The governor had called for thirty thousand volunteers; this looked like a good part of them. Every building, stable, or poultry pen or refreshment stand had been turned into a barracks. Meanwhile, where were the Enfield Blues?

That question was answered only a few steps inside the gate. The Blues had responded promptly to the governor's appeal and had secured perhaps the best quarters to be had. They were in Reception Hall, a big frame building where in peaceful years the annual state fair had housed administration offices and special exhibits. As the three latecomers entered, with Wash lugging packages and carpetbags behind them, greetings rang from room to room and from corridor to corridor.

Uniformed friends and relatives quickly surrounded

them and showed George and Billy and the Reverend Mr. Jesse Page where to unroll their blankets. Suppertime was at hand. Wash, the skillful, unpacked a hamper to prepare a meal for his master and himself. As darkness closed in, fiddle music sprang up in a hallway. To George it seemed festive, homelike.[15] Everybody seemed happy and healthy.

". . . found all the boys well in camp," Billy Beavans finished jotting in his diary.

Taps sounded over Camp Ellis, tuneful and military and somehow plaintive. George lay down on blankets spread over straw. He was in the army now.

III

UNTIL WE ARE PREPARED FOR IT

Private George Whitaker Wills was not given to any great display of dash or self-dramatization, but he faced military adventure resolutely enough.

Like most Southerners he loved his family deeply. Even so briefly from home, he thought much and tenderly of his parents and his brothers and sisters. The Reverend Mr. Wills had nine children and was on warmly affectionate terms with all of them. George's oldest brother, Richard, was also a Methodist minister, riding circuit on the North Carolina coast. His sister Martha, married to Jesse Page, was three years George's senior. Younger than George were Brother Eddie, fourteen and disappointingly careless at schoolwork but with an almost copy-book zest for work in the broad home fields along Rocky Swamp east of Brinkleyville; two favorite sisters, seventeen-year-old Lucy and twelve-year-old Mary; and three "little girls," Harriet and Cornelia and Agnes.[1]

George's mother, born Anna Maria Baker Whitaker, was of a family great in Halifax County. It traced back to a Revolutionary War colonel, before that to Colonial Virginia, and before that to the learned William

Whitaker, master of Saint Jude's College at Cambridge in Queen Elizabeth's day. For her George had a deep and respectful love, and Anna Wills may have indulged her son a trifle, because he had a queasy stomach and a susceptibility to colds. In a smaller family, with parents more foolishly indulgent, George might indeed have grown up a spoiled boy. As it was, he stubbornly picked and chose what he ate. For neither beef nor mutton did he have any relish, and not much for corn bread. He enjoyed fruit and vegetables, fresh in season from the Wills orchards and gardens, or from the supplies preserved for winter in the big home pantry. His taste for condiments—particularly pepper vinegar—bespoke a young epicure of sorts.[2]

He had been well educated under Professor John Beavans at Whitaker's Chapel and had achieved a clear handwriting, with the *f*-shaped Saxon *s*. He understood the use of unusual and even scholarly terms, though as a rule he wrote and spoke with a strong, vivid Carolina colloquialism. His occasional mistakes in grammar, spelling, or punctuation would seem to be careless informality rather than ignorance. Possibly this good schooling had been provided by his father in the hope that George, like Richard, might enter the ministry; George, however, was not utterly persuaded to so holy a life. He liked the society of both men and women, and he could enjoy a good joke, even when it was on him.

The company of Wash as his personal servant was like part of the home atmosphere. Wash was really brother Richard's property. They were of the same age, Wash and Richard, and as boys had rambled and played together on terms of affectionate equality, while Wash had alternately petted and supervised the younger George. Wash still supervised at times. That was a natural consideration in assigning Wash to "look after" the young soldier.[3]

George's half-dreamy thoughts of Brinkleyville turned frequently to someone not his relative, someone of slender, disdainful beauty. Miss Fannie . . . George's parents seemed to disapprove of their son's interest in her. Miss Fannie was a girl with a will of her own at that, and a tendency to coquettish tyranny. She was what some would and did call "independent." But might she love George after all? He could not be sure of that. Just now he was at Camp Ellis, and other assurances must be established.

He was glad to be made welcome by his kinsmen among the Enfield Blues. Kinsmen aplenty he had in that self-confident and dapper company, and close friends as well.

The Blues had no long history as Southern militia companies went—they had organized just after John Brown's Raid on Harpers Ferry in 1859—but they knew their skirmish and close-order drill and they represented the best blood of the Enfield community. Ever since early spring at home David B. Bell, the consequential cotton broker who was their captain, had called them daily to march, countermarch, and go through the facings and formations. Morning roll call resounded with names that recalled to memory Halifax County's colonial leaders—Arrington, Bumpass, Britt, Dickens, Etheridge, Glover, King, Parker, Pittman, Whitaker, Whitehead.

Private Johnny Beavans welcomed George almost as cordially as he welcomed his brother Billy. Johnny and George were of almost the same age. They had been classmates at Whitaker's Chapel Academy, had visited often in each other's homes, and in many ways their thoughts and behavior were similar. Like George, Johnny was in love; pretty Miss Laura Gunter had promised to marry him when the war was over.

An older private was John Simmons Whitaker, the brother of George's mother—"Uncle Sim," a sinewy bachelor of thirty-one, with blue eyes and a banner of dark beard such as would soon become popular with soldiers. Second sergeant of the company was sedate, forty-one-year-old William H. Whitaker, "Major" to his family and friends. Theodore Lucian Whitaker, another cousin, was fourth sergeant. He was robust and good-looking, something like an older Billy Beavans. And junior second lieutenant of the Blues was George's favorite uncle, Cary Whitaker.

Uncle Cary was six feet tall, with the blue eyes, fair skin, and dark hair of the Whitaker clan. His direct gaze, long face, square chin, and full lips added up to a thoughtful handsomeness. Like his brother Sim he had come to war with a beard, and this added years to his apparent age—at twenty-nine he was the youngest of the four officers who led the Enfield Blues. The dignified Captain Bell was thirty-four. The company's first lieutenant was another of George's family connections, thirty-one-year-old Montgomery T. Whitaker, a prosperous planter skilled with banjo and fiddle but less popular with his men than such gifts might suggest. A planter, too, was the senior second lieutenant, Francis Marion Parker.

Cary Whitaker had gone two years to the state university at Chapel Hill, had taught school and read law, and lately had served as county attorney for Halifax. He and his brother Sim lived together at Strawberry Hill with their mother, and were partners in farming and the operation of a supply house. Like most of his many relatives Cary Whitaker was a good Methodist but not a blue-nosed one. He could appreciate a pretty face and, on occasion, a nip of whisky. The only unmarried officer of the Blues, he had special love and concern for his nieces and nephews, and apparently he enjoyed the company of his relatives in the ranks more than that of his brother officers.[4]

Oldest man in the company, at forty-eight, was Private

L. Shearman. The youngest was Private Flavius Cicero Pittman, who at fifteen had followed his worshiped cousin
Oliver into the ranks.

The officers and most of the men were, for their time and
region, well educated. Many considered themselves even
sophisticated. One or two had traveled extensively, perhaps, though to others Camp Ellis was the farthest adventure from home in a young lifetime. Almost without
exception they were deeply religious, most of them Methodists or Baptists. It is unlikely that any of them had heard
of the amazing theories of Charles Darwin or of Pasteur's
early rationalization of the causes of fermentation and
decomposition. All were eager to get to the front, and none
doubted that the war would terminate in a prompt and
gloriously overwhelming Southern victory.

Reveille brought them tumbling into the pleasant dawn
of Monday, April 29, with chuckles at other companies
who perforce had bedded down in rougher quarters.

One such company the Blues hailed readily, the Halifax
Light Infantry[5] from their own county seat, with as
captain James Whitaker, yet another of the ubiquitous
and patriotic family connection. The Edgecombe Guards[6]
excited jealous admiration; under Captain John L. Bridgers they had helped to seize Fort Macon on the coast from a
single unresisting Yankee sergeant. Over at the stables,
grumbling because they had been obliged to sleep on
straw, were the Charlotte Grays,[7] of which no enlisted
man had yet celebrated his twenty-first birthday. Here
and there newly enlisted country boys gaped at the Jews
in the ranks of the Grays, but such comrades-in-arms did
not seem exotic to George Wills and the others from
Enfield; their own able ranking noncom was Orderly
Sergeant Jonas Cohen.

A second company from Charlotte had a fascinating
name, the Hornet's Nest Rifles. Also present for duty was

the Orange Light Infantry from Hillsboro, including a number of state university students who had joined without waiting for the end of term.[8] One of them George recognized with pleasure—Cousin Spier Whitaker, from home in Enfield. Almost everybody, it seemed, was going to the war.

There was, however, little time to lounge and gaze and swap compliments. Drill, came the orders of Colonel D. H. Hill, who commanded at Camp Ellis. Drill three times a day, beginning before breakfast.

At Sergeant Cohen's command the Blues formed a single file, tallest man at the head, the next tallest man covering him, and so on until the shortest of the whole company stood at the rear.

"Front!"

They faced left, toward Sergeant Cohen.

"In two ranks, form company! Left face!"

They were a file again, this time with the shortest man at its head. In front of him now stood old Second Sergeant Whitaker.

"March!"

The short man faced front beside Sergeant Whitaker. The next man obliqued left into position and faced front behind the first. The third and fourth moved up, forming another file, with the others following in turn. When all had taken position and faced front, the company was in double file.

The right half of the company thus formed was the first platoon, the left half the second. Each platoon was further divided into two sections of about twenty-five men each, in charge of corporals. George, Sim Whitaker, Jesse Page, and the Beavans brothers found themselves together in the first section of the first platoon, by reason of height. Officers stepped into position—Captain Bell at right of his company, First Lieutenant Montgomery Whitaker in rear of

the second section of the second platoon, Second Lieutenants Francis Parker and Cary Whitaker behind the
centers of the first and second platoons respectively. The
third and fourth sergeants held positions in the file closers.

Now they split into squads, each with a noncom to
drill it.

"Forward—march!"

"About—face!"

"Eyes—right!"

"Forward—double quick—march!" [10]

The Enfield Blues did passably well at all this by reason
of those drill sessions at home, but some of the companies
formed and marched raggedly, under green officers and
sergeants. These were taken over by pink-cheeked cadets
from the North Carolina Military Institute at Charlotte.[11]

Breakfast, and a new parading of the companies, to hear
an officer read out the list of units that would form North
Carolina's first regiment of volunteers.[12]

"Orange Light Infantry . . ." Good for you, Cousin
Spier!

"Warrenton Guards . . ." Two companies in camp
from Warrenton. This must be the better of the two.

"Hornet's Nest Rifles . . ." A man's bound to like that
name.

"Enfield Blues . . ." Gentlemen, isn't it hard to keep
from raising a cheer for yourself?

"Lumberton Guards . . ." They're from down yonder
in the turpentine country.

"Duplin Rifles . . ." A company about as old as the
Blues, with a good captain, Tom Kenan.

"Charlotte Grays . . ." Some of those youngsters will
have to learn to use a gun before they can use a razor.

"Thomasville Rifles . . ." From somewhere to the west,
before you get to the mountains.

"Granville Grays . . ." Neighbors from the next county to Halifax, and some of us know Captain George Wortham.

"Columbus Guards . . ." That's another good name.

Smoothbore muskets were issued to these chosen companies. Gunwise Lieutenant Parker did not admire such weapons, but anybody had to admit that they were better than none at all. Back to drill, with an extra strut to the fortunate ten units, pouting disappointment evident among others.

Manual of arms proceeded at once. The men executed the shoulder, the trail, the carry, the reverse. At command they simulated the intricate process of muzzle-loading, in nine successive operations.

"Load!"

George Wills dropped his musket butt to earth between his out-slanting toes. His left hand grasped the barrel below the muzzle, his right hand moved to the cartridge box belted at his hip.

"Handle—cartridge!"

Up came his right hand, pretending to grasp an imaginary paper cartridge so that his teeth could catch its tip.

"Tear—cartridge!"

A quick, abrupt motion, as though to rend the bitten paper and expose the powder inside.

"Charge—cartridge!"

Dumb show of pouring powder down the barrel, disengagement of the ball from the paper, pretense of dropping the ball into the bore. Then George's right hand grasped the head of the ramrod, right elbow close to his side.

"Draw—rammer!"

Out came the slender rod from its clamps beneath the barrel, like a sword from its sheath. George reversed it to left so that its head entered the muzzle.

"Ram—cartridge!"

The rammer drove home, as though pressing the charge down.

"Return—rammer!"

It came out again and back into its clamps.

"Prime!"

George's left hand raised the piece and his right hand seized the small of the stock. He moved his feet to face half-right, his left hand sloped the musket across his body, while his right hand thumbed the hammer back to half-cock, then slid to the pouch and simulated the taking of a cap and pressing it down upon the nipple.

"Shoulder—arms!"

He faced front again and shuttled the piece up to slant upon his right shoulder, still at half-cock. The loading was accomplished.[13]

A pause to rest before dinner, and speculation as to who would be colonel of the new regiment.

That, of course, was up to the captains and lieutenants. They would elect their field officers, just as they themselves had been elected by the men of their several companies. But most soldiers felt that it would be Colonel Hill.

George Wills and the others had seen Daniel Harvey Hill standing at the door of his office or sitting his horse to observe and direct the instruction of troops. Colonel Hill wasn't really a great deal to look at. He was scrawny and no more than middling tall, with big eyes in a pinched face, the sort of face that bespeaks bad health. His spine was weak and he suffered from dyspepsia. But his military fame was enough for a giant. Graduating from West Point in 1842, he had served as an artillery officer in the Mexican War and had been brevetted major for headlong gallantry. Later he had resigned from the regular army, had taught at Washington College in Virginia and at Davidson in

North Carolina, and recently he had been superintendent of North Carolina Military Institute.[14]

He had published textbooks too. Some of the younger soldiers must have studied the school arithmetics Colonel Hill had turned out during the 1850's, with Yankee-baiting humor in the examples: "The year in which the Governors of Massachusetts and Connecticut sent treasonable messages to their respective legislatures, is expressed by four digits. . . ." [15]

A devout Presbyterian, Hill prayed daily and abstained from liquor and tobacco. He did not curse, nor did he need to. Plain, decent dictionary words were sufficient on his sharp tongue when he put a slow or argumentative soldier in his place. All in all, D. H. Hill acted and sounded like somebody who could help you win whatever fight he got you into.

Next day drill continued. Some of the gaudy militia tunics were doffed and put aside, for Adjutant General John F. Hoke prescribed either gray or blue blouses. He was a thrilling stylist in orders of the day, was Adjutant General Hoke. Between drills and details and guard mounts the Blues read his posted exhortations:

> . . . The decree for our subjugation has gone forth; the time of our trial has come; the blow will soon fall; we must meet it with the whole energies of the State; we must show to the world that North Carolina will maintain her rights at all hazards.[16]

That evening, his third in camp, George Wills wrote home to his sister Lucy such items of news as he thought might interest a politely reared girl of seventeen. He described the railroad journey with its overnight break at Goldsboro, plumed himself and his friends on being in good quarters, and spoke of "lively times in the camp," in intervals of those three drills daily. And there was news of a move toward the inevitable fighting in Virginia.

"We will stay in Raleigh a week or so before we start north," George set down; then, lest the home folks worry: "We have the assurance that we certainly will not be led into battle until we are prepared for it."

Loneliness descended upon the boy soldier as he wrote. "Give my love to *all*," he wound up, underscoring the last word of this adjuration. "Tell Pa and Mother, I wish I could see them again. As ever your very affectionate brother George."

At the bottom a postscript about kinfolks in the ranks with him: "Mr. Page says he will write to you to morrow. John Beavans sends his love to you." [17]

IV

LESS FEAR IN EACH PASSING DAY

That fate-ridden April came to an end the day George
wrote, and May brought summery heat upon Camp Ellis.
In crowded quarters, with open wells and sketchy sanitary
arrangements, the soldiers became sick by dozens. "Cramp
colic," they called the griping pains in their bowels. George
Wills felt a touch of this ailment, but he answered roll call
and stood guard on May 9 for all that. He had been bred to
do his duty, even twenty-four hours of alternate sentry go
and reserve detail, hard on a tall, thin boy with a misery in
his belly. He continued to disdain the coarse rations issued
him. A visitor from home lugged in two big boxes of the
things George liked to eat, and Wash cooked and served
and did the dishes.[1]

Miss Fannie was still in George's mind and heart.[2]
Perhaps he confided in his chum Johnny Beavans, who felt
similar doleful tenderness toward Miss Laura Gunter of
Enfield.[3] Billy Beavans, sensitive and thoughtful enough,
but older than these teen-agers and with something like
emotional safety in the number of girls who reciprocated
his admiration, naturally would grin at the moonstruck

solemnity of George and Johnny. He wrote in his diary something that he, at least, thought was poetry:

Camp Life

When the young enter Camp
They soon become homesick
Not fond of taking a tramp
Until they forget they *are* sick.

After they remain awhile
Their troubles pass away
And they will begin to find
Less fear in each passing day.[4]

What these couplets might lack in grace and inspiration they made up in sound appraisal of what happened to the Camp Ellis recruits. They grew used to duty and discipline. The smoothbore muskets balanced familiarly in their hands. They were becoming soldiers.

Meanwhile that hasty initial organization of the First Regiment of North Carolina Volunteers fell to pieces. Some of the chosen companies could not show the required strength and perforce gave way to other and larger ones. The Enfield Blues were kept, and the Hornet's Nest Rifles and the Orange Light Infantry. To these, by general order of May 9, were added the Edgecombe Guards, conquerors of Fort Macon's lone sergeant; the Southern Stars from Lincolnton, commanded by the adjutant general's kinsman Captain W. J. Hoke; the Burke Rifles and the Buncombe Rifles, mountain militia; the Randalsburg Rifles and the La Fayette Light Infantry.[5]

Grinding drill and confinement behind board fences wearied some men to desperation. "There is some talk of our getting off from here next week and it is good news, too," George wrote home, "for I reckon every man is tired of this place, cooped up as we are, it is a wonder that we don't get sick more than we do."

This was only mild complaint. The Enfield Blues were well disciplined, and on good terms with their officers. Men in other companies chafed under what they considered tyranny. One mountaineer quarreled violently with his captain and shot him in the thigh. The officer went to the hospital, the mutinous private to the guardhouse.[6]

Daily new volunteers crowded in, trailed by baggage-laden servants. Several of the unassigned companies—the Halifax Light Infantry, the Warrenton Guards, the Granville Grays—left on the morning of May 11 for Weldon. There, near the Virginia border, they would form the nucleus for another regiment. Men of the First bade them soldierly farewells and promised to meet them at the seat of war, wherever that turned out to be.[7]

Drill proceeded that day, though one of the Blues fell out of ranks, wrung with "cramp colic." Sergeants snapped out the orders. The company officers were absent, voting for regimental commanders.

Hill was colonel, as everyone expected. His two late associates at the Military Institute, Charles C. Lee and little James H. Lane, were chosen lieutenant colonel and major respectively. Lee was a West Point graduate, Lane had been a brilliant student at Virginia Military Institute.[8] Such leaders promised well for discipline.

Part of that discipline took the form of a court-martial for the hot-tempered private who had wounded his captain. The Enfield Blues speculated as to what would happen to the fellow.[9] Less savage and more immediately tragic was the case of Private James Hudson of the Hornet's Nest Rifles, who died that same day of pneumonia in the Camp Ellis hospital. His company escorted the coffin to the train and fired a solemn salute from its new muskets. "Highly respected," said the Raleigh *News* of Private Hudson.[10]

Captain Bell divided the Blues into messes. George Wills ate with his relatives, of course—Uncle Sim, Billy and Johnny Beavans, and Jesse Page. Sim Whitaker's shiny, black body servant Turner[11] helped Wash with the duties of extra cookery, though Turner was never as proficient as Wash. George felt young and lonely, as Cousin Billy's verse suggested. He finished his letter to Lucy:

> When you write, let me know what they are doing on the farm. Give my love to *all*. You must all pray for me that I may keep right while here and that I may be brought home again. Give my love to *all*. Your most affectionate brother
>
> George

Probably Wash carried this letter home, for he had a family errand. He may have taken another letter, as well, to Miss Fannie at Elba Academy. For all her caprices, or possibly because of them, Miss Fannie held George's heart. Her own written coquetries troubled her lover.[12]

Sim Whitaker and several others also headed for Enfield on leave, perhaps to ease the tensions acquired behind the palings of crowded Camp Ellis.[13]

On May 13 the Blues were sworn into military service for six months.[14] A few thought this might be too long a time for whatever had to be done to the presumptuous Yankees. Up in the Northern states volunteers were enlisting for only ninety days. Two days later the First Regiment was paraded by Lieutenant Colonel Lee at four o'clock after drill, to be mustered in as a complete unit.

The boys of the Charlotte Grays had been added again, as a tenth company. A justice of peace from town importantly administered the formal oath. A Charlotte newspaperman, watching, called the regiment "the finest-looking body of men ever assembled in the State." Undoubtedly it was.

But, almost at the moment of muster came a final change in organization. The melancholy Randalsburg Rifles could not show a full complement of men and were detached and their place taken by the Fayetteville Independent Light Infantry. This company, the oldest and one of the proudest in all the South, was first organized in 1786 and had rivaled the Fort Macon exploit of the Edgecombe Guards; on April 23 it had helped to occupy the United States arsenal at Fayetteville, confiscating precious stores of arms and ammunition and splendid machinery for manufacturing more. Because it had stood guard after this triumph, it had arrived late at Camp Ellis. Officers and men of the Independents strutted like gamecocks, with elaborate plumes on their broad-brimmed hats.[15]

Colonel Hill named one of his former Institute cadets, J. M. Poteat, as regimental adjutant. The surgeon was Dr. Peter Hines from Craven County. From the Hornet's Nest Rifles two privates were promoted, John Henry Wayt to be commissary and Edwin A. Yates to be chaplain. Chaplain Yates was a Methodist and becomingly stouthearted. "I intend to fight as well as pray," he announced.[16] While waiting for action he did not shirk his fair share of camp duty.

Now at last the companies were assigned to permanent order in the regiment. The Edgecombe Guards had the honor designation of Company A. The Hornet's Nest Rifles were Company B, the Charlotte Grays were Company C, and the Orange Light Infantry Company D. The Buncombe Rifles, Company E, were designated the color company and proudly hoisted as regimental flag the secession banner sewn from red, white, and blue silk dresses by the Woodfin sisters of Asheville.[17] The La Fayettes came next as Company F. The Burke Rifles were G, the Fayetteville Independents H, the Enfield Blues I, and the Southern Stars K.

On the very next day came news, highly exciting. They were going to Richmond, where an army gathered swiftly to oppose the invasion launched by that shadowy figure of menace, Abraham Lincoln.

Two days' rations of meat and bread were issued to the La Fayettes, the Fayetteville Independents, and the Southern Stars, and on Saturday, May 18, these three companies departed with Colonel Hill amid a new storm of cheers in camp and at the depot.[18] Impatiently the others awaited their own orders to follow, slackening in their energetic colonel's absence the stern regime of drill and fatigue duty. On Monday evening cannon boomed at Camp Ellis— word came that the convention at the State House was ready to vote North Carolina out of the Union.[19] Next day as Lieutenant Colonel Lee marshaled the remaining seven companies for the northward trip, the news was confirmed. Every delegate had signed a soberly worded ordinance of secession.

At the railroad station Raleigh ladies pelted the soldiers with bouquets and exhorted them to heroic deeds. Some of these fair spectators were seen to shed tears—not so the soldiers, and emphatically not so Private George Wills, marching with the tall men of the first platoon of Company I.[20]

Wash had arrived from home, bringing more provisions and family news, in time to pack luggage and join in the move to Virginia. George found time to write to his father. He felt ready to do credit to the Willses and the Whitakers, the communities of Brinkleyville and Enfield, the county of Halifax, the state of North Carolina, and the whole embattled South. This spirit, he hoped, would find echo among his loved ones.

"Tell mother she must cheer up, it isn't [like her?] to be low spirited," he urged. "I am getting along finely, she must wait until danger comes to be low spirited." [21]

At eight o'clock, after sunset of Tuesday, May 21, the train brought them into Petersburg below Richmond.

Virginians were out to welcome them in, as North Carolinians had been out to wave them away. Two spruce militia units, the Cockade Cadets and the Home Cavalry, were drawn up at the depot to greet them. The platform, the floor of the depot building, and the walks outside teemed with applauding citizens. From the porches and windows of a big hotel opposite the depot leaned Virginia girls in hoop skirts and secession bonnets. Cary Whitaker and Billy Beavans, always sharp-eyed for pretty faces, must have been ready to gesture greetings to these. Again flowers were tossed into the ranks—somewhat wilted, but gay for all that. More welcome still were "snacks nicely done up in paper," eagerly received by hungry soldiers who had eaten but lightly on the train.

The cordial greeting of the Virginia troops was tinged with something of envy. The North Carolinians made a brave appearance with their splendid uniforms, muskets, knapsacks, and canteens. "Without drawing invidious distinctions," frankly noted a Petersburg journalist, "we must say that this is the best equipped regiment which has yet made its route through our city." [22]

At eleven o'clock, with drowsiness overriding swagger, the regiment took another train, rode twenty miles to Richmond, and well after midnight fell in for a march of a mile and a half. The Blues, officers and men alike, felt agonizedly weary. "A hard time," confessed the usually active and cheerful Billy Beavans. Worse was the case of his messmate George Wills, who had come away from Camp Ellis with a stone bruise on his heel and could set only his toe to the ground.[23] At last they reached Howard's Grove,[24] a pleasant wooded hill above the James River, where the other three companies already had gone into camp. Gratefully they ducked into tents ready set up for them.

Doubtless everybody slept soundly, but neither the Confederate Army nor any other in history has ever respected late slumberers. They rose to bugled reveille at dawn of May 22. Colonel Hill immediately formed the regiment to perform the manual of arms. A gallery of Richmond ladies and gentlemen had turned out to watch in the sunrise.

Already Hill was being called "Old Hawkeye" by his men. He gazed sharply from wing to wing of the regiment as it executed the shoulder, the order, the carry. Suddenly his voice rose, dry and harsh.

"That old man in the rear rank of Company I is too slow," he accused.

Lieutenant Parker wanted to turn and look, but dared not shift his eyes from the front. He guessed that the slow handler of the musket must be Sergeant W. H. Whitaker, in the file closers. "Poor old Major," he muttered under his breath, but he might have saved his worry over the aging second sergeant. When the drill was over and the regiment dismissed, it developed that Hill's "old man in the rear rank" was in reality one of the teen-agers, probably still yawning from the train ride and the late hours.[25]

At nine o'clock the Blues mounted guard in what Billy called "very pretty weather." George took his post with the others, stone bruise and all.[26] During the rest of the morning, the afternoon, and all night they paced their beats in turn.

Of Richmond, wondrously bustling that spring of 1861 with war a new and pleasurable excitement, Blues and the rest of the regiment saw little just then. George and Uncle Sim and the Beavans brothers, walking their posts with musket on shoulder, made out only distant roofs and steeples. Nearer at hand were massed the tents of a neighboring regiment—from Tennessee, they heard—and beyond this and in other directions more tents and more flags.

There were thousands upon thousands of troops, dwarfing the mobilization at Camp Ellis.[27]

The Blues completed their tour of guard duty at nine o'clock the next morning, May 23. George limped into town to buy a length of oilcloth, as a ground sheet for damp weather.[28] After that, nothing to do—until sudden new orders:

"First North Carolina will proceed to Yorktown——"

George remembered that name from his school history. Cornwallis had surrendered there eighty years ago, at the end of an earlier War for Independence. It was to the east, on the shore of something called the Peninsula, a name to suggest yet another war, with Napoleon the great figure in it. Sergeants supervised the striking of tents, privates and servants bundled up bedding and strapped down the lids of mess chests and food boxes. The column marched back to where the train waited, then rolled away to a wharf downriver.

Crowded aboard the steamer—privates from luxury-loving homes were miffed because they must jam into the stuffy hold while officers, perhaps not their social equals, had pleasant deck accommodations[29]—they sailed for hours. A bit of tragic news filtered from company to company. Private Julius Sadler of the Hornet's Nest Rifles had fallen between two of the cars on the way to the steamer and had been killed instantly.[30] Another of the Hornets gone, before anyone had so much as heard a Yankee musket go off; too bad.

They sailed all night and most of the next day, and after dark of Friday, May 24, tied up at Yorktown. It was George Wills' nineteenth birthday, the first he had ever spent away from home, and he was glad to find a place to spread his blankets in one of the waterfront houses where Captain Bell billeted his men. At dawn he wakened again, fell in with the Blues, and marched a quarter of a mile from town. Wearily the soldiers pitched their tents. "We had been worried so much we felt very little like working," confided Billy Beavans to his diary.[31]

But they were near the enemy. Somebody pointed southeast toward Hampton, twenty-six miles away, where Federal troops had landed by regiments. And on the shore of the York River's estuary, gangs toiled to entrench a battery of cannon that would command the Yorktown anchorages. Far out, but in plain view, lay a steamer flying the Stars and Stripes. That was a Federal ship-of-war, Carolinians were told.

The talk of imminent action banished any impulse to relax and close tired eyes. George Wills stared across Tidewater swamps and thickets, thrilled but not daunted. This was the post of danger and of honor, between the enemy and Richmond. He and his friends would hold that post. It was what all the drill had been for, the loading of a musket in nine times, the handling of cartridges, the fixing of bayonets.

"Our colonel and his men are ready for and expecting a fight," wrote somebody to his home newspaper in Charlotte, "in which case you may listen for a good report from the gallant First Regiment." [32]

A good report, naturally; who back in North Carolina would listen for a bad one?

V

THE GOD OF BATTLES IS ON OUR SIDE

The next day was Sunday and, in a regiment led by praying officers, there were in the morning only necessary details of guard and garrison.

At ten o'clock Chaplain Yates stood up to preach. Colonel Hill himself lined out the opening hymn, Presbyterian fashion. The chaplain spoke feelingly of the death of his comrade Julius Sadler, and some of the Hornet's Nest Rifles shed tears.[1]

Afterward there was time to get acquainted with other units of the garrison—Virginians these, two regiments of infantry and one of artillery, and none of them to excel the First North Carolina in smartness of appearance or soldierly behavior. Commander at Yorktown, Colonel John Bankhead Magruder was an impressively handsome figure, with sweeping mustaches and showily gracious manners. He had been an artillerist in the Old Army, notable for his mannerly sumptuous hospitality, and into the Confederacy he had carried a taste for theatricals. Folks said that he had formally challenged the Union general at Hampton, squint-eyed B. F. Butler, to settle things by personal combat.[2]

Yorktown, site of ancient heroisms, was disappointingly small to George Wills as he strolled to trace the line of Cornwallis' entrenchments and to gaze from the height above the water. George was particularly interested in certain raised troughs, like aqueducts. He was told that Cornwallis had meant to fill these with powder, to blow up the town if Washington penetrated his defenses. "Ingenious," pronounced George.[3]

The Long Roll sounded that bright Sunday afternoon.

Staccato, sustained, blood-churning, the drummed signal meant action, the enemy. Officers and soldiers tumbled into formation, spreading out in line to defend camp and city. George found his place in ranks. Behind him he heard Wash's excited voice.

"If any of you fall, I want the gun," Wash pleaded. "I feel as if I could kill a few Yankees before I go home."

But no enemy ventured from the silent thickets. Standing in line of battle, muskets loaded and at the ready, the Enfield Blues saw Colonel Hill's mounted figure cutting across their front. Reining in, Hill raised his voice to address the regiment.

The Long Roll had been sounded, he informed them drily, to see how quickly they would respond. He then ordered a brief session of drill—not much, for it was still Sunday—and reassembled them for a final word before dismissal.

"You have made a great improvement," he said drily. "You formed in ten minutes, that did very well; but you were just eight minutes too long."

Monday saw a resumption of drill thrice daily, with additional labor at making breastworks. Few of the Blues liked this plebian business with ax and spade, but they were country-bred and adept at using tools. Not so, various soldiers from the towns; Louis Leon, a slender Jewish private of nineteen with the Charlotte Grays, gashed his tree so ineptly that he was given the ignominious task of carrying water for better axmen.

Another Long Roll was beaten after dark on the 29th, no deliberate false alarm this time. Swiftly taking position with his musket, George Wills was properly inspired by the shouting of Colonel Hill: "If the Yankees never learned double quick before, they'll learn it tonight!"

But again no hostile advance showed in the gloom, and the tense formation relaxed. The men lay down on the hard ground and slept without removing their clothes. Many were disappointed that there had not been action.

"I, for one, would have as soon seen them as not," George wrote to his mother. "I thought as the Colonel said, we were pretty well prepared to give them a small portion of hot lead and steel." [4]

A volley of hot lead from muskets, then steel at grim thrusting distance—a thought that both intrigued and chilled. But it was back to ax and spade next day. Headquarters issued a call for volunteers to dig new and improved entrenchments a mile from camp, and the whole regiment responded with patriotic fervor. When the job was done, the hands of the men were blistered. They favored stiff muscles and dabbed at dirty faces. [5] George Wills developed a distaste for spadework that he was never to lose.

No sooner were the new works completed than, on the last day of May, the regiment was ordered southwest toward enemy-held Hampton. Two companies only remained to garrison the camp, and one of these was the Blues. George felt slighted and forsaken. Would the war begin, hot lead and cold steel, without him?

He wrote home: "We are all lonely . . . and it is much to our sorrow, too, as we wanted to go with the rest, but it is not as we say, or our Colonel either, but the commander of the place here."

His loved ones, however, must not echo such feelings. "You must all be cheerful and not grieve over us," he finished, rather inconsistently, "for we are too cheerful ourselves to be grieved over. Pray for us at all times. We hope to see you again. May heaven's choicest blessings attend you all. Good by."

That evening the eight companies that had advanced toward Hampton came back, having marched ten miles in three hours, without once discharging their muskets. They told the Blues that some twenty-five hundred Federals had been reported to their front, but had not been seen. At four-thirty the next morning Colonel Hill roused his men to drill before breakfast, then set them to digging again. He organized them further for battle. Companies A and K, the flank units, were assigned as skirmishers. The other eight were divided into four battalions, each commanded by a senior captain. The fourth of these included the Blues and the Independents, under Captain Wright Huske.[6]

Newspapers began to arrive from North Carolina. With two Cumberland County companies in the regiment, a paper frequently seen was the Fayetteville *Observer,* whose editor had a son in the ranks of the proud Independents. One issue included an entire page headed IMPORTANT TO SOLDIERS—RULES FOR HEALTH. The advice sounded authoritative:

> Sun-stroke may be prevented by wearing a silk handkerchief in the hat. . . .
> A bullet through the abdomen (belly or stomach) is more certainly fatal than if aimed at the head or heart. . . .
> Let the beard grow, but not longer than some three inches. This strengthens and thickens its growth and thus makes a more perfect protection for the lungs against dirt, and of the throat against winds and cold in winter. . . .
> Twelve men are hit in battle, dressed in red, where there

are only five, dressed in a bluish grey, a difference of more than two to one; green, seven; brown, six. . . .

The author of these grave precepts was one Dr. Hall, editor of the *New York Journal of Health,* but he was heeded for all his evident Unionism. Beards began to sprout everywhere among Yorktown's defenders. Billy Beavans, that sturdy romantic, achieved a thicket that lent maturity to his ruddy handsomeness. Sim and Cary Whitaker no longer were remarkable for their thatched jaws. But their nephew George Wills continued to employ his razor; his beard would not grow evenly.[7]

Cary Whitaker was concerned with supply for his men. Field uniforms to replace the blue parade gear were maddeningly slow in arriving from supply depots, and so Cary had written to Enfield, asking his older brother Lawrence to procure clothes there. Cary's cousin, First Lieutenant Montgomery Whitaker, dug into his own pocket to equip the troops.[8]

The grind of duty, alternate drill and ditch-digging, was not relished. But on the morning of June 6 came an exciting new order: Roll blankets, pack three days' rations, and prepare to march.

Three days' rations—only two days' rations had been ordered for the move from Raleigh to Richmond. Billy Beavans had a premonition of unpleasantness, and may have expressed it to George as they formed column with the rest of the regiment and headed southwest. Evening brought rain, while they slogged along thicketed trails. After dark, at the end of fifteen weary miles of tramping, they were ordered to fall out near an unpainted clapboard building. That was Big Bethel Church, said someone who knew. George and Billy and others slept on the wet ground, with rain soaking their blankets.[9]

Morning found them stiff-jointed and grumbling. There

was no coffee, complained Billy, not smiling just now. George, less prone to complain, nevertheless missed the invaluable Wash, who had been left in Yorktown. Ineptly George singed his coarse and scanty rations over an open fire. Hill, the indefatigable, set part of the force to throwing up breastworks, the rest to building huts of brush. Those who visited Big Bethel Church found its walls scribbled over with inscriptions: "Death to the Traitors!" —"Down with the Rebels!" Union hands had written those things, and by now must have dropped pencils to snatch up muskets. How close might the enemy be this very moment?

Around the church grew trees in sandy soil, with denser, swampier thickets around. Southward the ground sloped to where, on the road that led toward hidden hostile forces, a flat wooden bridge spanned a slow river.[10] Some Virginia cavalry clattered over that bridge to do picket duty on the far side. Another church down there was called Little Bethel.

Hill's earthworks zigzagged in lines east and west of the church grounds, with a redoubt facing the bridge to the south. Into this latter defense some artillerymen shoved howitzers. All day and all night of June 7 the labor went forward, relays of men plying the few spades, picks, and axes.

There was still no coffee for breakfast on the 8th, and the Enfield Blues munched hardtack—"ship biscuits," Billy Beavans called this fare. Some men smoothed earth on top of the finished works. Others, picked patrols wise at hunting and stalking, went southward among the trees to scout the Federals.[11]

Federals were there. Some men from the La Fayettes found blue-coats plundering a deserted country house. Up rolled a Virginia howitzer, with Lieutenant Colonel Lee in command, and routed the prowlers with a single shot. A second Federal party was sighted and pursued by the

Buncombe Rifles. Another howitzer, under Major Lane, dropped a shell among the fleeing Federals in sight of the Stars and Stripes waving over Hampton; and a prisoner was run down and brought in by the jubilant mountaineers from Buncombe County.

Back at the earthworks, curious Confederates surrounded this captive. He was described as "a stout, ugly fellow from Troy, N. Y." Questioned, he said that "he had nothing against the South, but somebody must be soldiers, and he thought he had as well enlist." [12]

However thrilling these events might be, rations continued short. "Nothing scarcely to eat!" mourned Billy Beavans to his journal. George Wills was momentarily elated at the arrival of coffee from Yorktown, but when he drew his ration he found that it was in the form of green berries. He parched it as best he could in a shovel, then pounded it between rocks, and boiled it. Others cooked bits of meat skewered on their ramrods, with indifferent success.

Men of several companies, pretending not to hear Hill's bleak edicts against foraging, stole out of the earthworks to look for food. Three of the Charlotte Grays caught a stray pig on the banks of the river, butchered it, and shared it with comrades. Louis Leon, though devoutly reared in the Jewish faith, partook with famished gratitude. Another soldier, trying to rob a beehive, was badly stung.[13]

On June 9, the Enfield Blues mounted guard over the ramparts, ill-fed and miserable. George Wills took his place without complaint save in his heart. The day of sentry duty along the defenses and among the huts and howitzers was sweltering and hungry.[14]

At three o'clock next morning, an excited bugle blew. The whole regiment woke and formed to march. Colonel Hill seemed to be planning a surprise advance. The column headed off across the bridge and down the tree-girt road in the dark, a mile, two miles, three. Then the muttered order to halt, turn, and march back.

The men heard that an old lady of the region had warned Hill that the enemy held the woods to the south in large numbers. The right-about had been executed within a few hundred yards of a strong Federal position.[15] Back at Big Bethel, Hill sent his men into the earthworks, swiftly placing them in battle order.

Two companies deployed outside the fortifications, D to the east and A in the woods just below the bridge to the south. The other companies occupied the breastworks.

The Enfield Blues lacked both captain and first lieutenant that morning.[16] Parker and Cary Whitaker, the junior officers, put their men in line behind the works west and north of the church. The gay Fayetteville Independents, stern-faced now, drew up at their left. Straight ahead of the position was swampy, close-grown forest, enough of it to mask a whole enemy corps. The works made an angle where the Blues stood, and at their right, to the north, a road ran through toward the church. A howitzer stood there, blocking the way, with a crew formed for action. Beyond the road and the gun waited Captain Hoke's Southern Stars; and a nervous glance leftward discovered more artillery facing south toward the tree-fringed river.[17]

The sun came up. Early excitement died down. Parker walked along his line. George Wills and Billy Beavans and the others gripped their muskets with a fine show of resolution. What breakfast could be secured was eaten without breaking ranks. The hour of nine came, with the cloudless sky already bright and hot, and dark blue figures emerged from the trees far to the south, with over their heads the bright flag of the Union.

An abrupt booming explosion—a Confederate howitzer had opened the battle. The shell burst among the advancing enemy infantrymen, throwing them into instant confusion. They scampered from view, back into the trees or behind two small houses. Muskets crackled, then more cannon spoke deeply. A shell dropped into the North Carolina camp, and another and another. The Confederacy's baptism of fire had begun.

Men flinched nervously here and there. Colonel Hill, staunch veteran of Mexican sieges and stricken fields, was able to joke from his position at the center of things. "Boys, you have learned to dodge already," he called out. "I am an old hand at it." Suiting action to word, he ducked away from a whizzing projectile, then shook an admonitory forefinger toward the woods where Federals lurked. "You dogs, you missed me that time!" he roared.

His words and bearing helped green troops to stand as the bombardment increased. The first battle of the war built its voice to a whole universe of deafening noise.

Artillery fire was augmented by volleys of musketry from the advance elements of the Federals. To one man the bombardment seemed "a perfect hail-storm of cannister shot, bullets and balls." Artillery horses were struck, thrashed around and screamed horribly, but not a soldier was hit.[18]

Sudden quiet fell after all this thunder. The Edgecombe Guards, skirmishing below the southern point of the works, apparently had repulsed the enemy there. A courier rushed orders to Captain Huske of the Independents, and the Blues saw this comforting adjacent force pulled from their left and hurried off to face a threat somewhere else. Then a mounted officer spurred along in front of the entrenchment.

"Who commands this company?" he shouted, and the Blues recognized the handsome spiked mustaches of Colonel Magruder.

"Second Lieutenant Parker," the senior officer identified himself, saluting.

"Lieutenant, deploy your men along this swamp as sharp-shooters," commanded Magruder, gesturing. "Protect them as well as you can and keep a sharp lookout to the front, as I expect an attack right in your front."

Parker must have scowled. To him, sharpshooters meant men with long-range rifles. "We are armed with smooth-bore muskets, sir," he protested.

Magruder swept this aside with a full-mouthed curse. "Your muskets are as good as any used," he snapped at the lieutenant. "Deploy your men, deploy your men."

Away he galloped again, and Parker obediently took the Blues over the breastworks and extended their line to cover the space previously held by the Independents. George Wills and his comrades stood at the ready, staring into the soggy woods. An attack right in their front, Colonel Magruder had predicted. The place seemed alive with overwhelming Union forces, creeping closer, closer. There was a tense silence, save for thumping hearts.

At last a voice spoke up. Private Jo Arrington, re-nowned as a company jokester, was uncharacteristically solemn as he addressed Lieutenant Parker. "Is it not a fitting time for a word of prayer?" he asked plaintively.

To Parker the suggestion sounded entirely reasonable. He looked toward the right of the line, where Jesse Page, Methodist minister, stood with musket ready cocked in the first section of the first platoon. At the lieutenant's word, Page agreed to address a God who, from His throne in heaven, surely looked with kindly partisanship upon the Confederate States of America.

Then someone else spoke. This was Oliver Pittman, who may have felt a double responsibility with his wor-shiping cousin Flavius at hand. "Lieutenant," he ven-tured, "would it not be well to watch as well as pray? I will do the watching."

Thus self-appointed, Pittman mounted the breastwork

and from that elevated spot stared into the trees while Jesse Page spoke impromptu a soldierly prayer that comforted his brothers-in-arms and was remembered for forty years afterward.

Oliver Pittman's survey of the dubious swampland discovered no hostile movements. The Blues held their position outside the works. Eleven o'clock came, and more bombardment from several directions, then yells from westward—a charge was being repulsed by the companies on the opposite side of the defenses. At the same time, firing broke out from the south. Bullets spattered the trees and the earthwork where the Blues stood.[19] Jimmy Whitehead, seventeen and nimble, ducked as adroitly as D. H. Hill himself when a ball whistled close to his ear. But nobody fell.

At the right of the Blues, where George Wills, the Beavanses, Jesse Page, and Sim Whitaker stood among the tall men, no threat showed. At the opposite end of the company line, men may have been able to see confusion and struggle to the south. The musketry rolled intermittently, with punctuating roars of cannon. The Edgecombe Guards had slid westward across the road and were driving enemy back from lodgment beyond the bridge.

A howitzer hurried along behind the breastwork where the Blues were deployed. Shortly afterward, its voice rang out to scold unwelcome visitors away. Then the gunfire ceased. It was one o'clock.

Orders came to relax and ground arms. The Enfield Blues were told that the battle had been won without their firing a shot.

They learned that no more than half the regiment had so much as pulled a trigger to drive back a superior force of Federals. But gratifying praise came to the Blues from Hill—had they not remained at their post, exposed to danger? Would not the slightest faltering anywhere have disrupted the steadfast defense of the works around Big Bethel Church? ". . . the constancy and discipline of the unengaged companies cannot be too highly commended," Hill was to write in his official report.[20]

The first battle was over, with the enemy in full flight. Soldiers wandered over the ground they had held victoriously. Almost at the foot of the eastward line of works lay the body of a Union officer, who had fallen dead at the head of his charging troops. The Independents had gone to that point from their earlier position beside the Blues, and Private Buhman of the Independents disputed with Private McIver of the Charlotte Grays the honor of having brought down this brave foeman. The marshy open ground farther to the west was dotted with bodies. Among these lay knapsacks and cartridge boxes thrown away by the retreating Unionists. Jubilation—Old Hawkeye Hill had said the truth, gentlemen! The Yankees had learned double quick all right.

Southward lay other dead men, in gay uniforms that identified them as belonging to Duryea's Zouave Regiment from New York. The Carolinians rummaged in the knapsacks they picked up, laughing over home letters from New York and Massachusetts that asked if the "Southern barbarians" had been whipped out.[21]

Around one fallen form gathered long-faced gazers.

Private Henry Lawson Wyatt of the Edgecombe Guards lay dying.[22] He and four others had volunteered to set fire to a house beyond which Zouave sharpshooters were lurking, and a bullet had crashed through his head. Solemnly his comrades gazed at his blood-spattered face, peaceful in unconsciousness, done forever with war. This was death in action, different from James Hudson taken by fever at Camp Ellis and Julius Sadler crushed under the cars outside Richmond. Seven others were wounded, not severely.

Not wholly static had been the battle contribution of the Blues.

With the shooting over, a group of men appeared from the southwest, approaching the works. Sergeant Lucien Whitaker, with five men, had been sent the night before to watch a ford on the river, and had been almost forgotten in the excitement. Now he returned, with his patrol intact. You could count the soldiers—six—no, seven. Who was that seventh man?

He wore a darker uniform than that of the Blues, and he trudged under careful guard, a Yankee prisoner. The ford-watchers had held their isolated position, listening to the racket of the battle, and had caught a lone straggler near the water. He had surrendered readily. Congratulations rang around Sergeant Lucien, who grinned handsomely.[23]

As the Blues exulted, they looked toward the north, where the head of a marching column appeared. It was a Louisiana regiment, arriving just too late for the battle. Men of the victorious garrison fraternized with these reinforcements, gleaning various opinions.

George Wills, the impeccable of dress, deplored the appearance of the Louisianans. "They are the worst looking men you ever saw in your live," he scribbled a description for the home folks, "they all had on leggings wore red pants, with about three times as much cloth in them as necessary, and a long red bag for a cap, they burnt black as mulattoes." Briefer and kinder was the impression of a Virginia cannoneer: "A Louisiana regiment arrived about one hour after the fight was over. They are a fine-looking set of fellows." [24]

The Zouaves and the First North Carolina were ordered to march back to lightly defended Yorktown. Cavalry bivouacked on the field bought with the blood of Henry Wyatt.

Colonel Hill was generous with praise as he wrote his battle report. Every company commander present came in for commendation. And he took time to speak prayerfully to his victorious men.[25]

The Blues felt exhausted as they reached Yorktown again, but their spirits rose when they found good food waiting at their quarters. George did grateful justice to Wash's cooking, though his shaky digestion was troubling him again. His supper had the savory sauce of triumph. He wrote a letter to sister Mary:[26]

> We gave them a worse whipping than a set of men generally get, Colonel Hill says "If we work pretty well for two or three days we will give them a worse one than before."

Yorktown, now that George had returned from winning a battle, was no longer a strange, dubious base of operations. And the successful enduring of fire gave him sober confidence:

> We are beginning to feel that this is are home and are very well satisfied. When you all hear that we have been in a fight, you needn't believe it one third of the time, and when you find out that it is so, you mustn't be pestered until you hear from us, and then I know, unless Mr. Page, myself, or some one of our near relations gets killed, you will not be pestered, for the God of battles is certainly on our side, and our success is certain.

In a postscript, he addressed fourteen-year-old brother Eddie:

> Give my respects to the boys about there, and tell them, I hope there is a draft in the state, that it will get some of them; and more particular, *John Welles* and *John Hammill*. Be sure and tell them I would give twenty five dollars apiece to hear that they have been drafted.

VI

SO IT IS WHEN ONE OF US DIES

Billy Beavans was less recognizable as Smiling Billy after the return from Big Bethel. As brave and alert as any who had held place in the line beyond the ramparts, he had nevertheless the wide-open eyes of sensitivity. More, perhaps, than with most of his comrades he felt his elation tempered with solemn thoughts. Possibly one girl's face began to shine more clearly than others in his dreams. Back in Yorktown, weary and meditative, he suddenly stopped keeping a day-to-day record of events. And again he resorted to verse, an effort limping but self-revealing:

War

Notice how the troops go
From one Camp to another
With Yankees troden below
As our forces rejoice together.

Oh how we ought to lament
Over the sufferings of our troops
Provided they would repent
And forever tell the truth.

Just think the young gents
They are now in their Camps
Cannot see their sweethearts
Unless they get a pass to come back.

But their stay will be so short
They cannot reveal their love
Unless they at first make a report
And then bid good bye and be gone.[1]

More troops arrived at Yorktown, including recruits to swell the ranks of the various North Carolina companies. William Whitaker was another of the great Enfield family to report. Young Jimmy Whitehead hailed two relatives— James A. and Robert Whitehead. But in the midst of the greetings the Long Roll beat and the regiment formed quickly, the recruits falling in with their unaccustomed weapons.

Again it was a false alarm, shrugged away by George Wills and other veterans of Big Bethel, but a grim adventure to the newcomers. Nor did tales of the fight reassure these raw arrivals.

"One ball passed in two inches of my head," Jimmy Whitehead told his cousins. "The balls fell like hail."

These things James A. Whitehead wrote home to his father, the Reverend Mr. Laurence Whitehead of Dawson Cross Roads, glancing up from his penciled scrawl to stare at the Union gunboat hovering in the broad estuary opposite the Yorktown landings.

> We boys will see hard times, James prophesied. I have already see some. Make your self well satisfied about me, for I am doing what is right for my country. I have learned more since I left home than I did in all the rest of my life. . . . I have seen more than my pour tongue can ever tell. Richmond is a site to see more than you can think. . . .

The recruits were not as well provided with home delicacies as the original rank and file. James A. Whitehead disliked the rye bread issued to him—"mity sorry stuff," he described it to his family, and wished for corn pone.[2] But George Wills and the Whitakers fraternized with him, and there were prayers in camp at night, to make homesick boys feel better.

Wednesday came, and another Long Roll. The Blues scampered from their quarters to form line in the hot sun. George, ready in place, tried to hear what the officers were growling about. Suddenly a shot slapped the air, like a palm striking bare flesh. Somebody cried out in pain.

Was the enemy upon them? Staring, George saw two men fall struggling to the ground. Private B. F. Britt twitched and lay still. John Cherry writhed to get up, clutching his arm as it streamed blood. Then someone sprang at Robert Whitehead and snatched away his smoking musket.

Robert was hurried off to the guardhouse. Britt died while his comrades watched with wide, miserable eyes. John Cherry's wound proved serious but not fatal.

Robert had gone crazy. That was what his cousin, James A. Whitehead, was able to tell the officers. Shocked by the first alarm as the recruits landed, the boy had fallen prey to illusions. When the drum was beaten again, he thought himself surrounded by Yankees, and he had opened fire in blind panic.

The people at home must be told. James Whitehead did his best, though his hand trembled as he wrote:

> I think he will get well when he gets home. I have just give in my evidence and it will clear him. I am sure they will not send him to jail they will send him home soon. he is very easy controled. it hurt me worse than anything I ever saw in my life.

George Wills was shaken, too, but already he was
the veteran as he described the shooting to Mary:

> I can tell you that never did I have a more dreadful feel-
> ing than at that time. . . . This of course cast a gloom all
> over our camp, but it is gradually passing off; so it is when
> one of us dies, the world keeps moving just as it did be-
> fore.[3]

These tragic confusions did not prevent Chaplain Yates
from preaching a sermon that day, and there was a review
of the Yorktown regiments by Colonel Magruder. The
commander paused before each regiment in turn, deliver-
ing an address.

"I thank you in the first place for coming here," he told
the First North Carolina in theatrically ringing tones,
"and in the second place I thank you for your industry
as well as your valor in the recent battle. You have
crowned your heads with honor which never can be
blotted out in the history of the world; and you deserve
great place, and you will and shall get it." [4]

More briefly and comfortably, Lieutenant Colonel Lee
assured his men: "This place can't be taken."

More preaching on Thursday, and one drill session.
Then another review.

It took up some three hours of the hot bright afternoon,
and ended with Colonel Magruder pausing in front of
the Louisiana Zouaves. The sunburnt soldiers stood at
attention in their fezzes and red bloomers while the
commanding officer resonantly scolded them for killing
cows on neighboring farms to supplement their dull and
scanty rations. To George Wills, also in ranks with his
bowels again in disorder, it seemed that Magruder had
marshaled the other regiments near at hand for safety's
sake. The Louisianans had brought across the country a

reputation for poor discipline; they might even mutiny if admonished.

The Louisianans, possibly awed by the presence of so many other armed troops at hand, took their tongue-lashing in glum silence. For all their exotic dress and swarthy faces, they looked like fighters. Decided George: "I think if we had had them with us the other day, the New York Zouaves would have fared a good deal worse than they did." [5]

He and his Whitaker kinsmen continued to show friendly attention to James A. Whitehead, who was hungrily writing home for cake. The veterans stiffened James' backbone by talk of bravery at Big Bethel.

"We expect a mitey battle here soon," James warned his folks. "And when you hear of it you will hear of the death of a great many men. We are well fixed for a battle and seem to dread it a very little indeed." [6]

Jesse Page went to Brinkleyville on leave, and George sent Wash with him on an errand.[7] George's mess had difficulties with its cooking, the more so because they lacked utensils. Sim Whitaker fell ill, and George's worsening indigestion was complicated by headaches.

The papers, in Richmond and at home, rang with praise for the victors at Big Bethel. Governor Ellis, critically ill, asked of his legislature that Colonel Hill be promoted to brigadier general, and Carolina soldiers at Yorktown read of the flattering jubilation at Raleigh. Billy Beavans could appreciate verses in the Raleigh *Standard:*

> On, on, brave hearts, your cause is just
> And right and justice must prevail.
> As soon might straws attempt to stay
> The torrent wild—the sweeping gale—

As hirelings of the North drive back
Men with such hands and hearts as yours;
Go meet the invaders at their camp,
Let not their feet defile our shores! [8]

Two new companies augmented the First North Carolina. Captain Jesse C. Jacocks' command from Bertie
County became Company L, and that of Captain J. K.
Marshall from Chowan, Company M. The Fifth North
Carolina, Colonel Robert M. McKinney commanding,
also joined the Yorktown garrison. Even the post-Bethel
recruits looked upon these latecomers as raw and untried. "The first Regiment of N. C. is honored very high,"
noted James A. Whitehead proudly.[9]

On July 2, Jesse Page and Wash returned. George
turned out to welcome his brother-in-law. The unofficial
chaplain of the Blues was in high humor, telling stories
of Halifax County neighbors with a prodigality of comic
gesture. With him came a recruit—John Hammill, to
whom George had sent mocking messages about slowness
to enter the service.

The news Wash told his master was pleasantly homely.
The horses on the Wills plantation looked well, the barn
was full of corn. However, anxiety for George oppressed
Mrs. Wills, perhaps because of George's increasingly
stormy romance with Miss Fannie. Wash, the privileged
servant, had talked too much at home of his master's
affairs. For this, George reproached Wash, but consider-
ately voted against any additions to the mess, lest his
retainer work too hard. From Brinkleyville had come
extra cooking pots.[10]

Additional shipments of food pleased the Blues at
Yorktown. James A. Whitehead received a jug of apple
brandy from an indulgent uncle, and shared it with his
tent mates.

We have to get up soon in the morning and a little dram will help us, [he rationalized in a home letter]. We cant get a drop here. and I am glad of it too, for some would get drunk sure if they could get it. And I don't believe in that though I think a dram will help us here som in the morning . . . if a dram ever did a man any good it will here, for we have mity bad colds here indeed the air is changeable." [11]

July 21 brought reports of a battle fought on the other side of Virginia, at a place called Manassas Junction. An overwhelming Yankee invasion checked and routed, thousands of prisoners and mountains of stores taken—this, decided George, was "a grand affair," and he felt sure that "if they get one more good pop, Johns[t]on one and us one, that they [the Federals] would talk a little different from what they do now."

If this inland victory dwarfed the action at Big Bethel, the Blues comforted themselves with the expectation of more warlike excitement. "Gen. Hill thinks it won't be very long before we have an attack here, or at least he says it is bound to be some time," wrote George to his sister. He asked his mother to sew him a new pair of pants, and sent his love to all, as usual.[12]

He had reason for good morale and self-congratulation, though his home letters did not boast of what had happened. Some of the non-commissioned officers had been dismissed from the service, and new promotions included corporalcies for Sim Whitaker and George.[13] Two stripes on the sleeve, an increase in pay from $11.00 to $13.00 a month—a man could be forgiven for strutting a little.

The Federals were not bothersome, despite Hill's prediction. Many blue foragers and scouts had been captured by Confederate pickets, and the main body chose to stay close to its Hampton fortifications. But a sterner and stealthier foe was at hand.

Sickness broke out, perhaps because of the alternation of cool nights and hot noondays. The Enfield Blues saw half of their number in hospital beds by the end of July. In three days, July 26, 27, and 28, four of the Blues died.[14] And on August 3, George collapsed with a violent fit of shuddering fever.

His uncle Cary put him to bed in a cool tent, released Wash from mess duty to tend him, and wrote home to Brinkleyville.[15] The lieutenant soberly feared that his nephew might die, but by August 6 doses of quinine had partially subdued the fever and George was more comfortable, though weak.

The Reverend Mr. Wills hurried to Richmond by train and thence, by sailboat, to Yorktown. He found his son still abed and troubled by a racking cough. Jesse Page, too, was ill and in a hospital nine miles west of Yorktown. The sensible Mr. Wills was shocked at conditions in the camp.

"I have not time to detail many particulars," he wrote between visits to his son's bed and to the beds of others, "but say in a few words that much of the sickness might be avoided with proper sanitary regulations. First, there is great want of attention in Camp, and second, the men themselves are very imprudent."

Dr. Hines, the sole medical officer of the regiment, was swamped with his duties, and several private soldiers with partial medical training were helpful but lacked experience. On August 9, young James A. Whitehead died, the gorgeous experience of war at an end for him. On the following day, while Mr. Wills read the burial service over this young soldier's grave, eight other deaths occurred in the regiment. All this news the minister sent home by his friend, schoolmaster John Beavans, who also had been visiting the Blues.[16]

George fought free of his chills and fever but continued

weak, and his friends found refuge and care for him in the nearby home of a Dr. Coulling, a kindly Baptist preacher who was also a physician. There George convalesced, while his father returned to Brinkleyville; but the young corporal fretted at rumors of a coming battle. "I want to be there," he insisted to his mother, "if there is a fight over there I don't care about being absent." [17]

He was able to rejoin his regiment on September 4, and found that it had shifted Camp to Ship's Point, at the mouth of the Poquoson River some eight miles eastward. Colonel Hill had left to assume his duties as a brigadier, and Charles Lee and James Lane advanced one grade in rank to be colonel and lieutenant colonel respectively. Robert F. Hoke, who had been an energetic lieutenant of the Southern Stars, was now major. The new campground seemed healthy, and many of the men enjoyed the plentiful fresh fish.[18]

Greeted by his uncles and his cousins of various degrees of removal, George found that his worry over missing possible battle had been unnecessary. There would be war enough for everyone. On the day after Manassas, the Federal government had called for five hundred thousand volunteers, and all during August, Union armies had fought Confederates in Mississippi and Kentucky. Stubbornly the Yankees pocketed earlier losses and began to learn how to win. On August 29, a Federal fleet with troop-laden transports had overwhelmed Fort Hatteras on North Carolina's Outer Banks and seized Hatteras Inlet as a deploying point to the mainland beyond.

Meanwhile, the camp of the Bethel Regiment at Ship's Point was only temporary. On September 5 the commanders ordered another move, six miles inland to tiny Cocklestown between Yorktown and Big Bethel. Again supplies were short—"it was near like our Bethel fare," grumbled George of supper and breakfast—but the tents were pitched under the shade of beautiful trees. The new camp was named Camp Fayetteville, and on September 9 the regiment was marshaled for a review and a ceremony.

The ladies of Fayetteville, naturally vain of the First North Carolina's two companies from that town, had made a handsome battle flag for the regiment. By act of the state legislature, this banner bore the proud legend, "Bethel," and it had been brought to Virginia by an eloquent young spark named John W. Baker.

His speech had been written out beforehand, and was subsequently published in the columns of his home-town newspaper, but he never delivered it before the troops at Camp Fayetteville. Just before review time, Mr. Baker had been made welcome to what some called "Old Virginny Tangle-leg," and so copiously did he partake that he could scarce stand and speak. George Wills, at attention in ranks, had difficulty in stifling his merriment. He described the occasion to Sister Lucy:

> . . . tho he said he was here to represent the ladies of that place [Fayetteville], yet he did it very poorly. We thought when he was speaking, that he looked like he was tight. . . . Reading his speach, which he had written off, he spoke a good long piece over twice, then when he was through sit down and cried about it, this was some, wasn't it?

More abstemious, or better able to hold his Virginny Tangle-leg, young Adjutant Poteat rose in turn, his remarks having been written out for him by Colonel Lee.

". . . Something, perhaps, the regiment has done," Poteat wound up. "More, if the opportunity occurs, it will gladly do, to justify, if possible, the estimation which this gift evinces. The fair donors may rest assured that the regiment will return with the flag to North Carolina, if the regiment itself returns." [19]

At about the same time, elections were held for new officers of the Blues. Captain Bell had returned home and sent in his resignation. The men in the ranks assembled to mark their ballots.

Results were surprising to many, and distasteful to some. Second Lieutenant Parker, who had commanded under the hail of bullets at Big Bethel, was elected captain over Montgomery Whitaker, and ambitious Sergeant C. B. Corbitt became senior second lieutenant over the head of Cary Whitaker.

The amusement of George Wills at the liquor-muddled flag presentation turned to fury. "I think it a shame for men to do as our company has done . . ." he wrote home. "This is ridiculous, it was a foul play all the way by two or three in the company, who wanted promotion themselves."

But more than two or three had cast their votes for Parker and Corbitt. Both the defeated Whitakers contemplated resignation, but cooler-headed friends persuaded them to remain at their old ranks.[20]

George was disgusted, too, with beef on the daily ration.[21] He hoarded his dwindling supply of home-cured bacon, bought fish, and swore to eat dry bread before he touched beef. His messmate Johnny Beavans was less choosy, and had gained seven pounds. But dissatisfaction with company officers and food may have combined to make George stern on the day when a letter arrived from Miss Fannie.

"Overbearing" was George's word for his sweetheart's tone. He was a veteran now, not to be treated like that. He wrote her a sharp reply, bringing to an end the romance his family had never approved. Resolutely he turned his thoughts to the war and his part in it; off the North Carolina coast, a Federal fleet had swooped down and taken Fort Hatteras, and the officers who surrendered

were called traitors at Camp Fayetteville, where a fight
was still looked for. ". . . we poor fellows will have to
continue to work and fight hard, to keep up the name of
our state," decided George, and turned his thoughts to
getting a commission in the army.[22]

But again he was sick, with what the doctors called
pneumonia. As before, his father hurried to care for him.
The doctor prescribed opium, and by October 1, George
was eating well and wishing he was at home.[23]

Home was not far away in time. The First North Caro-
lina had enlisted for six months, dating from May 13.
Many officers were gone already. Lieutenant Colonel Lee
departed to command the Twenty-eighth North Carolina
Regiment. Captain Bridgers, who had led the Edgecombe
Guards to glory at Big Bethel, transferred to the heavy
artillery, and Captain Williams, of the Hornet's Nest
Rifles, was appointed produce loan agent for North Caro-
lina. The new captain of the Blues, Francis Marion
Parker, resigned on October 16 to become colonel of the
Thirtieth North Carolina. The men voted once more.
Montgomery Whitaker succeeded to the captaincy, while
Cary Whitaker leapfrogged his rival Corbitt to become
first lieutenant.[24]

Consternation attended an official pronouncement from
Raleigh. New musters of the North Carolina troops were
being designated as state regiments, numbered First, Second, Third and so on. The old names of the six-months'
volunteer regiments were changed, and the First North
Carolina heard that it would be called the Nineteenth.

Burningly eloquent was the protest launched at a meeting of the officers, in form of a resolution addressed to
North Carolina's officialdom:

> . . . *Resolved,* that having been the *first* regiment from
> North Carolina to enter the State of Virginia; the first regi-
> ment from any state to meet and repulse the invader; the

first regiment to receive the approbation of our countrymen by resolutions of their national and State councils;
that having been intrusted by the people of North Carolina with a flag upon whose folds is inscribed "The First
Regiment of North Carolina" by the hands of our coun-
try-women . . . we are not willing to surrender our name
to minister to the caprice of any one, or to subserve the
convenience of a few office clerks, and that we will never
submit to such an imposition until we have exhausted
every means of redress consistent with our efficiency and
character.[25]

This was a dying appeal. On November 8, the regiment
was reviewed by John B. Magruder, now a major general.
He bade them farewell with his habitual fiery eloquence.
That afternoon, six companies embarked for Richmond.

On the following day, a Saturday, the rest of the companies packed their equipment under cloudy skies and
marched off just before noon. By dark they reached the
steamboat landing. Rain began to fall. The Enfield Blues
found shelter in a tremendous haymow. Sunday's dawn
was cold and stormy as they boarded the steamer *North
Hampton*. They disembarked at Richmond at six o'clock
that evening, ate supper in town, and went into camp.

Close to discharge, men of the resolutely disciplined
Bethel Regiment sneaked through the line of sentinels all
the next day. A few waited until evening and secured
formal permission. Corporal George Wills had relaxed
his bleakness toward Lieutenant Corbitt—after all, they
were neighbors. They made up a theater party with Billy
and Johnny Beavans and Dick Hunter. Next morning, the
Blues drew guard duty.

The other companies began to leave. Home to Charlotte went the Hornet's Nest Rifles. The Buncombe Rifles
set their faces southwest for Asheville, carrying with them
the flag that had flown over the victorious regiment at

Big Bethel. The Burke Rifles went part way with them. The Southern Stars took their discharges. Those left behind felt restless, and several soldiers were drunk in camp. Billy Beavans, on sentry go, recorded a "lovely time" in his diary.

Next day, November 13, four more companies left, the Charlotte Grays, the Orange Light Infantry, the La Fayettes, and the Independents. The guard was relieved, with none to replace it. George Wills and the Beavanses idled that day and dined sumptuously at the Exchange Hotel in Richmond. At night they attended a concert.

Beautiful weather saluted the dawn of November 14, when the last four companies were mustered out. At two o'clock the Blues boarded a train for Petersburg and through, toward Weldon and home. The rising sun of the 15th showed them the welcome roofs of their town.

Back at Centerville Plantation, Billy and Johnny Beavans flung off their uniforms and put on old clothes. But, after visiting town again on the day following, Billy decided: ". . . it is very lonesome at home." [26]

George had reached Brinkleyville by then. Undoubtedly he showed no lonesomeness for his comrades in arms, or for Miss Fannie. He had a fine gift of restraint for so young a man.

VII

WOUND UP IN LOVE AS BY A CLOAK

If a sense of peace sweetened the autumn air of Halifax County, that sense was absent elsewhere. Young George B. McClellan, with splendidly organized and equipped Federal troops, had maneuvered Robert E. Lee out of the mountains of western Virginia, had cut all that part of the state from the Confederacy. Missouri, too, had fallen to the Union; its fugitive legislature, at Neosho, had voted on October 31 for a secession hard to implement in St. Louis, St. Joseph, and Cape Girardeau. Lines of blue, bristling with gun muzzles, tightened around the Confederacy from Chesapeake Bay to the Ozarks. Faintly but unmistakably the echo of shots sounded all the way to Enfield.

Uneasiness affected veterans who had seen the color of their enemies' backs at Big Bethel, and they could not be satisfied with fox-hunting and choir-singing at home.

Cary Whitaker did not resume his law practice. He headed for Raleigh, where Governor Clark promised him a captain's commission upon the raising of a new volunteer company.[1] Sim, who had been plagued by boils at Yorktown and Camp Fayetteville, oversaw the late au-

tumn work at Strawberry Hill Plantation. George luxuri-
ated in the home cooking at Brinkleyville, shrugged away
memories of Miss Fannie, and on November 22 ambled
over to Enfield to visit his Beavans kinsmen. There were
soldierly reminiscences, dinners with various aunts and
cousins, and calls on bright-eyed young ladies.[2]

Smiling Billy smiled again, on this pretty Enfield girl
and that. Johnny was gladdest, naturally, to see Miss
Laura Gunter. George, too, began to admire someone
named Miss Della. These victors of Bethel were readily
welcome everywhere and were stubbornly, if bucolically,
gallant.

Romance was formidable with protocol that November.
The young heroes had forsaken dingy uniforms for broad-
cloth coats, patterned vests, and flaring cravats to their
heavily starched white collars. Coquettishly admitted to
dim front parlors, they stammered elaborate compliments
and sat pawing through albums and lushly bound volumes
of poetry and essays. A sort of ecstatic misery dominated
such occasions, and Billy was inspired to verse that, in its
first line anyway, had a touch of distinction:

> Wound up in love, as by a cloak,
> And with hoarseness, fit to choak,
> Then he, she is trying hard to tease
> And she, he is so anxious to please.
> When alone with his love, he thinks and looks,
> Endeavoring to speak but he takes the books
> Turning over page after page, without relief,
> Look as if he was possessed of grief;
> But if he can once the subject break
> He can rip ahead at a rapid rate;
> Soon he will make her say yes or no
> At least before he takes his hat to go.[3]

Billy's own tender moments were hardly so awkward.
For Enfield, he was something of an intellectual, and was

reckoned a polished cavalier into the bargain. He felt more and more drawn to one in particular of his wide acquaintance among the ladies. Again he did well with a first line:

> Upon the verge of time I stand
> With my mind wandering from place to place
> And affectionately squeezing your hand
> With my eyes gazing in your face.
>
> I would soon feel as if I had forgot
> Every thing both of trouble and pleasure
> But of thee and the very spot
> When last I saw you and your treasure.[4]

It snowed on December 2, but not enough to keep hardy veterans at home. On the next day George Wills went with the Beavanses to take dinner at Strawberry Hill with Sim Whitaker. Uncle Sim, whose aspect was sometimes plain and practical, could exert something of quiet charm, rather like a more mature George Wills. He had plenty of company that snowy Tuesday. ". . . quite a crowd there at dinner for an old batchelor," applauded Billy's journal.[5]

The mild Carolina winter set in. On December 11, warm but with a hint of rain in the gray air, discharged members of the Blues attended the funeral of their comrade Dick Hunter, firing a military salute over his grave. Johnny Beavans was staying close to Enfield those days, seeing much of his cherished Miss Laura. Billy went to Hamilton for a stay, then to repay George's visit by a sojourn at the Wills plantation at Brinkleyville. On December 19 the two young veterans were entertained at a Brinkleyville boardinghouse, and probably Billy took an active part in the tableau staged there.

Christmas was happy, hospitable. Despite the war going on just beyond horizons to east, north, and west, there was plenty of everything country folk enjoyed. After the holiday, George again came to Enfield, bringing his sister Mary. They called on Whitaker relatives and stayed at Centerville. There were parties and dancing. Sweet, very sweet, was the sound of the violin, and in Enfield, at least, there was no war whoop. But young voices raised the choruses to stirring new songs—"My Maryland," "Bombardment of Fort Sumter," and "Yankee Retreat at Manassas." [6]

December 31 saw the sun rise and the air bright and mild. George and Billy took breakfast together, then rode over to Strawberry Hill for noon dinner with Sim Whitaker. There was an afternoon call at the home of another hospitable relative. The supper table at Centerville was graced by the presence of Miss Lizzie Addington. At night the three young men—George, Billy, and Johnny—headed for a party at the plantation manor of John R. Branch. Their ladies were there, too, to help watch the old year out.

But the last midnight of 1861 struck its chimes amid embarrassing tenseness in the Branch parlor. Something had happened. Both Johnny and George sulked—they "got bluffed out," as Billy phrased it—and fell heavily, scowlingly silent. Not, however, completely so. Each of them took occasion to quarrel with his lady.

Billy had no such unpleasant interludes. On the next day he resorted to his journal, good-humored as usual. The last space for entry was filled, but he found an empty page and dated it "Jan. 1, 1862," in pencil. Under this he made a note concerning what he felt was momentous history, worthy of inclusion in the same volume with brief notes concerning secession and Big Bethel:

> On the 31st Day of December 1861: Miss Laura Gunter and Brother fell out, and Miss Della and George Wills

came to the conclusion that they had better not stay in each others company any more!

George and Mary returned to Brinkleyville immediately after breakfast. There was a hint of coolness between George and Billy, possibly stemming from whatever happened at John Branch's party. Billy found more space on the page next his New Year's Day entry, for the jotting down of gravely considered resolutions for 1862:

Always keep sober;
Always treat everybody aright;
Always be kind;
Be good and quiet;
Be firm and sober;
Live like a gentleman;
Live with and around the young ladies without making too much of them;

And a final observation, no doubt with a wry cousinly snicker above the moving pencil:

G. W. Wills will henceforth and forever know how to conduct himself in ladies' society. That is better than he has previously! [7]

These quarrels of young lovers must have impelled George and Johnny to turn their eyes from home toward camps where soldiers mobilized and drilled.

After all, a young man in civilian clothes was not too happy around Enfield by the turn of the year. Old friends were going back into uniform. The Halifax Light Infantry was now a company of the Twelfth North Carolina Regiment, and the Halifax Mounted Rifles had joined the Third North Carolina Cavalry. Lucien Whitaker had become a lieutenant in the Twenty-fourth North Carolina. There would be bloody work for all these troops, for if matters seemed quiet in Virginia, the Confederate fortifications on Roanoke Island were under siege and, in Tennessee, Union gunboats closed in on Fort Henry. Cary Whitaker sought enlistments for his new company, and his young kinsmen listened to him.

Billy Beavans had lost his smile again in January, as sense of duty prodded him back toward the army. On January 23 he wrote to a young lady on whom he had called several times:

> After I returned last night it was some time before I could go to sleep; I have thought a great deal of this war with its hardships & cruelties but never so much as I did last night. It makes me sad to think that now when I could or ought to have a great deal of pleasure it is broken up by this horrible war; but I sincerely hope the time soon comes when we can have peace on our once glorious and prosperous land, when there will be some prospect of a young man taking care of his bride if he should be so fortunate as to get one;
>
> So I hope you will have a glorious time no matter where you are or what is the state of our country.
>
> Write soon to your very affectionate friend
>
> William Beavans[8]

This may have sounded to the lady very much like a declaration of intent to marry her. But Saint Valentine's Day, which may well have found both George and Johnny Byronically unresponsive, saw Billy Beavans enchanting another belle, Miss Priscilla Macon, with an acrostic verse:

> Perhaps you would like to hear from me
> Rise and endeavour to see
> If it is composed and penned by one
> So you are not outdone.
> Can I truly & sincerely say
> In this without any delay,
> Lo, with feelings of my heart

Lest we should soon depart
As my heart is ever beating
My love, your name ever repeating
At the beginning of each line dwell,
Continue until you find what it will spell.
Oh, yes, by that you can find
Now the subject of my Valentine.

Lest we should soon depart. . . . Billy, too, heard bugles sounding afar. For Miss Priscilla or for another girl, he wrote a scrap of rhyme, with something grim to it:

Soon to the war I expect to go
To help drive back the invading foe,
To join my comrades in the field,
Using the ball and cold steel
Whether it shall be that I on the battle field **fell**
Or survived, time only will tell.
Sickness may take me away
Let my soul no longer in this world stay

But no matter at what time,
You will be fresh in my mind.[9]

Awareness of danger and possible death could not keep him at home. Restlessly he wrote one more entry in the old diary:

Tuesday, March 5th, 1862: Very dull about old Enfield at this time; nothing wanting nothing doing.[10]

Billy's haversack may have been packed even as he wrote those words, and George's as well. Johnny Beavans composed his differences with Miss Laura, and tarried at home; but George, still acidly defiant toward the ladies who had displeased him, looked with Billy toward Camp Mangum, west of Raleigh, where Cary Whitaker gathered his recruits.

On March 17 they boarded the southbound train at

Enfield. From far places in the Confederacy, news of fighting tingled their ears. At Hampton Roads off Old Point Comfort, the ironclads *Virginia* and *Monitor* had fought to a jangling draw that revolutionized sea warfare forever. John H. Morgan's raiding cavalry had jabbed into the outskirts of Federal-held Nashville and had fallen back under a stubborn counter-assault. At Pea Ridge in Arkansas, a Confederate army had suffered a stinging defeat, and there was much less confidence in moves to recapture Missouri. And on March 14, New Bern on the North Carolina mainland had fallen.

Billy Beavans, dressed for his journey in a well-cut civilian suit, looked considerably more than twenty-two years old with his thick, carefully trimmed beard. George had whiskers of a sort, too, possibly grown in imitation of Billy's manly equipment. They thickened properly only on his jaws, and straggled feebly around his mouth. But he had saved a uniform from Yorktown days, and put it on, though it was tighter than it had been a year ago. Wash remained at Brinkleyville, to follow when his young master sent word.

As before, they stopped between trains in Goldsboro. Soldiers swarmed plentifully there, and George and Billy knew many of these. Hotels proved to be crowded, and Billy and George could secure only a dingy room, but they had a happy time with friends in uniform. They visited a photographer, and felt disappointed at the daguerreotypes he took, but paid for two sets. The next day, they went on to Raleigh, diverted themselves with a stroll through the town, then headed three miles west to Camp Mangum.

Captain Cary was there, and quartered his kinsmen in a log house—"very well for a soldier," declared Billy. Billy worried about his young brother, Absolum, sick at home, but was encouraged to learn that there were but two dress parades a day, morning and evening. Army doctors scowled over the condition of some recruits. Noting this, Cary Whitaker pointed Billy out to the examiners. "I'll take him, anyway," announced the captain definitely.

Passed by the medical examiners, the two newcomers drew their uniforms. There had been no such wealth of equipment at Camp Ellis or at Yorktown. Supply clerks gave each of them a dress uniform, a suit of fatigues, an overcoat, two shirts, two pairs of drawers, and two pairs of shoes. Then Billy and George reported to their company.[11]

Cary Whitaker's recruits were assembling slowly. Uncle Sim, George heard, was coming soon. Jimmy Whitehead, safe by two inches from death at Big Bethel, was at Camp Mangum. So were others of the Enfield Blues—James Etheridge, James B. Taylor, John Williams. But the bulk of the organization was made up of new men, not of the elite quality of the Blues. Some of them signed the muster roll with a cross.

Short of men enough for a full company, Cary Whitaker joined forces with Thomas A. Baker, who had been a young sergeant of the Independents at Yorktown and who now was ambitious for commissioned rank. Baker brought Cumberland County recruits, including another old Independent. This was Charlie Broadfoot, a nineteen-year-old like George. He had left the state university to go to war, and he became a friend of the Whitaker-Wills-Beavans group.

On the day that George and Billy were enrolled, the company elected officers.

Cary Whitaker was captain, of course, and Baker became first lieutenant. Sim, though still absent, was chosen second lieutenant. Of the four sergeants appointed by Captain Whitaker, the newly arrived Billy and George ranked at the top as orderly sergeant and second sergeant respectively.[12] William T. Gray and John Slaughter were third and fourth. All of these ranked from March 12, 1862.[13]

Sitting down to write to Maggie before he made out his company roll, Billy told of the adventures at Goldsboro and Raleigh, and said that he was sending the daguerreotypes:

> . . . The pictures we had taken were very poor, that is they did not look as well as we do, but we concluded that we had better send them. . . . Sis, I am getting on very well and as satisfied as could be expected of one [who has] just left his near relations and especially a poor sick brother. . . . I hope Mother is not much pestered about my leaving for I hate leaving bad enough any how; I hope she will become reconciled, for it is my duty to go to war, and do the best I can.

His spirits rose as he described the issue of plentiful new equipment:

> . . . Tell brother I have got more clothes than I know what to do with. . . . I tell you our men are rich one time.

As for George, he sent sister Lucy a copy of the picture of himself, though he, too, felt that it looked "hard," and that he might have done better sitting for a Raleigh photographer. He knew deeply lonesome yearning for his home, and for the absent Wash.[14] On March 20 he wrote to Lucy:

> As we are not yet formed into a Regmt, and are not in active service, it hardly seams that I am in camp, but suppose I am, at any rate am somewhere besides home. . . . What a place this is, tho it is a right nice place, and all this, yet there is no chance of hearing any news, for when the

news reaches us it is old, very old, and you know I love to hear news as well as anyone.

Election of officers stirred his ambition again:

> I expect to go to Raleigh to morrow, and have a notion of going to see the Gov. and see if he can't get me as adjt to the next Regm't, I have not mentioned it to anyone tho, and don't think I will do it. There is only one reason why I am anxious to be an officer, that is, these officers have so much privilege, and another thing I see so many who hold office, that I know are not as competent as myself.

The Eleventh North Carolina was organized, with many old Bethels as officers, and it acquired the flag marked "Bethel," over which drunken tears had flowed.[15] Shortly afterward, on the 24th, Cary Whitaker's men were mustered, as Company D, into the Forty-third North Carolina Regiment.

Junius Daniel, a Halifax County man and a West Point graduate, was chosen colonel, and Cary Whitaker was sent to call upon him with the news. Captain Thomas Kenan, a handsome point-bearded officer whose Duplin Rifles had been at Camp Ellis in 1861 and were now Company A of the Forty-third, was lieutenant colonel. Captain Walter Boggan of Company H from Anson County became major. Some remembered Boggan as second lieutenant of the Anson Guards at Raleigh in 1861, when his men swarmed out to frighten off a provost guard from arresting Boggan for drunkenness. Boggan had resigned shortly after that, but now he was back in service, with field rank.[16]

Wash came to Camp Mangum in early April, laden with supplies for Sergeant George Wills. These were cooking utensils; food such as George liked to eat; and razor, razor strop and brush—for George had given up the cultivation of a warrior beard such as was worn by his uncles and Billy Beavans. George exulted over Wash's biscuits, while Wash, certain of his privilege, grumbled aloud because Billy Beavans ranked above his master.

George, who at Yorktown had been a corporal while Billy had remained a private, may have felt pique himself, but he stifled it. "I am going to do my duty as I now stand," he vowed to Lucy, "and am also going to make myself *competent, by hard study* to make myself fill a *much* higher office than the one I now hold, and I have no doubt but that before the war ends (if I shall live to see it) I will have an appointment both to my taste and ability." [17] He expressed sergeantly suspicion of men who reported themselves sick. He himself made light of a cold, and asked that his mother make him drawers of a finer cloth than those he had been issued. As for Miss Fannie and Miss Della, he chose not to mention them. ". . . regards to the neighbors and *ladies* of my acquaintance generally."

On April 23, Company D bethought itself that it lacked a junior second lieutenant, and held an election accordingly. Out of thirty-eight votes cast, Billy Beavans got twenty-four. George, popular with the men, had been asked to run, but had refused to do so. He told Lucy why:

> I did not think it right for one friend to contend against another. . . . But you need not be too proud of your brother when he tells you, that not only could he have gotten the 3rd lieutenancy if he had let his name be run, but could have gotten the first Lieut. if it should be left to the vote of the company; and that too with some reason (I don't mean to say that our Lieut. are not competent, for I think they are certainly competent) but that I also (with the say so of our Capt, and some of the other most competent judges in camp) am competent (*except my age*) of holding even a higher position. . . . it is only to you and

the rest of the family, tho, I feel very proud to say this indeed, I would like very much to be an officer, but don't intend to make myself silly over it at all. . . . every dog, it
is said, has his day, so maybe I will have mine one of these.
. . . I have learned to be satisfied anywhere and with anything.[18]

But he wrote with considerable assurance, for there had
been salve for whatever hurt his pride felt. Cary Whitaker
promoted him to orderly sergeant, vice Billy Beavans
commissioned second lieutenant, which was a considerable
triumph for a boy not yet twenty years old.[19] From another
quarter came a different sort of vindication.

Miss Fannie, the capricious, had changed her tune. She
lived in Raleigh now, within a few miles of Camp Mangum. Icily, George declined to call upon her, even though
Uncle Sim urged him to do so. Thus ignored, Miss Fannie
wrote pleadingly to Maggie Beavans, sister of Billy and
Johnny and fond of George. Maggie, as intermediary,
appealed to the disdainful ex-suiter. His former sweetheart, said Maggie's letter, was contrite and humble, and
would like for George to take back the daguerreotype
he once had carried to Big Bethel and which he had
dramatically returned the previous autumn. Wise in coquetry, Miss Fannie might well depend on that portrait
to plead for her; it showed a lovely slender girl, blue-
eyed and fair-haired, such a princess as knights might
serve by fighting ogres and dragons.

But she was not dealing now with an awkward, unso-
phisticated country boy. Orderly Sergeant George Wills,
Company D, Forty-third North Carolina Regiment, had
traveled far and had seen much. He drew twenty Confederate dollars as his monthly pay. He had smelled powder
and had heard bullets whistle. Enemies had run before him
in the field. A company of soldiers obeyed his commands
and looked to him for instruction and administration.

Superior officers assured him that he could, and probably would, gain further promotion. And now Miss Fannie wanted to act as if nothing had happened between them. . . . Back to Cousin Maggie he returned a savagely mocking message, dashed down in a bold hand:

> You can say to Miss Fannie when you write to her, that I am much obliged to her for wanting me to keep the type, but that it pleased me to send it to her more than I could have been pleased otherwise. . . . You can also say to her, it suited me in another way, for since I became acquainted with this life I have become disgusted with the things that used to please me, that is, giving and receiving types from young ladies (I don't mean my relatives) running on so much foolishness with them, etc. Ha! ha! I want you to tell her all this, and then as much more in that style as you think I could put forth, for really they are my sentiments do you believe it? . . . for I have made the conclusion never to get married and I think it a wise conclusion, that these things you call wives are troublesome *critters,* ha! ha! but it is so.[20]

His written laughter echoed harshly, but not exactly merrily. He had been hurt, and he had hurt Miss Fannie in turn. She had no more power over him.

I have made the conclusion never to get married. . . . As a soldier in 1862, other matters preoccupied him.

For, at Yorktown on the Peninsula, McClellan was hammering the Confederate defenses to pieces. Shiloh had been fought and lost, in bloody desperation, early in April. On the 25th of the month, Fort Macon on the North Carolina coast had been gobbled by Federals. The siege of Corinth in Mississippi had begun on the 28th. And young men like George Wills were dying everywhere.

VIII

I NEVER BEFORE KNEW WHAT
SOLDIERING WAS

Captain Cary Whitaker began and flourished as a good company commander. His first thought was for Company D instead of for his popularity at regimental head-quarters.[1] Affectionately disposed, as ever, toward close relatives, nevertheless he was wise enough to refrain from showing them partiality. George had brief hopes of becoming regimental adjutant, but his uncle exerted no special influence on George's behalf. The post went to Sergeant Drury Lacy of Company B.[2]

Junius Daniel, having already accepted command of the Forty-fifth Regiment, declined with thanks the offer of the Forty-third. Lieutenant Colonel Kenan was chosen in his stead, and some disliked the possibility that Major Boggan would receive a like promotion. George, himself developing into a competent drillmaster, was grimly amused at Boggan's military clumsiness.[3]

"Well such a Major as we have," he wrote home. ". . . it is amusing to those who know better (tho, a great many of our *officers* don't know any better) to hear him drill a battalion, such commands, ha! ha!"[4]

But a majority of the line officers decided not to

advance Boggan. William Gaston Lewis, major of the Thirty-third Regiment, was invited to transfer as the new lieutenant colonel. Lewis had been a second lieutenant of the Edgecombe Guards at Big Bethel, and was known and respected by the Halifax men.[5]

Sim Whitaker returned from a visit to Enfield, bringing recruits. Among them was Johnny Beavans, to whom George had sent urgent messages; George was less familiar than before with the newly commissioned Billy, and wanted his chum.[6] Another reason for Johnny's enlistment was the draft decreed by the Confederate government that April, with all able-bodied males between eighteen and thirty-five liable to call. Volunteers were allowed to choose their own regiments. Lieutenant Billy Beavans gave creaky-rhymed notice to the new law:

> *The Draft*
>
> This thing you call a draft
> Is apt to make those Laugh,
> Who are exempt from Military duty
> Whether they be ugly or a beauty—
> But those who have to grab
> Are apt to feel very bad.
> When they reach over in the hat,
> Whether they draw a prize or blank,
> They look as if they had no life
> When they hear the sound of drum & fife.
> They think it is life or death,
> And then they draw a long breath.
> But when they draw a blank
> They are ready to play a prank
> At their own expense
> Or [on] the person [of] some one else.[7]

Maggie Beavans had written George another gently chiding message about the tearfully disconsolate Miss Fannie. Jack Whitaker, an eighteen-year-old cousin, also

touched on the subject in a letter. George was still savage
as he answered Cousin Maggie:

> You and Jack are just alike both after me about talking
> about sweethearts, well I have assured Jack, that I will not
> write to him again about them and now I will tell you the
> same, for since then I have become so *disgusted* with them
> generally, what do you think of that? [8]

The regiment entrained for Camp Holmes in eastern
North Carolina, as part of a mobilization against Federals
holding New Bern and the adjacent coast. Company D
pitched tents on sandy soil a few miles east of the
blockade-runners' lair at Wilmington. To some recruits,
the position looked vulnerable to attack. George remembered holding Big Bethel against outnumbering Yankees,
and snickered at such nervousness.[9]

Colonel Kenan exerted himself to secure arms for his
regiment. Muskets arrived in driblets, and he doled them
out to the companies. By May 9, Company D had forty-
four stand of arms, mostly Enfields with raised sights.[10]
There was constant drill, as at Camp Ellis and at Yorktown. Cary Whitaker's men wearied of it.[11] They longed
to be in Virginia where, if one could believe the papers,
the Confederacy scored bloody victories.

As orderly sergeant, George called the roll before sunrise each morning and then, secure in the sense that his
well-disciplined company could exist without him for an
hour, returned to his tent for a nap. Later he made out
his morning report—so many sick, so many absent, so
many on special detail, the rest marked for duty. Then he
strode forth, lean and towering. Impressive against his
gray sleeve were the three blue stripes and the lozenge
that bespoke the ranking noncom of Company D. He
supervised guard mount and oversaw company drill.[12]

On May 20, four days from George's twentieth birthday, the regiment completed election of all line officers, and Colonel Kenan drilled the Forty-third battalions. It was a long and wearying session. George was not low in spirits, but he thrilled enviously to accounts of how Stonewall Jackson's tough, tireless regiments flogged the muddled enemy up and down the Shenandoah Valley.

". . . if I had my way about it," wrote George to his mother, "I would have this Regm't ordered immediately to Jackson's command. I know them boys up there must lead a hearty life." And McClellan's advance up the Peninsula, overwhelming the works dug so painstakingly at Yorktown a year before, did not dismay the sergeant or his comrades. "Well it is thought (tho I myself don't know how it will be) that if we whip them at Richmond & Corinth, and Gen. Jackson keeps on in his course, the war can't last very long. . . ." [13]

For moments after dark on June 7, the war seemed suddenly close. The Long Roll sounded. Veterans of the Blues slid into line with swift assurance while the familiar frantic warning beat out on the drums. George was in the rear, with Johnny, now fourth sergeant of the company. Privates Jimmy Whitehead, James Etheridge, James Taylor, and John Williams stiffened the line as old battle veterans should. These seasoned soldiers grinned at strained faces and shaky knees among the recruits; such things took their minds off meager and unpalatable rations.[14] Later, friends at regimental headquarters said that Colonel Kenan had ordered the alarm to catch several men trying to sneak through the cordon of sentries.

George messed with the company officers, and lost his awe of Billy's shoulder straps. This favor must have been offered to the sergeant so that the skillful Wash could be detailed as cook, and George received $15.00 a month for Wash's services and shares of the food that again arrived from home.[15] But $15.00 would buy only an ounce of

quinine, increasingly scarce even among the blockade-
runners in Wilmington. This precious drug George gave
Wash to carry home to Brinkleyville, along with a letter
to the Reverend Mr. Wills.

That letter must have given the minister something of
worry. "I don't enjoy religion as I once did," confessed
George, though he added that he still tried to follow its
precepts and examples. Needs of the body sometimes
seemed greater than needs of the spirit. The mess fared
poorly on June 9, and George sent another note home,
urging, "You all must send enough good things by Wash
to give us one good dinner." [16]

Wash came back, laden with delicacies, on the evening
of June 15. He was just in time to help George pack to
leave for the coast. Men of Company D had been ordered
to cook six days' rations, but the commissary could supply
only enough food for a single day. The one wagon that
went with the company could carry only a few cooking
utensils. Glumly the mess abandoned most of the meat
and vegetables from Brinkleyville. Stubbornly Lieutenant
Sim held out for several firkins of butter. He and Wash
shared this burden between them as the regiment began
its march at seven o'clock in the evening.

Through the dark it tramped, weary and hungry, until
after midnight. Company D fell out in a churchyard,
and George slept soundly under a tree among the graves.
They were roused at seven o'clock—George noticed that
the churchyard grove was "pleasant"—and marched on
for ten miles under a hot sun. Worn-out, they reached
Fort Johnston.[17]

There new orders awaited them. They were put aboard
a train, and reached Petersburg in Virginia on June 26.

They were part of a brigade now. Tall, tawny Junius
Daniel, once offered the colonelcy of the Forty-third,
had been promoted brigadier general, and his command

included four other North Carolina regiments, the
Thirty-second, the Forty-fifth, the Fiftieth, and the Fifty-
third. This brigade, in turn, was attached to a division,
headed by Major General Holmes of North Carolina.
He was handsome in a grandfatherly way, self-important
and almost deaf. Parading the Forty-third, Colonel Kenan
introduced his division commander, who spoke as dramatically as had ever John B. Magruder. Impressed,
George wrote to Lucy about it:

> [General Holmes] commenced by saying *the ball had
> now* been opened, that we belong to a *N. C.* Division and
> to a *N. C. Brigade,* and that also the reputation of *North
> Carolina* depended upon us (that is, his Division) and
> that *we* (the 43rd) and one other the 45th were his main de-
> pendence of the 3rd Brigade, and if we *did do* wrong, all
> was lost. He said if there was anybody in the whole Reg'mt
> who wanted at that time either a furlough or a discharge,
> just step out of ranks and he would take the responsibility
> of giving him one, but every man that left that camp would
> be expected to fight to the very last, and if *any man* did
> show the *white feather* and he (Gen. H.) knew it, he would
> never return alive to N. Carolina. In fact the whole talk
> was a good one, and just to my notion exactly. I believe the
> 43rd stands pretty high generally (I mean every where).[18]

The ball had been opened indeed. Before Richmond,
Robert E. Lee marshaled his forces to oppose the mighty
threat that had rolled up the Peninsula under McClellan.
When orders came from Holmes' Division to march for
Petersburg on the night of the 26th, Mechanicsville had
been fought, bloodily but indecisively, and more action
was coming on the morrow.

The Forty-third bivouacked near Drewry's Bluff during the 27th and 28th, in "undergrowth so thick that
it keeps off the dew, and would almost keep off the rain."
Billy Beavans, ill with a sore throat, remained in charge

of the company's camp at Petersburg. Captain Cary Whitaker was sick, too, but stayed with his men as they
approached what seemed like certain serious conflict.[19]

On the 29th, a cloudless Sunday, Holmes' Division
crossed the James River beyond Drewry's Bluff and
marched eastward. It camped that night as wind and rain
came again, marched in the morning, and in the afternoon drew up in line of battle on a rise of ground. The
Forty-third stood in a road, its back to a rail fence. Into
position Holmes rolled six batteries of artillery, about
thirty guns. He hoped to disrupt a Federal retreat from
somewhere northeast, where the main Confederate force
was giving McClellan's unwieldy host a great deal of
trouble.

But to the southward flowed the James, and upon it
waited armed ships of war. These opened fire across clear
ground, with the long, lean shells called "lamp posts"
by dour soldiery. There were bursting explosions, like
a succession of volcanic eruptions.

This was sharp seasoning for raw troops. A patrol of
cavalry scouts scurried rearward through part of the
formation. Several artillerists cut horses out of the caisson
teams, mounted, and galloped away after the cavalry. The
Forty-fifth North Carolina, on which Holmes had de-
pended, broke and ran into some woods. The Forty-third
stood fast, and so did most of the other regiments, under
an hour-long hammering by the gunboats.

Nobody was killed in the Forty-third, and only a few
were wounded. But almost everyone was nervous, and
many were dismayed. The standing in line, with loud
racket all around, may have reminded some Old Bethels
of their own first experience of fire a year before and
some sixty miles eastward. George Wills, his feet planted
in obdurate refusal to stir from his post, suddenly found
his wide mouth twitching into a grin. Several of Com-

pany D's new men had thrown themselves down and thrust their heads under the fence rails, as startled ostriches are reputed to do. Perhaps their comical demoralization helped sterner-fibered men to endure the bombardment.[20]

At last came the triply welcome order to fall back. The brigade camped four miles west of the height, and slept poorly. Next morning, July 1, they returned to the exposed ridge where they had encountered the rain of shells, and there formed line again. A few miles to the east, the Seven Days roared to its blood-splashed conclusion on the slopes of Malvern Hill.

In Company D, at least, the men were eager for action —"looking for work to do," as George Wills put it— but no orders came to advance or retire. Again they endured heavy shellfire, the loudest in George's experience. All day they remained, and the sun went down on them still immovable in line. They slept by snatches where they were, still expecting and hoping to be sent forward. But in the gray dawn came news that McClellan's columns were in retreat.

Back to Drewry's Bluff marched Holmes' Division, knee-deep in mud. Nobody had been killed in the Forty-third, but exhaustion, soaked uniforms and lack of sleep brought on sickness. Both Cary and Sim Whitaker were ill from colds, as were many others in the company and throughout the regiment. George, to his own happy surprise, came out of the adventure feeling vigorously healthy. He wrote home to reassure his family:

> I came to the conclusion that I never before knew what soldiering was, but I have (praise be unto the Lord for it) been very well all the time, and have made out remarkably well. The summary is this. Since Thursday night last we have marched eight or ten miles a day slept from a third to

a half of each night and been in the rain all the time it was raining.

No word of self-praise for his coolness under fire; but he wrote at the top of the page, where the home folks would see it at once: "You needn't be afraid of my getting sick, as the life agrees with me so well." [21]

Another and fiercer triumph he might have felt had he known of another letter, sent on the same day that he slogged back through mire from the edge of the Seven Days. From Raleigh, Miss Fannie had written wretchedly to Maggie Beavans:

> Maggie, there is one thing in the history of my life which almost makes me miserable. I can never forgive myself for it—you well know what I mean, if not I mean the affair between George Wills and myself, I thought I never would mention it again, but it weighs heavily on my mind; and you dear Maggie is the only one to whom I could with safety confide my secrets, and long cherished sorrow, I have tried to banish this sorrow from my mind, but his voice haunts me wherever I go, *but just as I deserve,* how can I complain. . . .[22]

What George thought of that, if ever Maggie Beavans betrayed her friend's confidence by telling him, nobody could know. His heart was able to hide its own bitterness. With McClellan in flight from the Peninsula, Holmes' Division returned to camp near Petersburg. The surgeon of the Forty-third advised that the drill program be lightened in the hot weather. It was pleasant to sleep in tents under shady trees, but the town put high prices on delicacies that might relieve dull rations of poor beef and coarse meal. Shopping in Petersburg, George found that frying chickens worth six cents in Enfield brought a dollar each. Three onions or a quart of snap beans sold for a quarter. Butter was a dollar a pound. Shoes were ten dollars a pair. He longed, with watering mouth, for the home garden and smokehouse at Brinkleyville.[23]

Men of the Forty-third found time to make friends in the other regiments of Daniel's Brigade. George must have hailed old comrades of 1861—Louis Leon, for instance, was in Company B of the Fifty-third, a regiment commanded by another old Bethel, William Owens. Leon and others plumed themselves on romantic conquests among fair factory-workers at Petersburg.[24]

But the prize for gallantry went to a private of the Thirty-second—handsome, confident Joe John Cowand, who swept girls off their feet by squads and platoons. He contrived to engage himself to no fewer than six, and expressed his intention of winning six more. His undeniable personal attractions were complemented by luck and diplomacy enough to keep these charmers ignorant of each other. "Dancies," Joe John called them. In his own vigorous country idiom, "They lean to me like a sore eyed kitten to a Basin of milk." [25] Even Smiling Billy Beavans, for all his rhymes and shoulder straps, must defer to this supreme Lothario.

Johnny Beavans, single of heart and mind, dreamed only of Miss Laura at home. George thought rather of promotion, wondering if he might be commissioned lieutenant to drill the conscripts gathering in North Carolina.[26] He welcomed news that his father was coming to visit. "I hope you will fix up a lot of vegetables butter &c., and bring with you," he wrote.

When Mr. Willis arrived at Petersburg late in July, it was to find George racked with dysentery.[27] The surgeon gave the sick orderly sergeant opium and, as once before on the Peninsula, the father arranged for George to be cared for in a private home. George's host was a Mr. McIlwaine, and unweariedly kind. Captain Cary Whit-

". . . TO DO MY DUTY AS I NOW STAND . . ." George Wills as he looked shortly before he went to war with the Enfield Blues—thoughtful, intelligent, confident, self-respecting, with quiet humor ambushed behind his expression of young gravity.

"... WE WILL STAY A WEEK OR SO IN RALEIGH BEFORE WE START NORTH ..."
left to right: Billy Beavans, Sim Whitaker, Johnny Beavans, and Cary
Whitaker. This beautifully preserved daguerreotype shows the four soldier-
kinsmen very early in their service, probably while they were still at Camp
Ellis before going to Virginia. Billy, who has not yet grown his military
beard, wears a fatigue jacket over his duty blouse. Sim has a civilian coat,
vest, and shirt, such as he might have worn to church at home, with military trousers. On the top of his cap is the insignia of the First North Carolina Volunteer Regiment. Johnny has donned his overcoat, neatly caped,
for the picture, and Cary has strapped around his waist the sword belt that
bespeaks his lieutenancy.

"... WE GAVE THEM A WORSE WHIPPING THAN A SET OF MEN GENERALLY
GET ..." *right:* This map of the battlefield of Bethel is copied from one
drawn by William Gaston Lewis, a lieutenant of the Edgecombe Guards in
1861, and is in the map collection of the North Carolina Room of the
University of North Carolina. The position of Company I (the Enfield
Blues) shows at the upper left of the Confederate works. The field is mostly
flooded today.

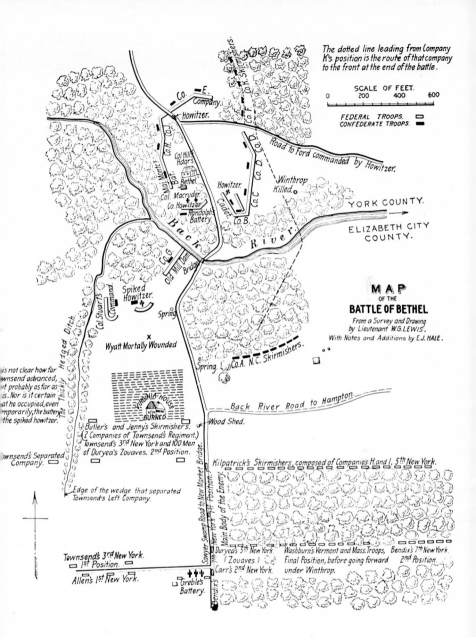

The dotted line leading from Company K's position is the route of that company to the front at the end of the battle.

SCALE OF FEET.
0   200   400   600

FEDERAL TROOPS. □
CONFEDERATE TROOPS. ▬

Co. F. (O.K. Skirmishers

Co. E.

Company.

Howitzer.

Co. H. Co.

Col Hill's
Hdqr's

Bethel

Col. Macruder
Co. Howitzer

Randolph's
Battery

Howitzer.

Road to ford commanded by Howitzer.

Co. C. Co. D. Co.

Co. C. Cedar

Co. B.

Winthrop
Killed.

YORK COUNTY.

ELIZABETH CITY
COUNTY.

Main Battery

Back

River.

Co. G.

Old Mill Dam Bridge.

Col Stuart's
Command

Spiked
Howitzer.

Spring

× Wyatt Mortally Wounded

Spring. Co. A. N.C. Skirmishers.

MAP
OF THE
BATTLE OF BETHEL
From a Survey and Drawing
by Lieutenant W.G. LEWIS'.
With Notes and Additions by E.J. HALE.

The Thickly Hedged Ditch.

is not clear how far
wnsend advanced,
t probably as far as
is. Nor is it certain
at he occupied, even
mporarily, the battery
the spiked howitzer.

VIRGINIA HOUSE
BURNED

Butler's and Jenny's Skirmishers.
(2 Companies of Townsend's Regiment.)
Townsend's 3rd New York and 100 Men
of Duryea's Zouaves. 2nd Position.

Wood Shed.

Back River Road to Hampton.

wnsend's Separated
Company.

Kilpatrick's Skirmishers, composed of Companies H. and I. 5th New York.

Edge of the wedge that separated
Townsend's Left Company.

Sawyer Swamp Road to New Market Bridge.

New York 1st Position.

Main Body of the Enemy.

Duryea's 5th New York.
(Zouaves.)

Carr's 2nd New York.

Washburn's Vermont and Mass. Troops,
Final Position, before going forward
under Winthrop.

Bendix's 7th New York.
2nd Position.

Townsend's 3rd New York.
1st Position.

Allen's 1st New York.

Greble's
Battery.

Bendix's.

Washburn's Vermont and Massachusetts Troops. Preliminary Position.

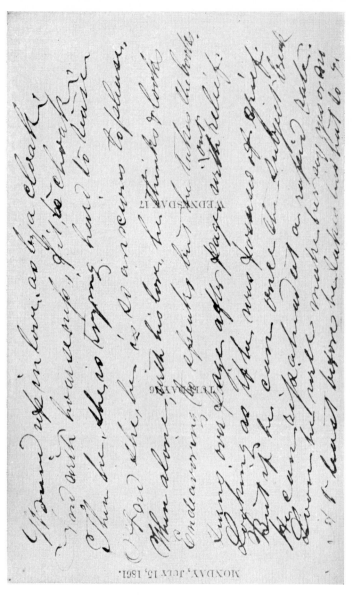

". . . WOUND UP IN LOVE . . ." One of Billy Beavans' verses, from his 1861 diary. He wrote it in ink, probably during his months at home between Yorktown and Camp Mangum.

"... THE PICTURES WE HAD TAKEN WERE VERY POOR ..." Taken in Goldsboro in March, 1862, on the way to join Cary Whitaker's company at Camp Mangum, these portraits of Billy and George originally were hinged together and belonged to Billy's beloved sister Maggie. Billy wears a sturdy civilian suit, and the beard he sprouted at Yorktown gives him a look of fierce maturity. George, whose rumpled uniform blouse probably survived from the Bethel days, did not long keep his scrubby mustache and side whiskers. Neither picture did its subject justice.

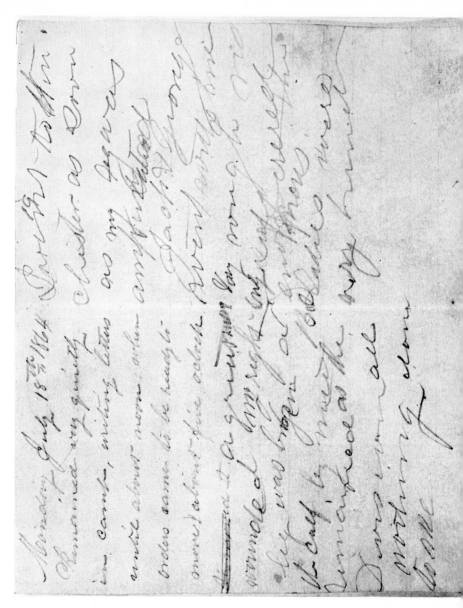

"... SUFFERED ENORMOUS ..." Billy was writing in his diary, neatly and without much worry, in the early evening of July 18, 1864. He broke off in mid-sentence to rush into battle, suffered a wound that shattered his leg, and shakily completed the entry as he lay on a blanket behind the lines. Next day he wrote again, gamely and agonizedly, of amputation without anesthetics, and found himself able to notice with gratitude the kindness of Winchester ladies who helped nurse him. Then his pencil trailed off the page and he wrote no more, ever.

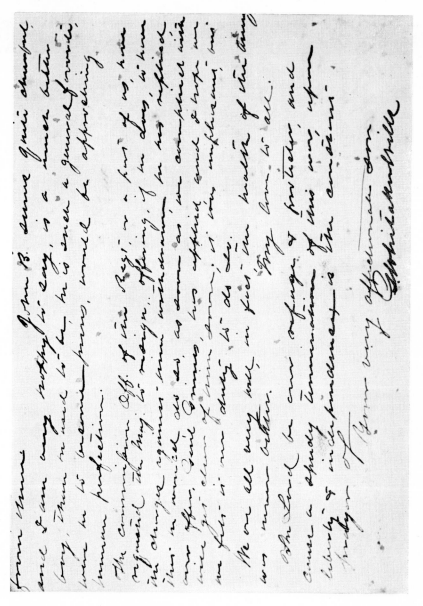

"... THE LORD BE OUR REFUGE AND PROTECTOR ..." The end of George's long letter of September 14 and 17, 1864, his last written message home. Meditative and confident, the young lieutenant wrote to his father of home thoughts, news of skirmishing with Federals, yearning for a family dinner, a word of praise for Cousin Johnny's cheerfulness, and a final prayer for divine protection and a victorious end of the war. Two days later he was killed in battle.

"... WHEN THIS WAR IS OVER ..."
right, a letter from Wash, the brave
and faithful Negro servant who followed George through more than three
years of advance and retreat and then
served George's younger brother Eddy
to the end of the war. Shaky in spelling, Wash nevertheless wrote a clear
hand and expressed himself well. This
letter was sent home from Goldsboro
where, on March 12, 1865, Wash and
Eddy paused among the boy-soldiers of
the North Carolina Junior Brigade for
a last fight with Sherman's overwhelming host.

below, a parole form such as was issued to officers and men of the surrendered Army of Northern Virginia at Appomattox. These forms, hastily
ground out on presses at nearby Lynchburg, were filled in and signed by
regimental adjutants. The parole shown was issued to General Matt. W.
Ransom. For line officers and enlisted men like Sim Whitaker and Johnny
Beavans, regimental and company designations were included.

aker made shift to visit his nephew often, advising him to rest and get well. But George yearned to be with his comrades. His reasoning in a letter home was, perhaps, original: "The reason I am so low spirited is, I think, because I am away from the noise and stir of camp, and have full time to think about *home,* to which I am very anxious at present to go." [28]

But while George fought back to convalescence, his brigade marched without him, to frighten back from City Point a fleet of Union transports that wanted to land an army on the bank of the James. Later the whole camp moved there, and on Tuesday, August 5, George left the hospitable McIlwaine home to rejoin his company. Wash carried George's knapsack as the sergeant trudged to City Point.[29]

The region seemed healthier than at Petersburg, but the water was not so cool, the Union pickets were five miles closer, and the regiment sweated grimly over the digging of trenches. George, still shaky from his illness and with an orderly sergeant's rating, did not touch a spade. But it was warm even when lounging, and he sympathized with his comrades laboring side by side with impressed Negroes, a total of six hundred men at work.

Food was scarce there, as almost everywhere in that part of Virginia. George's monthly $20.00 would scarcely meet his mess bill. But melons, peaches, and tomatoes were found to augment the meat and meal.

Several times that August, Daniel's Brigade moved to demonstrate against Federals still on the Peninsula. The maneuvers were fatiguing but did not result in major action. "War," some called this; others agreed with Lieutenant Colonel Lewis' summation: "We have marched & counter marched & fired on the enemy & have been fired at in turn." [30]

Elsewhere, though, fighting was hot and plentiful. In

permanent camp near Drewry's Bluff, Daniel's men heard
of a second stroke of lightning at Manassas, where Lee,
with Jackson and Longstreet, gave a terrible beating to
the overconfident, overrated Pope. Later they heard of
more battle, this time at Sharpsburg in Maryland, where
Lee and McClellan fought each other to a standstill on
the banks of the Antietam.

Wash managed to bake bread for the mess, using meat
fryings for lard. "Hard living," thought George Wills, but
in less than two weeks he added ten pounds to his gaunt
frame and wrote home that, at 148 pounds, he was "right
fat." [31] Winter approached, and he asked for a hat, an
overcoat, boots.

Late in September, Daniel's Brigade advanced on Suffolk, where the sudden appearance of heavy enemy forces
caused it to fall back without firing a shot. Complaints
at so fruitless an errand echoed through the army. But
George found the adventure bracing.

"I am very well now indeed," he informed his father,
"don't think I ever stood a march so well. If I could
always be as well, wouldn't mind going up to the Army of
the Potomac as I would be certain to stand it." But the
hurried troop movements had played havoc with foot-
gear. "I am about barefooted, my shoes can be mended
up however, so as to do very well for a month or so, I
will have them mended, but in the meantime must have
a pair made as soon as possible in case these should give
out sooner." [32]

Food continued to be a problem. Wash did miracles
with haphazard materials. On October 5 he, with the
help of Lieutenant Sim and Charlie Broadfoot, produced
what the mess called a "slice-potato pie." Captain Gary
Whitaker partook and relishfully praised the concoction.
George, the fastidious, declined a slice, fancying that the
pie contained soot. But he continued to gain weight for

all that. By the middle of October he weighed 156 pounds, more than ever in all his life before.[33]

Mrs. Wills visited camp that month. Her officer-brothers welcomed her, and George arranged for her to board with the family of a Methodist preacher near by. Wash headed home, just as November began and the nights grew cold.[34]

Autumn had colored the leaves of the trees, and now they fell. Sim Whitaker, skilled with the ax, made a log chimney for his tent and daubed its interior with clay. Soldiers off duty played marbles like schoolboys, shouting over scores or misses. There was rain by early November, turning to snow, with cold winds and cloudy skies.

The brigade started to build winter quarters. In Company D, these took the form of huts made by driving poles upright into the ground, stockade fashion. General Daniel remarked that the war would be over by Christmas, and that these shelters would not be needed. George had soldiered long enough to be skeptical. "I had certainly (rather) see that than hear talk of it, wouldn't you?" he inquired in a letter to sister Lucy; and, less certain than his brigadier of peace at hand, he asked for bedding to pad his cabin bunk. "A comfort will do better because I can lay on that, and it will keep my bones from hurting better on account of its thickness; for notwithstanding I am right fat, you must know I have large bones." [35]

Clothing and blankets arrived, and soldiers began to live in moderate comfort and quiet. On Sundays they dutifully attended preaching by the regiment's newly appointed chaplain, young Eugene W. Thompson. George, probably overcritical from his upbringing among ministers, felt that Chaplain Thompson's sermons suited "only the lower class of the Reg't," [36] but he did not backslide. To his brother Richard he sent $5.00 from his pay, to further "some good cause . . . to appropriate as you think best, to what purpose you choose." He and others of the company were vaccinated for smallpox around the middle of December.[37]

General Daniel's prediction was half right. Though the war went on, his men did not long use their snug huts. On December 15 they cooked five days' rations and marched to Petersburg. Next morning at eight o'clock they boarded a train for Weldon, waited there in an open field for chilly hours, and went on that night by flatcars to Goldsboro. Tentless, they squatted around fires made of stolen fence rails.[38]

Things were due to happen in North Carolina. Other regiments had also made camp around the town. Men of Daniel's Brigade visited these, and old Bethels found many of their former comrades in the Eleventh North Carolina.

Talk was sober among the veterans. "We came to the conclusion that at Yorktown we were playing soldier," reported Louis Leon, "but now there is no play to it." The weather, decidedly cold for the North Carolina Piedmont, helped with this realization. On December 21, Leon tried to wash in a stream and froze icicles into his hair.

Some provisions were more plentiful at Goldsboro than at Petersburg. The officers' mess of Company D bought potatoes for a dollar a bushel instead of four, as at their last station. Yet, on Christmas Eve, George wished hungrily that he were at home. Company D spread its blankets in the woods. It was dark and cold, but George managed to scrawl a few lines to sister Mary:

> Tomorrow will be Christmas, well you all must eat enough for me, as I can't be there to eat with you; I am cheated out of it myself altogether, though if I had remained at the Bluff would have a dinner there.[39]

IX

I BELONG TO GENERAL LEE'S ARMY

But conditions bettered in that cheerless camp. The regiment's baggage arrived, and quarters were made more comfortable. Fires blazed warmly as the new year came in. It must have seemed decades since the watch party at Branch's plantation manor.

Evidently there would not be immediate movement. Troops had been gathered in eastern North Carolina to protect transport lines along routes where Confederate commissary officers gathered stores of bacon, salt fish, and other provisions. Lieutenant Billy Beavans, who before the war had learned something of bookkeeping, evinced talent for paper work and organization. He drew an office detail in Goldsboro.

On January 3, a Saturday, Colonel Kenan issued passes to several members of Company D. Neither Captain Cary nor First Lieutenant Sim stood on rank with their non-commissioned kinsmen; Sergeants George and Johnny went with them to Goldsboro. The four met Billy there, and had a lazy, pleasant day.[1]

New conscripts in the company provided work for George and Johnny as drillmasters. Wash, meanwhile, wanted to go to Brinkleyville again—he missed warm-hearted, golden-skinned Leah. His master smiled teasingly as he granted permission, and handed him a note to carry along:

> When Wash came to camp the last time (from home) he said on acc't of his having so long a stay at home at that time, he would not ask for another furlough until March; he however has changed his mind since, and now says, he can't afford to stay away from his *wife* that long, so let me now introduce him to you (*Washington, the married man*). . . ."

With Wash went orders to find a turkey for the mess. Also: ". . . ask mother to send a cabbage or two, some pepper-vinegar (pretty strong with pepper) and a pound or two of candles." [2]

George himself went home on furlough in February,[3] a short ride on the train. Meanwhile, old Bethels at Goldsboro were gladdened by the news that Daniel Harvey Hill, a major general now, had been assigned to command of the troops in North Carolina. Hill was begging the secretary of war for more men—he had but the three infantry brigades of Daniel, Pettigrew, and Evans, with some slovenly cavalry under Beverly Robertson.[4] Nor were these brigades large; Daniel's command, as of February 20, counted 581 present for duty of 794 officers and men. Part of this force was lightly engaged in a demonstration toward the Federals at New Bern. Another move, toward Kinston, began late in the month. George returned from Brinkleyville in time to overtake his regiment. He was welcome in Company D because, on February 28, Captain Cary Whitaker had been detached to serve on a court-martial.[5]

The regiment camped at Kinston, less comfortably than ever before. The marshy grounds were named Camp

Tadpole by the Forty-third, and pickets were strung in
the muddy hollows from the Neuse River to the Trent.
Men with the main body had time to read, with under-
standable fascination, a posted order signed by General
Hill under date of February 25:

> Soldiers! Your brutal and malignant enemy is putting
> forth efforts unexampled in the history of the world. Hav-
> ing failed to subjugate you, he is maddened with the thirst
> for vengeance, and is pushing forward his foreign merce-
> naries to plunder your property and lay waste your homes.
> But his marauding hosts have been so often beaten and
> baffled that they are now discouraged and demoralized.
> . . . We must cut down to 6 feet by 2 the dimensions of
> the farms which these plunderers propose to appropriate.
> . . . Our cities, towns and villages are full of young and
> able-bodied skulkers, wearing the semblance of men, who
> have dodged from the battle-field under the provisions of
> the exemption bill. The scorn of the fair sex and the con-
> tempt of all honorable men have not been able to drive
> these cowardly miscreants into the ranks, so long as they
> can fatten upon the miseries of the country and shelter
> their worthless carcasses from Yankee bullets; but they are
> insensible to shame. But a day of retribution awaits these
> abortions of humanity. Their own descendants will exe-
> crate their memory when the finger of scorn is pointed
> and the taunt is uttered, "He is the son, or grandson, or
> great-grandson of the exempt and extortioner." Do your
> full duty, soldiers, and leave these poltroons and villains
> to posterity.
> All commanding officers are hereby enjoined to furnish
> the names of officers and men who distinguish themselves
> in pitched battles and skirmishes. Those so distinguishing
> themselves will be recommended for promotion and their
> names published in the principal papers of their respec-
> tive States.
> . . . Those who have never been in battle will thus be
> enabled to enjoy the novel sensation of listening to the

sound of hostile shot and shell, and those who have listened a great way off will be allowed to come some miles nearer, and compare the sensation by the distant cannonade with that produced by the rattle of musketry. . . .

Men who had served with Hill in 1861 considered these sentiments as characteristic rather than extraordinary. "Hurrah! For old Daniel H.," applauded George in a letter to Lucy, and paraphrased that part of the order that has special appeal for him: "He furthermore says that particular notice shall be taken, of both off's and men, and those who bear themselves *gallantly* should be so read out and recommended for promotion. Look out for my name as promoted for *gallantry*. Ha! ha!" [6]

But George only pretended to laugh at the notion of advance in rank. He tried, with his uncle Cary's help, to get a naval commission, but without success.[7] He was a good orderly sergeant in a good company, and grew better daily. Yet: "I have held the place I now hold as long as I want it. . . ."

Meanwhile, General Daniel appointed a board of field officers to examine all candidates for commissions in the brigade, and sent to Company D an order assigning Lieutenant Billy Beavans as brigade ordnance officer.[8]

Officers and regimental surgeons growled at the poor quality of new recruits. Physically and morally they were far below the old Bethel Regiment's standards. In the Fifty-third, several deserters were pursued, brought back and flogged on their bare shoulders.[9] The Forty-third had better discipline, and on March 8 its skirmishers fought stubbornly against superior numbers of Federals.[10] During subsequent jabs toward New Bern, the enemy outposts were driven in.

On March 20, George led a patrol of twenty to scoop in a drove of hogs almost under Yankee gun muzzles outside Kinston. He felt some disappointment because there

was no effort to stop his venture— ". . . nothing at all
to get up an excitement out of." The officers' mess ate
well of fresh pork, and Wash, trying out the lard, kept
the cracklings for his profit on the enterprise. Well fed,
George thought again of coming battles up north. He
would "prefer that our Brigade would be ordered to Va.
in the summer." [11]

From the Kinston region the brigade tramped north
across sand ridges and swamps. On March 30 it waded
for fifteen miles through clammy clay bottoms, and built
fires that night to dry wet clothes. The objective of the
march was Washington—Old Washington, that is, the
North Carolina town that was first to bear the proud
name. Yankees fled before the advance. On April 1, the
regiments formed line of battle three miles from the
town.

George and other sergeants cautioned their men to keep
muskets at the ready and cartridge boxes on belts. Big
guns and small boomed all that day, somewhere among
the trees. The siege of the Union fortifications began.[12]

Fire from enemy batteries repeatedly swept the position of the Forty-third. Men on picket wormed through
damp brush to look at the earthworks behind which
Yankees crouched and waited. But there was no major
infantry action. Far worse than any desultory shelling
by Federals was a cold snap. Company D shivered in an
open field on the night of April 4, under a wind that
blew cold enough for December. Sim Whitaker, racked
with chills, was put to bed in a house behind the lines.
George, toughening with hardship, shrugged off a threat
of similar shakes.[13]

Pettigrew's and Garnett's brigades helped in the siege.
Seven thousand Confederate infantry, with many guns,
invested Washington. Boys who once had thrilled to the
first crackle of muskets around Big Bethel Church felt

downright bored at the lack of heavy fighting; Louis Leon
sneaked off from easy duty with his regimental color
guard to join his friends on the advance picket line.[14] A
fleet of gunboats on the nearby Pamlico River belabored
the pickets with shells, but only two men were killed during the first two weeks of April. "They have thrown iron
enough at us to build a rail road track some distance,"
wrote an unimpressed officer of the Forty-third.[15]

Irksome, however, were the April rains that soaked
and muddied gray uniforms. The tentless besiegers draped
blankets over poles to approximate some sort of wretched
shelter. Food, too, was scarce—that was becoming the
active principle of Confederate service. Scraps of meat
and ill-baked bread were all that Wash could find to
serve the mess.[16]

The siege was lifted on April 18, when the high
command despaired of drawing the defenders from their
works or of mustering a strong enough attack to storm
the town. As the Forty-third withdrew, shells from Washington battered it ineffectually. Nobody in Company D
was hurt. Again George Wills and other hardened cam-
paigners laughed at the nervousness of recent recruits.[17]

Kinston was their new campsite, where it rained so
hard on May 6 that nobody had to wash his face on the
morning of the 7th. More desertions occurred, and flogging was thought too mild a punishment. On May 11 the
brigade turned out to see two deserters face a firing squad.
Louis Leon soberly recorded the incident in his diary:

> After they were shot, we marched by them and saw one
> was hit six times, the other four. Their coffins were by their
> sides, right close to their graves, so that they could see it
> all.[18]

Those who did not desert rejoiced at news of Chancellorsville in Virginia. Forty thousand under Lee had

driven an abject hundred thousand under Joe Hooker. But the joy vanished when North Carolinians heard that Stonewall Jackson had been shot down by his own nervous men. George wrote to Lucy:

> There is one thing I love to think of, whether it is true or not I can't tell, it is this. Last spring we had to fight hard, very hard, and then were defeated. This Spring we hardly met before they give way. That makes me think the war will end one of these days . . . but it has made me feel rather badly on account of the wound of Gen. Jackson, who in my opinion is inferior to no one in this war.[19]

Must they sit dully or march blindly among North Carolina swamps while histoy was being made by steel and lead up in Virginia? George hoped not. He wanted to get into the decisive struggle.

At four o'clock on the morning of May 17, bugles dragged him and his comrades from their blankets on the pine straw. Cook all your rations, came the quick order; be ready to march in one hour. The brigade went by train to Goldsboro and stayed there that night. It was heading for Virginia, where the stoutest hearts longed to be.

But, when the regiment fell in to board another train in the morning, Company D was two men short. The Edge brothers, Joseph and Marshall, risked flogging and shooting rather than go to where they must fight.[20]

Their steadfast comrades went on to Richmond. Here and there a face glanced backward over a gray shoulder, yearning and sad, at what must be left behind. George Wills rode the rumbling car with but half his heart, for last spring's bitterly scornful farewell to romance had been forgotten.

Again a girl's face smiled in his dreams. Lulu, that was her name. Like Miss Fannie, she went to Elba

Academy with George's sisters. And she was lovely in his eyes, and her love was a true one, not fickle or vain like Miss Fannie's. . . .[21]

On May 19 the brigade paused at Camp Lee outside the capital. On May 22 the Forty-third marched for Fredericksburg.

The weather was hot, but the men of the Forty-third were in good shape. Under Lieutenant Colonel Lewis' prodding, twenty-six miles were accomplished that Friday, and twenty-six more the day following. At noon on Sunday, May 24, they reached Fredericksburg and camped on the heights from which Burnside's infantry had been slaughtered last Christmas season. Sixty-five miles in two days and a half—not bad; better than Daniel's other regiments, anyway.[22] They looked at scores of other camps around them.

Daniel's Brigade had been assigned to the division of Major General Robert E. Rodes, a blond-mustached Viking of a man. The Fiftieth North Carolina was transferred, and in its stead came the Second North Carolina Battalion.[23]

By virtue of Daniel's seniority in rank, his was the first brigade of Rodes' Division. Yet, by comparison with the other units, it was untried. Iverson's and Ramseur's North Carolinians, and the Georgians of Doles and the Alabamians under O'Neal, had fought major conflicts in Virginia while Daniel's troops had but skirmished. Men toughened on stricken fields were inclined to josh, even to sneer, at the new brigade, large and unpunished. Men of the Forty-third turned sullen. Give us a chance, they prayed.

A real battle was coming, or why did this large army gather? On May 25, George appropriated a sheet of blue-ruled paper from his sheaf of company stationery and hunted up an ink bottle. Then, to Lucy:

It looks strange to us, who have been used to a Brigade, or two or three of them, to see the no. of Troops around here, you don't ask for such a Reg't, but such a Brig. . . .

As he wrote, the baleful implications came and stared at young Sergeant George Wills. Miss Lulu, back at Elba Academy, had made life precious to him, but he did not flinch. A soldier saying had grown old in two years of war: Man born of woman and enlisted in Stonewall Jackson's army is of few days and short rations. Jackson was gone now, resting under the shade of the trees where the day was eternity and rations were short no longer. But there was still Lee; and Daniel's Brigade and Rodes' Division were in Jackson's old Second Corps, with Richard Stoddard Ewell to lead where Stonewall would have led. A trifle of fire touched George's pen:

> . . . tho it is more dangerous, yet I must say that I am proud to be able to say, I belong to Gen. Lee's army. . . . it is the general opinion, that the next move will be an advance by us, I think that will be the best way to go at it, and this will be the proper time, if any be proper.[24]

On May 29, Rodes' Division passed in review, and Robert E. Lee sat his horse beside Rodes.

Those who had seen Lee two years before at Richmond and on the Peninsula remembered a handsome black-haired man. Now the commanding general's hair and beard were gray.[25] His handsomeness had become a saintly beauty; but he looked old and worn, like the uniforms and illusions of the Confederacy.

Yankee observation balloons hung in the northward sky, watching the muster of men and weapons.

The bugles sang before dawn of Thursday, June 4. Over hasty fires the men cooked three days' rations. Away they marched [26]—George Wills, and Wash with his burden of cooking pots, and Cary and Sim Whitaker, and Johnny

Beavans, and Smiling Billy supervising the train of ordnance wagons, and the rest of Company D, and the rest of the Forty-third North Carolina Regiment, and the rest of Daniel's Brigade, of Rodes' Division, of the Second Corps under Richard Stoddard Ewell, and the First Corps under James Longstreet and the Third Corps under A. P. Hill, and the cavalry under Jeb Stuart, and Robert E. Lee at the head of the Army of Northern Virginia.

They went north, to invade enemy country.

X

OUR BRIGADE WAS IN IT GOOD

The Army of Northern Virginia that set its fierce face to the north numbered some 70,000 officers and men. These were gaunt, hairy warriors, enduring on the march, sure-eyed above the barrels of their muskets, and utterly certain that they could thrash anyone and everyone the Union could bring against them.

Jeb Stuart's 9,000 cavalry troopers were superbly mounted, dashingly led. The infantry, by contrast, seemed plodding, dingy and unshowy; but it was as good as ever, answered drum or bugle. By harshest experience it had learned to travel light. The road to glory, went another of those mordant army aphorisms, is not to be followed with much baggage, and long ago these men had forsaken spare shoes and coats, frying pans, sheath knives, waterproof ground cloths. That summer, Lee's representative infantryman wore only a shabby shirt and pants, a battered but defiant slouch hat, and shoes if he could get them. More than likely he had thrown away his cartridge box and carried his cartridges in his pocket. What food he might possess was crammed in a lumpy haversack. His canteen, looted from a dead Yankee at Manassas or

Fredericksburg or Chancellorsville, bumped his lean hip. Slung over his shoulder was a blanket roll. Unshorn, wolfish-eyed, tattered, he seemed all savage except for his bright-burnished musket, deadly at both ends.[1]

Men of the Forty-third and of Daniel's other regiments were, by contrast to their new mates, well equipped with shoes and uniforms. A few, like the insistently fastidious George Wills, still wore underwear and carried razors. As they began their march, Major Walter Boggan was detached to stay behind.[2] Not many felt that he would be missed in whatever action was to come.

With the Second Corps rumbled a string of supply wagons, with "U S" printed on most of the hoodlike canvas covers. The same initials showed again and again on the harness of the teams, on the breeches of cannon, on caissons and ammunition carts. These were captures from fields of violent triumph over the Union. Without them, Lee could not be moving into enemy country.

Ewell's Second Corps covered another sixty miles in four days, waded the swift-flowing Rapidan, and camped east of pretty Culpeper Court House on the night of June 7. There was a day's rest on the 8th. Then, at mid-morning of the 9th, orders hurried Daniel's big, fresh regiments toward Brandy Station, where Stuart's cavalry sabered it out with a column of pugnacious Federal horse. The advance guard of Daniel arrived just as the bluecoats, barely defeated, galloped away north again. The men of the Forty-third watched prisoners hustled rearward, destined for melancholy, hungry captivity in Southern pens. That night the regiment camped two miles from where flies swarmed the blood-gouted meadows around Brandy Station.

So swift had been that march from Fredericksburg that the infantry had outdistanced Billy Beavans' ordnance wagons. He reached camp at ten o'clock that night. All lay late again the next morning. It was past noon and brightly hot when the corps, with Rodes' Division at the head, moved northwest in the direction of Winchester.[3]

Winchester . . . the name must have echoed in George's ears, and in Billy's. Winchester had the character of a pleasant town. But men had fought bitterly there in 1862, and men were hurrying to fight there now.

Twelve miles Rodes led his troops by eight o'clock that night. In the early dawn they marched again, sixteen miles more with three streams to splash through, pleasant to tired feet. They camped by an old mill race beyond Flint Hills. Eighteen miles the following day, the 12th, over part of the Blue Ridge and across the head of the Rappahannock and both forks of the Shenandoah.[4] Ladies cheered them as they trudged through Fort Royal.

Ewell was after a Federal force at Winchester, some eight thousand commanded by Major General Robert H. Milroy who bore the reputation of barn-burner and plunderer. Before reaching Winchester, Rodes' Division, with cavalry in the van, turned west toward a Federal outpost at Berryville. On the 13th, Rodes approached the enemy position, but his inept cavalry scouts alarmed the Federals, who prudently ran away. Yelling rebels jumped over deserted breastworks and found themselves in possession of abandoned tents, baggage, and a plentiful dinner steaming in pots under pleasant trees.

Sergeant George Wills stood off with young Methodist austerity from direct plunder. Others, less scrupulous and very hungry, attacked the captured food—real coffee with sugar, beans and potatoes and other good things. Leftovers went into haversacks and canteens. Louis Leon, who had left the color guard of the Fifty-third to be a sharpshooter, was among the first into the enemy camp and heartily enjoyed the tasty spoils of war. Billy Beavans, too, brought in his wagons, and he and his drivers took "what was left in their camps worth having"—those wagons must have been stowed in every vacant corner with captured provisions.

Relaxing a trifle, George accepted from his friends a fistful of hardtack, then a pair of gloves and some spurs. He felt, perhaps, that these ceased to be plunder when they had passed through Confederate hands. The trees that waved over the captured tents struck him as beautiful. Some of those tents had belonged to sutlers. Had George been early enough, he might have snatched some toothsome prizes; no, he decided on second thought, he wouldn't have done that. ". . . it looks ridiculous to plunder as they do."

Others of Company D agreed with George on the beauty of the Shenandoah Valley. Some swore to return and live there when peace came. As for George, ". . . wished I had been born there, if it was not for the war." [5]

They camped four miles beyond Berryville. It rained hard that night, and dripping warriors wished they had brought those abandoned tents.[6]

Again behind screening cavalry, they advanced through the misty morning of the 14th. The rest of Ewell's Corps beat the Federals around Winchester and drove them pell-mell eastward toward Martinsburg, but Rodes' men saw only swiftly departing blue backs ahead. Too bad to have missed sharing the victory—Ewell had taken 3,358 prisoners,[7] twenty-three guns and a number of wagons, and had lost only some 269 of his own forces. Twenty-five miles Rodes accomplished that day, and after dark chased the Union rear guard from Martinsburg. Billy Beavans flashed his ready smile at pretty girls in the town. Others, less romantic, were chiefly impressed by the food offered them by citizens.[8]

By June 16, they were on the banks of the Potomac, waiting for the rest of the Second Corps. The taste of victory made bearded lips smack. Town after town had been taken, with almost no effort. Some felt that these successes equaled those of Stonewall Jackson a year before. But there was valiant disappointment, expressed by Lieutenant Colonel Lewis and echoed in the ranks: "Our brigade as usual has not been engaged, the enemy running whenever & wherever we met him." Would the Forty-third never get a chance to show what it could do? [9]

Rodes called a halt by the river. Some of his shoeless men dabbled their feet at the brink. Other divisions of Ewell's Corps were crossing. Company D stared across the river to Maryland. Beyond Maryland was Pennsylvania. They'd go there, the boys from Halifax and Cumberland counties—the word had come from the generals. To unthinkable Pennsylvania where the Yankees would be shamed into making a stand.

On the 17th they waded over, knee-deep in the Potomac, and paused all day in Williamsburg. Meanwhile, behind them and screened by the Blue Ridge, Longstreet's First Corps looked through Ashby's gap. East of there, at Aldie, the cavalry under Stuart skirmished with the increasingly troublesome squadrons of the Union. A. P. Hill with the Third Corps was still farther back, at Culpeper where the Second had camped ten days earlier. And the whole blue Army of the Potomac was hastening northward, trying to locate and face the strange sudden threat of Lee to its home soil.

Meanwhile, farther away, the shoe was very much on the other foot for the Confederacy. Vicksburg's bomb-pelted defenders counted their percussion caps and their morsels of bread inside Grant's grappling clutch. In middle Tennessee, W. S. Rosecrans' army maneuvered to drive Bragg back upon Chattanooga. And the Southern gunboat *Atlanta* was captured that day in Wassaw Sound on the Georgia seacoast.

Now, at Williamsburg, came orders for most of the supply wagons to turn back. Billy Beavans' ordnance train, with arms and ammunition, would stay with the invasion. So would ambulances and commissary wagons, but Cary and Sim Whitaker sent their excess baggage to Staunton. George Wills felt vigorous and elated, and in his ears rang an unforgettable war song. Hurriedly he penciled a note home:

> We are now on the shores of "Maryland my Maryland" . . . Tho. we have had some hard marching, yet if I can keep the health I now have and nothing else happens to me, I wouldn't take anything for the trip, for it will learn me more than I could otherwise learn. . . . I will write to you again as soon as I can, hope to tell you something about Penn. by that time.[10]

All day of the 18th, too, the Second Corps rested. Williamsporters gathered to stare at the invaders. "The people are mixed in their sympathies," wrote Louis Leon of the Fifty-third. Again Leon, as on the 19th they marched through Hagerstown: "Here the men greeted us very shabby, but the ladies quite the reverse." That night they reached the banks of the Antietam, crimson the previous September with the bravest blood of two armies, and crouched under trees and in the lee of fences for the next two days, while hard rains fell.[11]

June 22, bright again, saw them on the road at eight o'clock in the morning. Ewell split his corps once more. Rodes' Division and part of Johnson's headed straight up and across the Pennsylvania line. Before noon their column swung through Middleton and on to Greencastle. They entered a beautiful broad valley, the Cumberland. High mountain ranges lifted toward the sky on either hand, and between them rich lowlands cradled the prosperous green farms of the Pennsylvania Dutch.

No love was lost between these industrious country folk and the spare, hard-faced Southern infantry. Up at regimental headquarters, Lieutenant Colonel Lewis decided: "They are a coarse, uncultivated set & bent entirely on making money." Sharpshooter Leon was able to smile at bleak stares from the Greencastle sidewalk: "I am willing to swear that no prayers will be offered in this town for us poor ragged rebels." Trying to buy food, Leon found doors slammed in his bearded young face. One Greencastle lady was an exception to the rule. Either a Southern sympathizer or naturally sorry for a hungry boy under whatever flag, she fed Leon and a comrade, but refused the Confederate scrip they offered in payment.

George Wills, not readily disdainful of anyone, was impressed with the fat lands and magnificent barns, but missed his favorite item of landscape: ". . . their quantity of land is so limited, that they haven't the woodland to spare for groves, but have a small yard without trees." And as flavory as any conversation between Carolinian and Pennsylvanian was that of Wash with a buxom old farm wife.

She suggested that he slip away from his master and the Confederacy and stay in Pennsylvania as a free man. "Are you treated well?" she asked solicitously.

"I live as I wish," was the brown man's reply, courteous but boldly prompt. "And if I did not, I think I couldn't better myself by stopping here. This is a beautiful country, but it doesn't come up to home in my eyes." [12]

Noon of June 24 found them in Chambersburg, a town of ten thousand. "There are a plenty of men here— a pity they are not rebels, and in our ranks." Again no friendly smiles for the frightening tatterdemalions with their bright muskets and bushy faces. Daniel's Brigade camped beyond the town, rose at midnight and forded cold waters that wakened the drowsiest shamblers. At Shepherdsburg by the next dawn, welcome orders for a day's rest. Men off duty strolled through the little town— "flying around," Billy Beavans called it—and compared the landscape with that of North Carolina's mountains and plains and coast. June 26, and the brigades bored on north and west, joining the rest of the Second Corps and fanning out into line of battle as they approached Carlisle.

Military barracks were there, and troops in blue. These made no more resistance than the Federals encountered below the Potomac. They fired a futile volley at long range, then scurried through the town and away. Into Carlisle strode the Southerners, and their advance parties met frightened civilians.

Those bluecoats who had fled so swiftly were only two raw regiments of Pennsylvania militia. But they had fired muskets—would the town's captors vengefully sack and destroy? Good-humoredly, George and others assured them of the contrary. Robert E. Lee had forbidden anything like that. Made happy by this news, Carlisle's residents were generous with food and drink.[13]

Daniel's Brigade found quarters in the deserted barracks. Company D threw down its sketchy possessions indoors for the first time in weeks. "It looks like a pity to destroy such pretty property," confessed George Wills, and came out to watch a detail from the Thirty-second Regiment raising the flagstaff that had been cut down by the fugitive Pennsylvania militiamen.

The staff in place again, the Thirty-second's color sergeant raised his regimental flag, bright, new, and clean. A special story went with that flag. Before the Army of Northern Virginia had started for the Potomac, some ladies had sewn the starry cross and presented it to President Davis, who in turn had given it to Lee. From the commanding general it had passed on to Ewell. Ewell had given it to Rodes, who had conveyed it on to Daniel. That brigadier bestowed it on the colonel of the Thirty-second. Having completed this somewhat apostolic succession, the flag ran triumphantly to the masthead at Carlisle and fluttered brightly against Pennsylvania's blue summer sky.

A band struck up music—"Dixie," then "The Bonny Blue Flag." Voices, variously tuneful, sang in chorus:

> "We are a band of brothers beneath a Southern sun,
> Fighting for the liberty our brave forefathers won,
> And when our rights were threatened, the cry rose
> near and far,
> 'Hurrah for the bonny blue flag that bears a single star!' "

In keeping with another Southern tradition, there were speeches. General Ewell, a bald cockatoo of a man with a wooden leg, chirped out a few words that he hoped would inspire. He was followed by handsome old Brigadier General Isaac Trimble of Virginia. The magnificent blond Rodes spoke in his turn, and finally Junius Daniel. Everything the generals said was greeted by storms of applause from the listening troops, and certain Carlisle townsfolk clapped hands as well. Food, drink, music, oratory—this was almost like the war young men had expected in 1861.

George Wills was frankly enthused. "I felt like going on to N. Y. on the occasion," he scrawled on the torn leaf of a ledger to sister Lucy, and added that Carlisle civilians were hospitable to men of Company D. "Those that happen in the right place fare splendidly," he wrote. Billy Beavans, his teams unhitched, was treated with whisky, and ice water to mix with it.[14]

Except for picket and provost duty, there was nothing much to do for the next three days. Joe John Cowand, the Thirty-second's prince of heartbreakers, felt lonesome for his many Virginia sweethearts, and for someone else, too—his pretty-cheeked cousin Winifred at home in Bertie County. He, too, found a pencil and a bit of paper to tell her about life in Carlisle Barracks: "I am in Yankeydom fairing finely Plenty of something to go on but a long wais from home and I cant tell you when you will be hearing from me again. . . ." [15]

Rumors crawled through the divisions. Rodes would lead on to Harrisburg, capital of Pennsylvania. Refreshed by rest, elated by effortless victory, soldiers rejoiced in the prospect. On Tuesday morning, the hot, bright last day of June, they were inspected. The inspecting officer found that Company D mustered three officers and fifty-three men for duty, with nine sick, four under arrest, and four absent without leave. He approved of the company's good discipline and appearance and the condition of its arms and clothing. Inspection over, they marched again.

But Rodes headed them south. The whole Second Corps was going south, toward a rendezvous with the rest of the army. Thousands of feet kicked up dust clouds on the Baltimore Turnpike. Through Holly Gap they moved, through villages called Papertown and Petersburg. Seventeen miles from Carlisle they bivouacked, at the crossroads hamlet of Heidlesburg.[16] The rest of the army gathered at other points, the corps of Longstreet and A. P. Hill, and from somewhere was riding the cavalry of Stuart. Not much of a place, Heidlesburg, just a few houses. But seven miles along was a real town. Sizable. What was its name again? Gettysburg.

At six o'clock, shortly after dawn of July 1, the Second Corps was up and moving through Heidlesburg and through little Middleton beyond. Rodes' Division led.

Nobody was particularly apprehensive. "We marched without thinking any danger was at hand," wrote Billy Beavans of that morning.

Until, up ahead, the dull fierce boom of cannon.

The Third Corps had approached the western edge of that town called Gettysburg, and was fighting. Rodes halted his own column and drew aside from the rutted road to let wagons roll rearward. Only Billy Beavans' ordnance train would accompany the advance.[17] That means business, boys. . . . Forward again. Closer, with the guns yelling more loudly, and another halt.

The Forty-third found itself on a rise of ground near a roadside farmhouse. Wheat fields spread goldenly to left and right. Men in the ranks looked two miles southeast, downslope into the streets and yards of Gettysburg. At the edge nearest them stood a big house, almost a mansion. Behind this and to its left loomed the tower of a college building.[18] Beyond the town rose tree-tufted slopes and heights, and nearer at hand, between the houses and their own position, grew a belt of green timber. Among those nearer trees showed blobs and patches of blue, the uniforms of Federal infantry, lots of Federal infantry.

The great voices of artillery shouted, faster and angrier. The advance regiments of Rodes' Division began to deploy, muskets lifting to the ready. Shells burst among the formations. Over the heads of the gray infantrymen shrieked back the answering bombardment from their own guns.

"About 11 o'clock," summed up Billy Beavans, "our brigade was in it good."

All the brigades were in it. Rodes strung three of them across his front from left to right—Doles, O'Neal, Iverson, more than a mile from wing to wing. Again Daniel took a reserve position, his regiments drawn up one behind another at the right, while Ramseur's Brigade, more North Carolinians, supported the left. Real fighting began just ahead there. The rain of big shot and small at Bethel on the Peninsula, the flailing from the gunboats during the Seven Days, the in-and-out exchanges on the North Carolina coast, were nothing to what this would be. Captain Whitaker and Lieutenant Baker and Sergeant Wills stood tense with Company D, waiting to move close to their work.

The sun climbed to its noon above grimy clouds of powder smoke. Cannoneers sweated to serve their roaring pieces. To Daniel's regiments came new orders—shift into line behind Iverson. The Forty-third took place next to the Thirty-second, which was on the right flank. Leftward, in order, were the Forty-fifth Regiment, the Second Battalion, the Fifty-third.

Half-past one, and Iverson's men began to advance. They had boasted, Iverson's men, of helping to shatter the Yankee charge at Fredericksburg, of playing a bloody part in driving Joe Hooker's right wing from Chancellorsville. As these bore leftward along the road toward town, Daniel's own line double-quicked to catch up, support Iverson's right flank, and look toward the west. Other forces should be arriving, to make the advance unbroken from horizon to horizon.

In front blazed and rattled the enemy muskets. Daniel's line had moved a mile from its starting point, and was beside Iverson instead of behind. Loading and firing as they advanced, men of the Forty-third heard their company officers howling orders to move by the left flank, past the next two units in order. Facing quickly, they hurried to a new position between the Second Battalion and the Fifty-third Regiment, a place where, suddenly, all the shells in all the world seemed to be bursting at once.

Company D and others at the right of the regiment staggered under these explosions. Men fell, limp or struggling, but grimly the others kept their ranks. Nobody broke for cover or courted mocking laughter by a dive into flimsy shelter. Another order, shouted along from captain to captain:

"Forward!"

A concerted yell, and a rush at the noise beyond the smoke, and Yankees were falling back before them.

Pluckily, steadily, the Forty-third pursued. It reached a deep ditch with grassy lips, where a railroad was in process of construction. On the far side were thickets. Trapped against the ditch, some bluecoats dropped their muskets and threw up their hands. The Forty-third and other regiments scooped up prisoners by scores.

From those thickets across the cut burst more enemy troops. Two batteries of guns poured a thundering succession of volleys into the left of Daniel's Brigade. Again, on order, the Forty-third shifted position to help bolster Iverson's abruptly crumpling line. Its sister regiments scrambled across the cut and smashed into the woods, routing the Federals lodged there. The Thirty-second stormed a height of ground farther west, taking more prisoners and snatching up flags thrown down by frightened Yankee color sergeants. A final scrambling advance took the rest of the brigade across the obstructing ditch and into position behind the embankment of another railroad just at the edge of town.[19]

It was evening now. Tired soldiers mopped from their sweaty mouths the black powder smudge of bitten cartridges. Daniel had taken 2,100 officers and men into battle, and nearly a third of these had been killed or wounded. Among the fallen was Lieutenant Baker of Company D. But, reckoned exultant Carolinians, the loss of the driven foe was heavier still. Best of all, there could hardly be any more lofty patronizing of an untried brigade.

For Iverson's proud veterans had broken against bloodily resisting foemen. Lots of them had surrendered, and the Federals had almost flanked and obliterated the rest. Only Daniel's left, the Forty-third and the Fifty-third and the Second Battalion, had stemmed the tide, had stubbornly hammered out a victory against odds. And who hadn't heard about the Twentieth North Carolina, Iverson's regiment when he was colonel? It had lost its flag to the enemy, and the Forty-fifth had got the flag again, with the Yankee who had taken it. Captain Galloway of the Forty-fifth had handed it to one of the Twentieth—here, son, here's your flag back, take better care of it. Let Iverson's heroes comb that one out of their tangled whiskers! Come to think of it, some folks said Iverson hadn't done so almighty well at Chancellorsville, after all.[20]

Along Gettysburg's northern outskirts lay Rodes' victorious brigades, gobbling rations and counting casualties. They had been hurt, but not crippled. They'd still go forward, if Lee wasn't holding them back until all his army was up. Well, tomorrow they'd finish what they'd begun today. Give the Yanks a twenty-devil whipping on their own dunghill, set them running the way they'd run at First and Second Manassas, at Chancellorsville, at Winchester, and just now north of Gettysburg. After that—it might be Washington, Philadelphia, even New York or Boston. Even the final victory. Boys, nothing they've got can stop us now.

XI

FOUGHT WELL AND WAS
COMPLIMENTED

Little patrols of the knowledgeable, deadly sharpshooters stole into Gettysburg by sunset, picking up stragglers from the Federal retreat that had streamed clear through town. On the field that they had won, Daniel's men slept soundly, with dead bodies for company.[1]

The worst punishment had been endured by the Thirty-second and Forty-fifth regiments and the Second Battalion, but nobody of the Forty-third could complain of having spent the afternoon in boresome security. The whole regiment had been galled by fire, it had faced and fought and beaten superior numbers of the enemy. And nobody had faltered, or turned from the close-driven glare of danger. Bravery had abounded everywhere. With two of Company D, that bravery had been conspicuous. Captain Cary Whitaker and Sergeant George Wills had been admired by superior officers.[2]

Gray dawn saw the brigade up and moving to the right and around, upon the north end of the height it had helped to seize on July 1—Seminary Ridge, Gettysburgers called it. At a strong point they halted again, with less

impatience than they had felt twenty hours earlier, and
formed to support elements of A. P. Hill's Corps. Riddled
but not crippled by battle, Daniel's Brigade[3] was still
larger than most of its fellows in the Army of Northern
Virginia. Indeed the Carolinians were proud and somewhat boastful as they lay on their muskets and talked
of how they had helped to win the northern edge of
Gettysburg.

By the rising sun's hot light they watched a battery
unlimber for action against Yankees on the frowning
height below the town and opposite Seminary Ridge.
Firing began and was noisily answered. That was Cemetery Ridge over yonder. Appropriately named, maybe?
Loudly and sustainedly, Confederate and Union guns
tried to shout each other down. Shells burst among the
deployed companies, and wounded were borne away.

". . . the cannonading was warmer and harder than
ever I heard," decided Billy Beavans for all the brigade,
as he watched Hill's troops in front, and Longstreet's to
the right, advancing against a blue threat in the hollow
between the ridges. Common soldiers were bound to
wonder what was going on while they waited. Hadn't
they whipped the Yankees yesterday afternoon? Weren't
they going to whip them again today? Why couldn't
General Lee give orders to——

General Lee was there. He rode to the front on gray
Traveller, with staff officers behind him.

Lee's dark, wise glance probed the action beyond and
below. He had not chosen this battleground, with the
Federals yonder on that string of high places. Stuart had
been off glory-seeking with the cavalry that should have
informed Lee of the enemy's whereabouts. And, after one
day of promising success, this second day wore on to disappointments—Ewell loitering in Gettysburg at the left of
the line after having broken and turned the flank there,

when he should have grabbed strong points below the town; Longstreet, who had never wanted to invade, showing his dissatisfaction by glumness and slowness amounting nearly to rebellion against his commander.

As Lee reached the flank of the Forty-third, soldiers faced toward him and, one after another, dragged the old slouch hats from their unkempt heads.[4] Nobody spoke or cheered; it was somewhat like being in church, for all the thundering bombardment and the bright blood on the grass. Lee's presence stiffened the spine of every man who saw him. Youngsters far from home turned to him as children turn, for leadership and compassion and miraculous victory. "Our father, Lee. . . ." So he was named in the heart of Sharpshooter Louis Leon of the Fifty-third.[5]

All through the day the Forty-third watched from where it waited, while the battle went on across the valley and toward the south, at points called Little Round Top and Devil's Den, the Peach Orchard, and the Wheat Field. It settled nothing, that fighting, everything was still to win or lose tomorrow, July 3. Meanwhile, Daniel's men endured bombardment on Seminary Ridge as cattle endure a storm. Thirsty, they held their supporting line, and hungry and sweaty; and rising gunsmoke veiled the sun as it dropped behind their backs to the western horizon. A bright full moon rose in the sky above Cemetery Ridge across from them. By its light they were advanced at last, as though in line of battle.

Cannon flashed on Cemetery's dark brow. Shells burst to right and left, groping for victims. Pace by pace, the regiments of Daniel descended into the shadow-clotted valley. Again the voices of the officers:

"By the left flank—march!"

In column now, they trudged away through Gettysburg's outskirts, taken yesterday with their own hands, and beyond to the eastward. More Confederates waited in the moonlight, lines of them ready for battle, hard, bearded, ragged men with their shining muskets in their practiced hands. And off to the south and the west, the position from which Daniel's Brigade had come, guns still whooped in the night.[6]

The force which Daniel joined was gazing toward the two knobs at the northern end of Cemetery Ridge below Gettysburg, containing those heights in the curve of their battle formation. Billy Beavans came up behind his brigade with the ammunition wagons. He had refused to quail under the shells that had pelted around those loads of explosives. At three o'clock in the morning, Daniel's men sprawled along the edge of a roadway and slept by snatches.

Dawn was early, clear, with the sun's first edge peeping at the shabby gray left shoulders of the Forty-third. At command of Thomas Kenan they rose, formed, deployed, and moved up the eastward slope of knoblike Culp's Hill, where the division of Edward Johnson clung tensely to an upward-staring position seized on July 2. On the tree-covered crest above them waited a line of Federals, stiff and stubborn. Again big guns began to boom, building into an ear-assailing antiphony as yesterday and the day before.

A brigade up ahead scrambled to its feet and advanced. After it came Daniel. Kenan led his regiment splashing across a creek, struggling through brush and between scattered boulders. The Yankee batteries struck from above as with clubs. The men started to climb.

As the brigade ahead slowed up, like Iverson's north of Gettysburg on the first day, Daniel moved to the left and into the first line of the uphill advance. Through belts and thickets of trees his regiments strove. Nearer they scrambled, nearer, with volleys ripping into them from behind a rough barricade of felled trees at the lip of the crest.

Then, suddenly, they were there, and the Federals sagged away from the makeshift works. Kneeling behind the logs, the North Carolinians poured Minié balls into the fading enemy line and endured a new tempest of shells from beyond.

Men fell here, dead and wounded. Muskets strove, defiantly inadequate, to give cannon a proper reply. Over in the Fifty-third Regiment, Louis Leon's ramrod stuck in the overheated barrel of his piece, and he flung the jammed weapon down to snatch another from a comrade fallen at his side. At deadly point-blank range, he and others fired into the enemy. But such an unequal fire fight could not go on, the small shot against the great. The Confederates must fall back or go forward. Who would hesitate in choosing which?

The Forty-third held the line at Daniel's left. Next to them were Virginians, the brigade of George Steuart. These swept forward at command. Kenan, too, scrambled over the logs, and after him poured the left of the Forty-third's line. The men fired as they advanced, and saw a blue formation melting in front. But, before the right wing of the Forty-third was clear of the crude breast-works, Steuart's command faltered and fell back to shelter again.

Not so Kenan. He halted his men, half in and half out of the encumbering mass of logs. A Federal battery less than a quarter of a mile away opened on them with grape, shell, and shrapnel.

Then they saw their friends and brothers fall to left and right, heads smashed, bodies severed, arms and legs blown away, "almost as fast as the leaves that fell as cannon and musket balls hit them." The terrain here was, in some measure, a more thicketed miniature of what they had seen from Seminary Ridge the day before. They held one rise of ground, the enemy another, with a dipping depression between. For either side to charge would mean a rush forward, down, then up, over scattered boulders and impeding timber clumps. Such an advance would partake of the suicidal. The two forces blasted away at each other murderously.

Kenan was down, in front of his men, and members of his staff dragged him back behind the captured breastworks. Lieutenant Colonel Lewis took command, among squads that grew smaller and smaller up and down the line. In lulls of the firing, soldiers in the works or in front of them could hear wounded comrades begging for water.

Noon came and passed, and still they fought. Billy Beavans was dragging the ammunition up to them somehow. George Wills, the tall sergeant, directed the fire of his company, and himself used a musket to deadly purpose. Those still on their feet saw the enemy line dwindling too. Death seemed everywhere, bleakly impartial in his choice of blue victim or gray.

But the Federal batteries were the deciding factor. Nobody could face that unreturned cannonade forever. Word came to fall back. Down the hill retired the Confederates, bringing with them such of their wounded as they could carry. Weary and decimated, still they took a new stand at the foot of the hill, firing upward at enemy positions among the trees on the slope.[7]

There was an effort to pursue them. Skirmishers in front of the new line encountered Yankees stealing through cover, and as afternoon wore toward dusk there was fighting at close quarters. Some parts of the skirmish line were shot to pieces. And all the time the din of other battles struck from elsewhere. West and south of Culp's Hill the Confederacy had receded from its high tide—Pickett's charge that topped, but could not take and keep, Cemetery Ridge. And east and north, Stuart's cavalry and the Yankee mounted brigades under Gregg sabered and pistoled each other to a standstill.

Night came, and rain fell on shelterless survivors. Fagged, sullen, hungry, they tightened their powder-crusted lips and stayed where they were. Some, perhaps, could sleep, weariness overcoming the noise and clammy downpour, the confusion and the sense of danger. At midnight Daniel moved his men away, through the streets of awed Gettysburg, to rejoin their division and take a position at the right of the main line. It was almost where they had paused so triumphantly on the night of July 1. They lay down in the mud, and the rain beat upon them.[8]

At last they could look around them for surviving friends, and count the holes in the ranks where other friends would march no more.

For Company D, George Wills reckoned a light loss compared to that of some other units. Lieutenant Baker was wounded. W. R. Carlisle and J. R. Gammons had been killed. Jonathan Hill and S. C. Wheeless were breathing their last. Others were wounded, but would recover. One private was missing—G. A. Manning, left in the enemy's hands on Culp's Hill. The regiment had suffered 147 casualties, and in Daniel's entire brigade of 2,100 a total of 916 were marked killed, wounded, or missing.[9] All along the Confederate line, regiments licked their wounds. Facing them, the Yankees recorded their own staggering losses.

Who had won? Nobody, perhaps, thought some. "Both sides got the worst of the fight at Gettysburg," sententiously decided Gaston Lewis,[10] now commanding the racked Forty-third in the wounded Kenan's place. Many officers and men, Northern and Southern, might be disposed to agree with him.

Next day, quiet after all the apocalyptic tumult. No guns, no headlong charges.

Wagons rolled off in long lines, laden with the wounded. Kenan went in one of those wagons, and Baker in another, with all the suffering thousands. Some, past all suffering, would lie where they had fallen. Company D hastily buried its dead. Over in the Thirty-second, Joe John Cowand had been killed, with fifteen Virginia girls and a pretty-cheeked Bertie County cousin to weep for him. Of the Fifty-third's sharpshooter squad, only Louis Leon and John Cochran were still on their feet.[11]

Rain began to fall at noon, spattering the fresh graves and churning mud under the ambulance wheels.

When the cloud-masked sun set, Lieutenant Colonel Lewis ordered his regiment to be ready to move. Another long wait and, by midnight, they started gropingly off along a road southwest, at the head of Rodes' Division.

Morning found them still moving. Billy Beavans' ordnance train overtook them on the squashy-wet road. At midday of the 5th they paused west of the little town of Fairfield and bivouacked, tired, soaked and hungry. Dawn was clear, and the men of Daniel's Brigade paused to watch other units move past.[12]

They would be the rear of the army now. Longstreet and Hill had gone ahead, the Second Corps would follow. To right and left of the road Daniel deployed them across a green valley, and the pursuing Federals came up, swiftly spreading into line to give battle.

At once the Confederate rear guard opened fire. The oncoming bluecoats brought their own muskets into play. "Surrender!" yelled a Federal officer, charging near, but he and his men backed up before murderous volleys. Slowly the two lines drew apart. Another dogged advance by the Yankees, again a slowing up before a skirling burst of musket fire. A second time the space widened between the lines, and Daniel formed column to march after the army.[13]

Traversing Monterey Gap in South Mountain, Company D heard unhappy news. Union cavalry had rushed the ambulance train on the evening of July 4, had cut off some of the wagonloads of wounded. Colonel Kenan was in enemy hands. So was Lieutenant Baker,[14] and so was Surgeon William T. Brewer, who once had dosed George's dysentery with opium, and who had ridden with the wounded of the Forty-third. On strove the infantry through mud and mire, reeling with fatigue and faint with hunger, but still fighting away the Yankees who pressed from behind.

George's tall spare frame wilted. Wet clothes and utter weariness sickened him to the point of exhaustion. Billy Beavans, riding near, saw his friend's plight and beckoned him to ride in one of the ammunition wagons. Other officers were similarly compassionate. More than once the rear guard saw a general trudging through the mud, leading his horse on which sat a sick or fagged private soldier. And the commanding general himself was close to the fighting. They saw, and Leon wrote: ". . . our father, Lee, was scarcely out of sight when there was danger. We could not feel gloomy when we saw his old gray head uncovered as he would pass us on the march. . . . I care not how weary or hungry we were, when we saw him we gave that Rebel yell, and hunger and wounds were forgotten." [15]

Reaching Hagerstown in Maryland, they fell prone to rest. All day July 7 they fought back to energy. Company D bade good-by to Billy as he headed his wagons toward the Potomac at Williamsport.[16] Cannon roared to westward, where the Union army sidled close again.

But Lee's retreat was slower now. He would not break and run. The Potomac River, knee-deep at this point

twenty days ago, had grown swollen and swift with heavy
rains. Lewis turned the Forty-third to throwing up breastworks, part of a line behind which the whole army would
defend the wagons and the crossing. There were no assaults on that position, and very little firing.

With rest and food, the Army of Northern Virginia
lifted its head again. There was no overwhelming sense
of defeat or disaster. George, back with his company, was
still weak but ready to fight if ordered. Writing home, he
spoke for a whole army still very much in the field:

> Our Brig. fought well and was complimented by Gens.
> Lee, Ewell & Rodes. . . . I don't want you to think for a
> moment from this letter that I am at all discouraged but
> on the other hand am in good spirits.

The tall young sergeant could spare concern for home
affairs, even while he eyed the enemy threat beyond the
new breastworks. His young brother was on his mind:

> I suppose it is now time for the schools to commence
> their terms again, so I hope you have concluded to send &
> probably [have] sent Ed. off to one of them. If you have
> not, I hope you will send him as soon as you get this, we
> all are willing to make sacrifices for him, and indeed I will
> promise to pay for his tuition.[17]

On the 11th the regiments paraded, while the adjutants
read a new general order, signed by Lee:

> After long and trying marches, endured with the forti-
> tude that has ever characterized the soldiers of the Army
> of Northern Virginia, you have penetrated the country of
> our enemies, and recalled to the defense of their own soil
> those who were engaged in the invasion of ours.
> You have fought a fierce and sanguinary battle which,
> if not attended with the success that has hitherto crowned

your efforts, was marked by the same heroic spirit that has commanded the respect of your enemies, the gratitude of your country, and the admiration of mankind.

Once more you are called upon to meet the army from which you have won on so many fields a name that will never die. . . .[18]

That sounded like action to come. The ragged rebels would not flinch from action, especially under orders from Robert E. Lee. But there was no general engagement, though skirmishers had their exciting moments on July 12 and 13. Again rain, and a retirement through ankle-deep mud to the very banks of the Potomac. Once again Daniel's Brigade rear-guarded the army.

A single pontoon bridge tossed and trembled on the swift-running waters. Across this Billy Beavans urged his wagons, just before dark of the 13th. During the night the infantry waded across. Upstanding men like George Wills and Cary Whitaker sank to their armpits. Smaller soldiers, like Louis Leon, found the water lapping their chins. Men carried their guns and ammunition above their heads. They floundered ashore at last, more weary than ever.[19]

"We went six miles further, and I honestly believe more of us were asleep on our night's march than awake," wrote Leon in his journal. "But, still, all kept up, for the rear was prison."

The brigade halted at last, not far from where Billy Beavans had unhitched. In the first hint of rainy dawn, groups of soldiers built fires and tried to dry themselves. A few hours later they resumed the march across wet Virginia soil, and the downpour washed from seedy uniforms the mud of Pennsylvania and Maryland. That night they slept, wet and drugged. On the 15th they completed only five miles, and on the 16th only eight, coming to Darksville at noon.[20] There they bivouacked, their fagged bones absorbing the sweetness of doing nothing.

Company D could count its losses now. These were reported to Orderly Sergeant George Wills, temporarily in command.

For sickness had racked the weary regiments. Cary Whitaker had been detached to serve as adjutant for the brigade, replacing the ailing Captain W. M. Hammond. Sim Whitaker, too, was ill, and gone to the army hospital at Staunton. George, back on his feet, glowered fearsomely at those who whined about hardships and dangers, but he himself wished silently for home faces and voices. He wrote to his father:

> Whenever Gen. Lee thinks proper (for I want surely to be governed by his wishes) I am ready and anxious to go where I can see and hear somebody from home; I don't know when I ever did want to see you all worse than I do now, therefore just as soon as we get to a place fit, I want you to come to see me.
>
> I feel grateful to the All-Wise-One for his care of me during the many dangers I have passed through, and feel that I have never served Him as I should. . . .
>
> Pa I am almost discouraged sometimes when I hear how the lower classes, which you know comprises most of our army talk but I take courage by thinking fear of military power will probably keep them.

Pride in what had happened at Gettysburg and afterward possessed him as he continued:

> If Gen Lee could have driven the enemy off those Heights the 3rd day the south would have been more complete than any time since the war [but] that he couldn't do, and our supplies were nearly exhausted, we had to flee back toward the Potomac which he took his own time about. You will see from the papers that we were in line of battle at Hagerstown two or three days. We had a splendid position but couldn't get them to attack so con-

sequently recrossed the Potomac it (the recrossing) is said by old troops to be one of the boldest things they ever knew.[21]

Again, no word about his own conduct. But, elsewhere in the Darksville bivouac, Lieutenant Colonel Lewis drafted his report for the Forty-third, raw no longer since that three days of unflinching courage under scalding enemy fire. "Where all acted so well," he summed up, "it is difficult to particularlize for good conduct, but . . ."

Two officers he mentioned for gallantry. Among the enlisted men, two more: "Sergeants Grier, Company B, and Wills, Company D, behaved remarkably well."

Junius Daniel made his own list of conspicuously valiant subordinates in the brigade. This included Cary Whitaker, noted for "bravery and coolness." And Ewell, for the Second Corps, wrote: "The following non-commissioned officers and privates are honorably mentioned for gallantry. . . . Sergeant Wills, Company D, Forty-third North Carolina . . ."[22]

These praises by his commanders must have drawn George's long body even more proudly erect. Businesslike and casual, the sergeant-commander of Company D gave Wash permission to visit home. Let the faithful servant bring back a new shirt and a pair of drawers, and several pairs of socks—most of George's supply had shredded in the muddy marching. Still refusing rations of beef and mutton, George lived on bread mixed of flour, salt, and soda stirred up in water. Despite this cheerless fare, he wrote to sister Lucy that he was in good spirits, and counted himself fortunate to be alive. And: "May the good Lord keep you all, and may we meet again, in the country's peace and freedom, is the prayer of your devoted brother. . . ."

XII

FALLEN IN LOVE ON SOMEBODY ELSE'S PLANTATION

Billy Beavans had secured a notebook, probably in Pennsylvania where such things were easier found than in paper-starved Virginia. Characteristically, he wrote on the first page the name and address of a Northern girl who must have admired him, gray uniform and all:

> Miss Amanda White
> Amboy Street   First Home
>   Below Columbia Avenue
> East Side   Philadelphia
> Penne.

Wars just don't last forever, both Billy and Miss Amanda White must have reflected. When peace dawned, such young men and women might do something toward achieving conciliation between the sections.

More businesslike, Billy set down a record of arms in the hands of Daniel's various regiments, and in the wagons. The Forty-third, for example, had 503 rifled muskets. Then, a matter of the utmost importance to soldiers in the field:

RECIPE FOR THE ITCH.—Take one wine glass of fresh unslacked lime, two of flour of sulphur, and ten of water. Put in a porcelain kettle and place it over the fire, stirring it all the time with a wooden paddle until the sulphur disappears on the surface of the water. Then bottle it up closely and it is ready for use. Wash the patient well with warm water, then saturate every part of the body with the fluid; in half an hour wash off in warm water again. Put on clean linen and you are cured.

Billy's sentimental versifyings, so frequent in the war's first year, would hardly belong in the same book with that useful item, and he included none. However, he continued his writing with a history of the Gettysburg campaign as he had seen it, from the advance in support of Stuart at Brandy Station to the final march westward from Darkville.[1]

If he had ceased to compose verse, Billy relished music as before. Again he listed songs he liked:

She, Forever
Love, Good Bye
On to Richmond
When this cruel War is Over
Dew Drops
No Surrender, by T. H. Taylor.

He was messing with the brigade staff now, and Company D saw him only on social visits.[2]

On July 20, the Second Corps fruitlessly pursued a Federal force toward Martinsburg, moved beyond to Winchester, and eventually, by way of the Shenandoah Valley, to Madison Court House by July 29.

There was time to recognize that Gettysburg had been a defeat, and not the only one to befall the Confederacy. Vicksburg had fallen on the day that the wounded had been captured at Monterey Gap. Raiding northward, the flying cavalry chief, General John Hunt Morgan, had been captured. Ebb tide had set in for Southern fortunes and for Southern morale.

That brought a mood of meditation, a sense that life was short, uncertain, unhappy. Throughout the whole Army of Northern Virginia, men turned to thoughts of religion. They flocked to their chaplains and to visiting preachers. There were series of devout prayings and sermons, of the nature of a revival—not so shoutingly emotional as earlier civilian camp meetings, but earnest for all that. Chaplain Thompson, in the Forty-third, began a great work of conversion as the Forty-third set up a new camp near Orange Court House, and in two weeks swept many previously doubtful and backsliding listeners into a profession of faith. George, who once had thought the chaplain uninspired and coarse in his pulpit manner, was rejoiced. ". . . he is a working man," George described Thompson to his father, "and worth a good deal to the Regt. . . ." [3]

Spiritual consolations may have helped make the survivors of Gettysburg more cheerful. George, turning to physical thoughts, wished he could get somewhere within reach of a bacon issue.[4] As for the Shenandoah Valley, where once he thought he would have liked to be a native: "This is a great country, as I have written before, and the scenery is sublime, but I must acknowledge to you that I am heartily tired of this now, and am perfectly willing to look upon some less beautiful for a short time at least."

Lee concentrated his forces against a possible advance by the enemy. Men returned from hospital, stragglers rejoined their regiments, and deserters were herded back. The sturdy North Carolina troops, irked with reports of Union sentiment in their home state, called a convention to make public their own views. George went as a delegate from the Forty-third, and voted in favor of a resolution declaring sharply for continuing the war.

Wash, too, came back to Company D, laden with boxes and parcels. Dolefully the mess threw away chickens spoiled en route, but vegetables were washed in a cold stream and thankfully devoured. And Wash had home news, too, frankly spoken as always. The loyal and staunch servant who had disdained flight to freedom in Pennsylvania spoke with contempt of timid stay-at-homes. George, fresh from voting at the convention, passed on these observations to Lucy:

> Wash says no matter how many conscripts they call for, there will then be a lot of men home, who will remain there, says they are flying around and there is no war there yet.
>
> I wish some plan could either be hit upon to get them off, or to make them feel public censure, one of the two; I do not think when this war does end that the men who stay at home, with no excuse, ought to be looked upon as those in the army, and I for one will go in to put them down, too. Croakers & deserters ought to be hung on the same scaffold.

More lightly, and with a touch of playful mystery, he finished:

> Marrying and giving in marriage, being the order of the day, I want you to say to my numerous sweethearts, I wish when they commence at least one of them would wait for the war to end, ha! ha! reckon you will be tho like Wash, and not know who to tell.[5]

After a month in camp at Orange Court House, the Forty-third had arranged things in soldierly fashion, and praise trickled down from high levels of command. Rumor had it that it was considered the best regiment in the entire army, saving only the Eleventh North Carolina, inheritor of the Bethel flag and the Bethel tradition. George, still commanding the company with all officers away, was pleased, "though I had rather have been *first.*" On August 31, the inspector general of Rodes' Division ordered a review, and liked what he saw.

Company D mustered thirty-eight for duty out of seventy-one, but this half showing was soldierly and smart. The inspecting officer paused to address Sergeant Wills, bracing to attention in front of his men. D had the best muskets in the Forty-third, which had the best in the division. "I was rather proud of that," George understated his feelings in a letter to his father.[6] With Virginia gardens flourishing, rations were better, too. Wash sliced tomatoes and boiled fresh corn for his master.

Sim Whitaker returned from sick leave at Enfield,[7] to family joshing about romantic rumors. Sim had something to say about another romance, too. George's heart glowed to hear his uncle speak of Miss Lulu, "the elegant and refined manners and good disposition of my new sweetheart. . . ."

The good humor was diluted by sad news. Lieutenant Baker had died in enemy hands. Company D voted for new officers. Sim Whitaker was advanced to the first lieutenancy, as he deserved, and Orderly Sergeant George Wills, conspicuously gallant at Gettysburg and for some weeks acting commander of the company, became Second Lieutenant George Wills. He did not say much of his joy at this final crowning of his hopes, but his morale rose high and his spirit was strong.[8] Johnny Beavans, doubtless lonesome for Miss Laura, moped; George, with a commission, good rations, and his own love warming him, cheered Cousin Johnny up. On September 8, Cary Whitaker left on a fifteen-day furlough, and on the day following the Second Corps passed in review before General Lee. Present with the commanding general were Ewell, Early, Johnson, and Rodes of the Second Corps, and the insistently dashing Jeb Stuart of the cavalry.

At dawn of September 14, the Second Corps formed column and by seven o'clock was marching. It completed twelve miles to Morton's Ford on the Rapidan and heard firing from somewhere. In the morning there were reports of skirmishing close at hand. The whole army took position along the stream.[9]

The view from the Forty-third's new bivouac was at once forbidding and beautiful. Ramparts of red earth extended along the south bank of the river, with artillery posted thickly on every advantageous rise of ground. Farm homes dotted the valley, and fields of vigorously ripening corn covered the bottoms. Afar toward the west rose the Blue Ridge, festooned with fleecy clouds; and just beyond the Rapidan, shallow and narrow just here, could be seen the line of Federal pickets, small as tin soldiers, stretching off into the distance both ways. Farther north still, the white tents of the enemy clustered on distant green slopes like flocks of sheep.[10]

Two such armies in face of each other meant action to come, and lively action. Batteries of guns began to scold each other, as if in preparation. Some of the men cowered from the prospect of battle, and desertions became distressingly frequent. On September 16, Rodes' entire division paraded to witness what happened to deserters.

A band played a funeral dirge. A chaplain prayed over the kneeling prisoner. Then the man was bound to a stake, and the firing squad sent its volley into him. Finally, regiment by regiment, the marshaled witnesses walked past to have a look at close quarters. Eight bullets had smashed through the slack body.[11] Similar shootings were being conducted across the river by the Yankees. These stark measures lessened the number of desertions on both sides. Even hard autumn rains and no tents found the rank and file of the Forty-third remaining steadfast.

"In speaking distance of the Yankees," Louis Leon noted in his diary as he did picket duty on September 20. Two days later, he ventured to the brink of the Rapidan, fraternized across the brown trickle with a bluecoat of the Seventh Ohio, and exchanged a home newspaper for one from the North. Leon, small, sure, grown expert with his musket, had found himself as a scout and a sharpshooter. He declined the ten-day furlough offered to all Jewish Confederates for the New Year's holidays, and on the 26th helped with the building of cabins against the increasingly chill weather.[12]

Young Lieutenant Wills, sitting down that same day to write to Sister Lucy, thought of other things than war. Maggie Beavans and kindly Mammy Leah had made a final attempt on behalf of the disconsolately repentant Miss Fannie. But with George it was too late now, far too late, for any reconciliation:

> Tell Cousin Mag. & Leah, it isn't worth while for them to get a certain young lady's regards for me. I am certainly out of it now; don't care whether I see or hear from her, or not—have fallen in love on somebody else's plantation now.[13]

The thought was as snug in his heart as were Miss Lulu's letters in his pocket. Like Johnny, George thought of marrying when the war was over. Even a double wedding may have entered his mind. On the margin of another home letter he wrote, dreamily happy:

> Laura and Lulu
> Laura and Lulu
> Johnnie and George

News of a Confederate victory at Chickamauga, River of Death, trickled in to cheer the army. Therefore, Lee assumed the offensive.

The sun dropped down on October 9 as the regiments formed for marching, swiftly and silently. Off moved the thin gray ranks in the dusk, westward below the river, along muddy roads. Men splashed and floundered in puddles. A pause for rest after midnight, and at dawn all were up to march again. They waded across the Rapidan at Liberty Mills, camped, and on the 11th forded the Roberson River. They must be near the enemy—orders were passed forbidding the men to sing or talk as they slogged through brushy hollows and under the shadow of ridges. The sound of firing rose away to the westward, where cavalry were fighting. On October 12 the infantrymen moved through pretty Culpeper, stripped off shoes and pants to wade the ice-cold Hazel, and completed twenty-five miles. In the afternoon, within a mile of Jeffersonton, bluecoats bobbed up in front of Daniel's Brigade.

But the check was only momentary. A yell and a rush by the fierce Southern infantry, and the opposition melted away through town. On the far side, the brigade formed line of battle and moved swiftly forward. Still the enemy retired, across the Rappahannock and through the town of Warrenton. Pressing swiftly, Daniel scooped up Union stragglers.

The forward movement continued through Warrenton on the 13th, and the men held position beyond all day and all night. At four o'clock the next morning sharpshooters moved ahead of all brigades in the Second Corps. At daylight the men in line of battle heard a volley.

Again an advance through brush and timber, with no stubborn stand against it. George drew his saber to conduct his first battle as a commissioned officer. His shipwrecky digestion was plaguing him again, but he kept his place in front of his troops. Company D poked into thickets and behind trees, flushing demoralized Yankees from hiding, singly or in bunches. Scrubby-looking men, decided George; many were grizzled oldsters, others seemed boys in their teens. The young lieutenant ordered these captives bundled off to the rear, and moved on. When a halt was called at last, the enemy continued to flee from in front, but sharp firing resounded to the right.

There the Third Corps had met stiff resistance. Ewell changed the direction of his own victorious divisions in the direction of the new fight, but the Federals fled there, too, just as the Second Corps arrived.

Again on the move, the men heard that this battle would be called Bristoe Station. More cold autumn rain fell hard as the regiments camped on an open field. What place was this? Manassas, where twice before Confederates had beaten the invader. It was a comforting thought, however soggy the ground under the blanket.

October 15 they paused at Manassas, alert for a Union threat that did not come. On the following day, headed back for the Rapidan, they destroyed railroad, bending red-hot rails over blazing bonfires of crossties. And on October 17, in camp near Warrenton Junction, George snatched time to write home.

Dysentery wrung his bowels, as so often before, and weakened his knees, but he had not fallen out during march or battle. He permitted himself a slight boast about that. Cary Whitaker and Johnny Beavans, too, were ill and had difficulty keeping up with Company D. Even patient, sinewy Wash complained dolefully and wished for rest in snug quarters.

Tired and wet, the Second Corps crossed the Rappahannock on a pontoon bridge, and the Forty-third threw down its blanket rolls near Kelly's Ford. It was bitter cold, and men scrambled for turns at axes with which to build little huts. Company D's captain and the elastic Wash shrugged off their sapping illness, but George and Johnny still ailed.[14]

That stubborn griping of the belly made George the happier to claim a fifteen-day furlough the first week in November. While the rain ceased and the sun brightened the reds and yellows of autumn foliage, he headed southward, and away for Halifax County and Brinkleyville.[15] There he could put his booted legs under a family dinner table heaped with harvest plenty, and exhibit his glory of shoulder straps and sash and saber to elegant-mannered, starry-eyed Miss Lulu.

XIII

HARD, HARD TO BE A GOOD MAN

George was back on November 21, still with twinges of misery in his guts,[1] to hear of the fighting that had gone on without him.

His comrades had returned to the camp below Morton's Ford on the Rapidan, and the tale they told was of Federal assault both cunning and resolute. On November 7, just after George left for home, the Long Roll was beaten on the Rappahannock. Across Kelly's Ford, from high ground on the north side, poured a strong blue column.

A rush to intercept, and Daniel's Brigade reached the ground to find that that the enemy had made a successful crossing. Two brigades of Confederates were smashed. That night sharpshooters like Jimmy Whitehead and Louis Leon crouched within a hundred yards of the blazing bivouac fires of overwhelming Union forces while the main army was forced to retreat clear below the Rapidan.[2]

It was a clear and baleful defeat, almost a disaster. Nobody of fair mind could deny that the Yankees were brave and aggressive and well led. The day had passed when two forces could blast away at each other all day, as at Big Bethel, with only a handful of casualties to count.

Company D, with the rest of the army, built new huts along the Rapidan for winter quarters. Cold weather added to George's sufferings, but he sensed battle coming, and refused to report sick. He had missed one fight when he had been needed; the next would find him present, with arms in his hands.[3]

It came on November 27 when again a torrent of blue infantry approached the crossings of the Rapidan. There was a clash of battle lines in rough, semi-wooded country south of the river, back and forth over land threaded with chilly streams. The Forty-third and most of Rodes' Division were spasmodically engaged that day, slept part of a chilly night, and advanced and retreated in rain on the 28th. In the evening they threw up breastworks behind a stream called Mine Run, and on the following day it developed that the enemy had dug its own line of entrenchments opposite. Artillery exchanged shells on the 29th, but there was no infantry action. On the 30th, pressure on divisions of the Second Corps relaxed. By night of December 1, the Confederates prepared for a determined attack, but in the morning found that their adversaries had retreated across the Rapidan once more.[4]

Back at their huts, Lee's soldiers slumped gratefully into shelter. They had skirmished for nearly a week, with scanty sleep, almost no rations, and cold weather night and day. George, who had not been well at the start of the campaign, was so nearly exhausted that he could barely write to his father on December 3.

He mourned the death of one old comrade from Bethel days, the sharpshooter Jimmy Whitehead. For his own safety, and his ability to drag himself back to his camp, he thanked "the mercy of the All-Wise-One." He reported to

Dr. William T. Brewer, the regimental surgeon who had been captured at Gettysburg and had returned to duty through exchange.[5] That acrid medical man had disliked his captivity. ". . . says he was treated miserably by the authorities, but could get what he wanted from the citizens, says the wounded Yankees that fall into his hands may take care for their limbs, for upon the slightest wound he will take them off."

Brewer sent George to the divisional board of medical examiners, who saw that he was in precarious health and approved for him a thirty-day sick leave. Barely able to rise from where he sat, George wrote to his brother Richard on December 8 that he would be home by the first of the following week. Wretched as he felt, he was able to think tenderly of Miss Lulu, and to write restrainedly to his brother Richard of a romantic hope:

> You may think me silly, but I really wish that I could look forward to a time when, and to someone who I could call *wife*. I think my life would be spent better, and be more pleasant, were this the case than at present, but Alas! provided I escape the sickness and fall of war, I fear it will be years yet before that much desired time shall come, for really the war begins now to seem to me like a ball, no end to it.

The death of brave Jimmy Whitehead still grieved George. He wondered if he would see Richard at home, and spoke of his earnest wish to "be as good as brother, but find it hard, hard to be a good man." [6]

Wash escorted his tottery master away to North Carolina, and there George went to bed at once. Friends and relatives called—surely Lulu came over from Elba Academy to visit her interestingly invalided lover. Home nursing and home cooking strengthened George somewhat, but by Christmas he was obliged to ask for an additional month of sick leave.[7]

At the plea of Richard, absent at Monticello, North
Carolina, for the holidays, the family spent New Year's
Day in prayer. Soon thereafter George was able to be up and
to go out on mild, fair days. News came that the Forty-
third had been transferred from Daniel's Brigade to aug-
ment a force marshaled against Federals who held the
North Carolina coast. Cary Whitaker visited home on the
way across the state. So did Billy Beavans, on furlough
from duty as Daniel's ordnance officer. On January 19,
despite windy cold, Billy and Maggie Beavans came to
visit at the Wills plantation.[8]

On the next day Richard Wills married Miss Lou
Norman. It seems to have been a fairly elaborate wedding
and reception, and to make it a happily hospitable
event must have taxed both the ingenuity and the resources of the Wills family to the utmost. Even in Halifax
County, wartime want stalked. Bacon, butter, corn meal,
flour, and pork were scarce and exhorbitantly priced. [9]
Sugar did not exist in a refined white form, and molasses
was used instead to sweeten coffee substitute of okra seed
or dried sweet potatoes. Clothes had long since worn out,
and were almost impossible to replace—very probably
Miss Lou was hard put, even with resewing and borrow-
ing, to appear in a bridal dress. But the Confederacy had
not run out of music or cheer. Not yet.

By the 27th, George was sufficiently recovered to visit
Centerville Plantation in return, accompanied by Sister
Lucy. Two days later, Billy and George called at Strawberry Hill to see Captain Cary, and then George went
home again. Apparently the activity of travel and visiting
weakened the convalescent, and he found himself still
unable to endure great or continued fatigue. Once more
he went to bed, while Billy returned to Virginia in
mid-February and Cary joined the Forty-third in Kinston.
Jack Whitaker, undoubtedly stirred by the sight and

example of his soldier cousins, enlisted in Company D on February 12.[10]

Mr. Wills began to treat his son with a preparation called Deem's Pills. They must have been effective; within ten days, George showed a gain of strength, and his skinny frame added four or five pounds. George's parents pleaded that he ask for an extension of his furlough, but George heard afar the beating of drums. On February 23 he and Wash headed for the camp of the Forty-third, just now turning its attention toward a Federal garrison at Plymouth.

Maddeningly, George felt a return of shaken weakness. He insisted on doing some sort of duty. Sitting at company headquarters, he supervised the making out of payrolls and other records. Jack Whitaker, new to the army but a good penman, did the actual writing. By February 28, George protested that he felt better and shook his head when friends advised him to apply for another furlough. He was an officer, his business was to lead men into battle. He fretted because he feared that he would miss the coming struggle and confided as much to understanding sister Lucy:

> There is no doubt, I suppose, about now returning to Va. in a month or so. I am so afraid, except there is a great change, that *then even,* I will not be ready for service. I don't know what I shall do if I am not, for I can't bear the idea of being left behind.

His back ached as he wrote, but his appetite was good. He asked Lucy to send a turkey by Johnny Beavans, who was on leave at Centerville. Lieutenant Sim, too, was burdened with delicacies as he arrived at Kinston on March 16.[11]

That same day George assuaged a feverish thirst by eating snow that fell on the camp, and four days later was able to report that he had gained an additional five pounds. And, again to Lucy: "Tell mother, if she please, console herself & Pa about my not coming home, I am doing as well here as I did there. . . ." [12]

By April 2, with rumor of a battle definitely coming, George pained Wash by refusing to ask for more sick leave.[13] Billy, relieved of his duty with the brigade, rejoined Company D.[14] The commander at Kinston—it was Major General George E. Pickett, the perfumed and ringleted chieftain who had charged and almost captured Cemetery Ridge at Gettysburg—waited for a special and formidable ally against Plymouth, the ironclad ram *Albemarle*.[15]

George swore to sister Mary in a letter written April 6 that he was much improved and ready for duty. In a postscript he cautioned his younger brother Ed against embarrassing Richard and his bride as they cuddled; but Ed had other things on his mind. The seed corn of the Confederacy was being called to the mill of wartime service. Seventeen years old now, Ed joined a company of teen-age recruits under Captain W. R. Williams, and before the month was out prepared to report to camp at Weldon. There he heard high praise of his lieutenant-brother, but was shocked at the efforts of his comrades to utter manful, soldierly oaths.[16]

At Kinston illness flowed over George again, despite his efforts to discount it. Weakened, he perforce returned to Brinkleyville and languished miserably, while the comrades headed into the battle. Plymouth fell to Pickett's force, and the Forty-third won golden opinions under Lieutenant Colonel Lewis. George must have raged—missing that glorious action in North Carolina. More maddening, there was a resumption of war in Virginia. As May followed April, the Forty-third was hurried back to Daniel's Brigade in time for the terrible battle of the Wilderness. Day after day the fighting continued, dubious among bullet-gashed trees, where Ulysses S. Grant, the new Federal commander, swore stubbornly to fight it out on that line if it took all summer.

And the Forty-third was brave in the Wilderness too, and at Drewry's Bluff and at the Bloody Angle and at Cold Harbor; all those actions without Lieutenant George Wills.[17]

The month-long battle wound up a Confederate victory, but news came of friends and kinsmen who had fallen in action.

Lucien Whitaker, shot in the spine, was reported dying, but refused to die. He came home semi-paralyzed, and made a partial recovery. John Hammill, teased by George in 1861 until he joined the Enfield Blues, was terribly wounded in the face. George Cherry, another family friend, lost a leg.[18] General Daniel had been killed almost in the moment of hard-fought success at the Bloody Angle. And others, so many others. Every man was needed in those riddled ranks.

With the end of May, George once more got his feet under him. Still not healthy, he refused to mope longer at home. With habitual care he donned his uniform as a Confederate lieutenant, the uniform still clean and new because he had had so little chance to wear it. His sword had been mislaid somewhere around the house, but he would not delay to find it. He and Wash burdened themselves with food and clothing and set off for the front in Virginia.

Above and east of Richmond they came to Cold Harbor, still stinking with unburied dead. Near the Mechanicsville Pike a system of battered trenches was held by the victors in the battle. The bony ragamuffins who welcomed George and Wash were hard to recognize as comrades.

George had been with the Forty-third for only two brief periods since early November. In his absence the regiment had exhausted itself to win distinction on the North Carolina coast and in the Virginia Wilderness. Just now it rested, having skirmished heavily and successfully with the enemy that morning, and nursed the wounds of May.

In Company D, no more than thirty grimy, wryly exultant men were on duty. Most of them wore only the last rags of shirts and trousers. They hailed their returned lieutenant with hairy grins.

Clustering around him, a gallant and filthy pack, they gazed with mock disgust at his natty uniform. Gold braid and commissioned rank did not abash men who had done their bloody part in repulsing the stubborn Grant and his swarms of assault troops.

"Those clothes are too clean for this place," declared one unbathed ruffian.

"That man looks too nice for this service," elaborated another, whose own recent service had included absolutely nothing of niceness.

"The sooner he gets those clothes dirty the better," offered a third.[19]

But it was affectionate, comradely derision, and George took it as such. Looking this way and that, he missed familiar faces. Cary Whitaker was gone, commanding the regiment, for Lewis' brave capability in the capture of Plymouth had won him a brigadier's star. Lieutenant Sim led Company D. And Johnny Beavans and Jack Whitaker had been wounded, were gone to the hospital in town.

Promptly George was told not to pity these bullet-pierced kinsmen. Day after day of facing a skyful of bullets had given the company a new philosophy; a wound, if not permanently crippling, was even a blessing of sorts. It won for a man some respite from the crushing toil and deadly peril of the battle lines.[20]

Casualties had riddled rank as well as file. Longstreet was severely wounded, Ewell had collapsed so utterly that he had had to be replaced as commander of the Second

Corps and A. P. Hill, though present for duty with the Third, was in poor health. And Jeb Stuart had been killed at the head of his cavalry—"I had rather die than be whipped," he had choked out. Daniel was gone, too, and into his place had stepped scowling, strong-bearded Bryan Grimes. Other dead included six brigadiers. Beside Longstreet, eleven general officers had been wounded, and two had been captured.

But the bullets hadn't struck home on one side only. George heard of the daily charges by Federals, line after line of them, and of how these were mowed down by cool, unerring volleys. Enemy prisoners said that Grant's casualties had been tremendous, and George expressed the hope that after a while all the Yankees would be killed.

"They are like ants, though," commented Billy Beavans, much more soberly than usual.

Up to regimental headquarters went George, carrying a fresh uniform for Cary Whitaker.[21] Gratefully Uncle Cary put it on at once. George was welcome, said Cary— only fifteen or sixteen officers remained to the Forty-third after the month of battles.

Cary, it developed, held only temporary regimental command, as senior captain. Thomas Kenan, in a Northern prison, still ranked as colonel. Incompetent Major Boggan remained on the rolls as senior field officer of the Forty-third; but wise superiors kept him on a detached assignment and employed the able Cary instead. Maybe Boggan would resign. Officers and men of the regiment hoped so. Then Cary would be promoted as he manifestly deserved.

On that same day clothing was issued to the troops who had guyed George for his neatness. Gratefully they discarded their tatters. And the officers' mess enjoyed the provisions George and Wash had brought with them.

At night there was heavy firing in front, and George

was sent to command the line of pickets. It lay close to the enemy, close enough to be smashed and obliterated should the Federals advance; but there was no advancing by those badly used boys in blue. George dozed once or twice, and by dawn had finished his tour of duty without incident.

Next day he wrote to his mother. He was hungry for asparagus soup but felt well. With somber hope he viewed the military situation:

> Grant will, after a while, come to the wise conclusion that we *cannot* be whipped, and not having any Army scarcely, as he will not have, will stop this very extended fight, and then possibly will commence some talk about having an end to this war. The Lord grant it, is the only response I make.
>
> The Yankees say, this fighting every day, is killing up their Army fast enough and if something isn't done they will not have anyone to fight with after a short while, from all I can learn, there is no doubt in my mind that Grant has lost since the 4th of May, every man of 100,000, when he makes these repeated attacks upon our breastworks with his from 5 to 10 lines of battle there is no doubt but that they are mowed down by *thousands,* I may venture to say.
>
> Tho our loss in fact is not at all to be compared with the Yankee, yet I must say this killing and wounding some every day is certainly doing great damage to the army. Oh how much I wish and pray for this fighting to stop, and everything again in peace and quiet.

That same day saw some fighting along the skirmish line, and on June 6 the whole Second Corps moved back to a reserve position. The weather was fair and warm.

Johnny recovered enough to leave the hospital for home, and carried back some luggage belonging to Cary Whitaker and George. Cary presented George with a handsome saber captured from the Federals at Plymouth, to replace the one left at home.[22] George wrote to sister Mary to send back asparagus and other vegetables by Johnny, and took a veteran's interest in news from Ed at Weldon:

> Tell Ed. he and his company are not half fixed up as they should be, if I were there as he is I would live more like home than that. soldiers life will not be half so hard and he will be much *better* satisfied. I want him to go to work, fix up his tent, a shade to sit under, with benches or stools, and by all means, something to boil his meat in and have no more fried meat. . . .[23]

Sunday, June 12, and George had been with his regiment a week and a day. He went with Uncle Cary and Uncle Sim and Smiling Billy to hear Chaplain Harding of the Forty-fifth preach. The text was the Twenty-third Psalm: *Though I walk in the valley of the shadow of death. . . .*[24]

George ignored twinges of stomach ache as he lay down that night. He woke to the voice of an officer in the dark. It was three o'clock in the morning. Around him men were rolling their blankets, donning their dusty hats. The regiment formed, behind another regiment. The whole brigade marched away.[25]

Where? The Southside Railroad perhaps? Or elsewhere along the Richmond-Petersburg defenses, to face some sudden Yankee concentration.

Dawn found them tramping along a road heading westward. Not only their own brigade appeared in the first light, but the whole division, and other divisions, the entire Second Corps. And there were strings of canvas-topped wagons, and rolling artillery.

"It soon became evident that our destination was the valley," wrote Cary Whitaker that day in his diary.

He meant the Shenandoah Valley, where General David Hunter of the Union threatened Lynchburg. He and Sim and George and Billy may have remembered Chaplain Harding's text of yesterday.

XIV

STILL THE WILL IS HALF THE MAN

The Second Corps traveled swiftly again, as with Jackson in the great day of Second Manassas and Chancellorsville, as with Ewell to Gettysburg. But it was less than half as large as when George Wills and his comrades had crossed the Potomac a year before; its new commander, the bold and profanely eloquent Jubal Early, had no more than eight thousand infantry, with six batteries of artillery. These reduced forces were superbly led. The Viking Rodes was now senior division commander. The other two divisions were headed by John B. Gordon, a handsome ramrod of a man who had shone at Gettysburg and in the Wilderness, and by Stephen Dodson Ramseur, a brave and brilliant young North Carolinian who sprouted a new beard to grace his increased rank and reputation.[1] Grimes was an able successor to Daniel. Cary Whitaker, riding in front of the Forty-third, looked as though he ought to be a colonel. Maybe he would be, if ever Boggan would resign and clear the way for Cary's promotion.

Twenty miles west of Cold Harbor they camped in the middle of the road they traveled. Next day saw them up and on the way shortly after sunrise, afflicted by the clouds of dust their feet kicked up, but making time for all that. They went twenty-two miles and fell out wearily near Louisa Court House, to cook rations for another day's journey. On the 15th, it was a brief march, seven miles only, but the dust made breathing unpleasant.[2] Passing through Louisa they heard with delight that three days earlier Wade Hampton's cavalry had driven from there a larger mounted force of Federals under Sheridan.

George Wills was keeping up, and so was Jack Whitaker, returned from hospital with a half-healed arm just in time to join Company D. Fighting against a new attack of dysentery, George wondered if the water he drank was bad for him. "Is it not hard to be only a half man?" inquired Dr. Brewer, never too kind to patients, as he handed out pills to George. "I think it is a good question," replied George, "still the *will* is half the man." [3]

The 16th saw twenty-five miles of ground pass under their tired but determined feet. Here was fruitful farm country. Wheat fields and potato patches encircled fine-looking country houses. The corps camped within six miles of Charlottesville, and were told that General Hunter was closing in on Lynchburg; also that, in Georgia, Joe Johnston had defeated Sherman.

The men knew now that they were hurrying to engage Hunter, and were eager for battle with that lively Yankee despoiler. "If he doesn't mind he may find himself about wound up before he thinks of it," jotted Cary Whitaker in his diary. Of the report of Johnston's victory, he decided temperately: "The rumor wants confirmation." [4]

George wrote home to sister Lucy that night, assuring her that he was well and keeping up with his company. He wanted to comfort his family: ". . . when I think of you all at home how concerned you are for me, and the many hardships I could miss by being with you, it some-times gives me the blues almost (not *quite* however), yet

I would not have it to say that I missed this march for anything, hardly." He could congratulate others absent, however: "John is missing it now isn't he? If he has a *good* wound, it is fortunate for him."

In Charlottesville next day, townsfolk treated the marching infantry to ice cream and cherries.[5] Gordon's and Ramseur's divisions boarded a train and rolled off. On the morning of the 18th, Rodes' men followed on another train. D Company sat on a flatcar, with dust sifting through beards.[6] Rolling into Lynchburg at four o'clock that afternoon, they heard big guns boom and were told that the enemy was but two and a half miles away, threatening the small garrison under Breckenridge. The Forty-third stacked arms in a pleasant grove on the edge of town.

Wakened at two-thirty in the morning, Cary Whitaker led his regiment east of Lynchburg, among the saw-toothed hills that overlooked the houses. But the Federals were pulling away from in front of the advance. Toward the village of Liberty the Confederates pursued, loudly cheered by the farm folk. On either side of the way sprawled butchered cattle and sheep and the carcasses of dead horses—Hunter's cavalry and artillery had shot their worn-out stock and replaced them with fresh animals from the farms. Homes had been plundered for food, too. "Demoralized," the Virginia citizens called Hunter's men. The pursuit was headlong, and covered twenty-three miles that day. Fast as Early's men moved, the Yankees moved faster in retreat.

Gordon and Ramseur caught up next day, and Rodes' regiments walked over the bodies of Union soldiers left on the field by the still-fleeing Hunter. Again the citizens shouted welcome and told of depredations. George and Billy frowned over stories of looted kitchens and slaughtered cows and horses. The Confederates themselves made a long march fasting. Company's D's hungry soldiers munched green apples, and several fell out, ill and exhausted.[7] That night they paused below a mountain ridge where Hunter was said to be making a stand.

Rations came up late at night, but not in quantity— only trifles of meat. "Bread! Bread!" shouted hungry men the next day as Rodes and Grimes rode by. George sympathized, but felt happy in a sense of regained health. The cherries he had eaten seemed to comfort his bowels.[8]

Hunter, still shy of close fight, retired from the mountain. The Forty-third hastened in an effort to cut off the enemy at a gap in the range. Elsewhere some cavalry from Lynchburg fought, taking prisoners and guns. Good, as far as the cavalry was concerned, but what about the Forty-third?

There was no catching up with Hunter, and on the 22nd the fagged troops were allowed their first day of rest since leaving Cold Harbor. Rations arrived at last, enough of them this time. In a pleasant stream near their camp Company D bathed and washed clothes.

George himself scrubbed gratefully in the cool running water, then sat down to write to his father. He was disappointed at not having scourged the enemy for despoiling the country:

> Sunday (19th) the Yankees having gotten the word of our being about, put out; and since then, Sunday, Monday & Tuesday we were pursuing them close up, and marched about 65 miles in the three days and only missed cutting off a large portion of them by only two hours . . . was quite unwell when we started and for the first two or three days, thought I should probably have to give up, but on the contrary commenced to improve, and am now perfectly well and yesterday was one of the best marching men in the Regt.[9]

As George finished writing, Billy Beavans brought him an assignment to duty at Rodes' headquarters. When the expedition moved toward Lexington on the 23rd, George commanded the guard that shepherded a column of doleful Union prisoners.[10]

Early had virtually stripped Lynchburg of its defenders, and now he had some fourteen hundred men with which to stalk his prey. Hunter had vanished, but Federals still garrisoned several Valley towns. The column moved toward Lexington.

The corps slogged past the female seminary at Botetourt Springs, and Cary Whitaker, at least, was disappointed to see no beauties among the young ladies who came to wave.[11] They reached Lexington by morning of the 25th.

George was back with his company now. Marching with the rear part of Rodes' Division, he and the others heard music up ahead—slow music, a dirge. The order came back for field officers to dismount, for the men to reverse their muskets as they marched. Down the street moved the regiments, one behind another, and finally they could see what it was all about. They were passing the grave of Stonewall Jackson.

Every officer doffed his hat as he passed the simple mound. Its wooden headboard had long ago been chipped away by souvenir hunters, but the Confederate flag fluttered there, and a profusion of summer flowers had been heaped. The men rested briefly in the town, and ladies appeared with cups of milk and slices of bread.

Jackson's grave, these ladies reported, had been guarded respectfully by Federals during the recent occupation. This courtesy had not included the Virginia Military Institute, where once Jackson had taught; the buildings had been burned, and so had the home of Virginia's governor John Letcher.

"What a pity," breathed one lovely girl to Cary Whitaker, "you were not here a fortnight ago." Then, after a winning pause and an eloquent look: "But I know you would have come if you could." Billy Beavans, too, basked in fair smiles.[12] The march was resumed, and they camped eight miles north of town. Hot weather was forcing many men to straggle.

Wearily the Second Corps toiled northward along the Valley through the villages of Brownsburg, Newport, and Middlebrook. Milk, butter, and cherries were the chief produce of the land, and were offered on all sides by the people. Some of these diluted their hospitality by complaining of General Early's failure to bag Hunter. "Of course each one knows exactly how it might be done," was Cary's ironic entry in his journal.[13]

In any case, Early had not failed everywhere. If Hunter had not cared to stop and fight, it would have been hard to catch up with him. The success lay in saving the crops of the Valley—the wheat was ready to cut now, to feed Lee's hungry troops arrayed in the Petersburg trenches against Grant, now fighting it out on another line than the one he had chosen in May.

George wrote to his mother on that 27th of July, about the impressively mournful parade past Jackson's grave, the hard marching—260 miles of it in two weeks, in hot weather and over rough country—and the kindness of Valley farmers: ". . . the inhabitants have from 5 to 12 cows that give 3 or 4 gal. per day. They furnish a good part of the Army with milk and butter, if I could get it all the time wouldn't need much rations." And he assured her again that he was strong and healthy. "Such weather & marching has caused a great many men to fall out, but we (our mess) are all up and doing well. Jack I believe, is like myself, commenced to improve on the march and is now perfectly well."

The next morning, too, they rested, cooking rations. At mid-afternoon they ambled through Staunton. North Caro-

lina farm boys gazed appreciatively at fine crops, ripe
for the cutting.[14] But Cary Whitaker scowled to see Union
prisoners sent to the rear in a stagecoach: "Can't see why
they are not made to walk."

On they went, fording rivers and eating miles of road.
Wash, the good forager, brought milk and butter for the
mess. On the 30th came word of General John Pope with
six thousand Federals up ahead at Martinsburg, "but,"
decided Captain Cary, "no doubt he is prepared if there
to skedaddle as soon as he hears our column is coming."
Some bivouac gossipers thought they were heading for
Maryland. Twice Confederates had gone there, and twice
had retreated. Would the third time be the charm, or
would folks say: "Three times around and out"?

If the men did not know, Early knew. Lee had told him
what to do after driving Hunter from Lynchburg; invade,
scare President Lincoln and General Grant, force the withdrawal of some of that great host of Yankees from around
Richmond. It would take brilliant maneuvering, tireless
energy, and a horse doctor's dose of luck. Early was ready
to trust to all three.

That afternoon, camped near New Market, George got a
sheaf of mail from home, letters dated June 11, 14, 15, 18,
and 19. Richmond papers arrived in camp, too, claiming
again that victory of Johnston over Sherman. George applauded: "Gen'l Joe is some, isn't he? that is right, kill
as many as possible without losing our men. I see the
Ex[aminer] thinks Grant & Sherman together must necessarily use up the Union nation after a while, tho they may
be like ants."

Like ants. . . . Billy Beavans had said that once, long
days and many miles back, in the Cold Harbor trenches.
Those ants swarmed everywhere, fanged with shot, shell,
and shrapnel. As men of the Forty-third rejoiced over
tales of purported victory, Sherman moved to outflank and

drive Johnston at Smyrna Station in Georgia, and, outside besieged Petersburg, Federal engineers drove an underground tunnel to blow up Lee's defenses. George did not know these things, and as he finished his letter he thought of something besides fighting. "Is mother going to put up many preserves?" he asked plaintively.

Twenty hard miles on July 1, anniversary of the charge into Gettysburg. Edenburg, Mount Jackson, and Woodstock were beads they strung on their line of march, and Billy felt better for the sight of pretty girls in Woodstock. The next noon the mess of Company D made a fair meal with cheese and butter found by Lieutenant Sim. That night, hungry again, Cary Whitaker and George went looking for a home-cooked meal. A housewife offered them supper for $2.00 apiece in coined silver. The ham was good, but the butter was rancid. "If I can't do better," sniffed Cary, "I had as well stop foraging." [15]

Winchester was in their front on Sunday, July 3. The Forty-third, still toward the rear of the column, heard shooting up ahead. The cavalry was chasing Yankees out of town. Winchestrians cheered as the infantry marched through at a fast clip. After twenty-four miles, camp at little Smithfield. Beyond was Harpers Ferry, and beyond Harpers Ferry the Potomac.

July 4, they fell out for a brief rest at Charlestown. George remembered that John Brown had been hanged there in 1859, the year the Enfield Blues felt the need of military organization. The Forty-third stacked arms in front of a handsome house. The owner flung open his gate to the soldiers, and his wife hurried out on the porch to distribute food. Every house seemed eager to refresh hungry marchers with meat, bread, butter, and milk.[16] Then, approaching along a railroad track beside the Shenandoah River, the army paused just outside Harpers Ferry.

Shots rang out in the sunset. Federals held the town. At

dawn, Grimes' Brigade went to the front, and the Forty-third deployed to lead the way in. But no enemy stayed to oppose them. The sharpshooters of the Forty-third, entering the streets, found that the retreating garrison had left most of the materials for a Fourth of July celebration behind them. George called it "a rich time generally, all kinds of good things, wines, ice-cream, lemonade, cakes, confectionaries." Billy Beavans sampled captured ale, porter, lager beer, and cider. Lager, too, came to the hand and the mouth of Cary Whitaker, and brandy and wine as well.

This wealth of food and drink half demoralized the famished Forty-third. Even some of the officers got drunk. General Rodes hurriedly ordered Cary to set a guard against rioting and plundering, and to arrest tipsy soldiers and others absent from their units.

The hot weather relented, as though in honor of the capture of Harpers Ferry. Falling out, soldiers admired the town and the surrounding hills. "Beautiful scenery at the Ferry," wrote Billy Beavans in his diary, between sips of beer. Cary, busy with the details of the guard, found time to agree with Billy: "The scenery around Harpers Ferry is very grand but had neither time nor opportunity to admire it." Adding to his troubles, the Federals had crowned Maryland Heights across the Potomac with cannon and sharpshooters, who fired at Confederates strolling downtown. George heard the shooting, and Billy noticed several wounded.[17] Cary, between chores, conversed with some ladies who professed Union sympathies but spoke proudly of Lee and Jackson. Walking along the street toward the ferry slip, he found himself under fire beyond the river. "Never wish to be on guard in a captured town again," he vowed.[18]

To George, sometimes critical of urban surroundings, ". . . the town is rather harder looking than I thought."

But he remembered that Thomas Jefferson had said that the scenery was worth crossing the Atlantic to see. "A good writer could certainly paint at such a place," he reflected, rather muddled in his notions of creative endeavor.

In the morning, relieved of provost duty, the Forty-third rejoined its division and moved away westward toward Shepherdstown.

Shells screeched across the Potomac and burst on the road, some close to the marching men but not close enough to stampede war-seasoned veterans. A courier galloped by with reports that the bluecoats were massing to recapture Harpers Ferry, and the regiment halted in place for several hours. It was a welcome rest on a hot day, and more welcome still was the later word that the attack would not materialize.

Around sunset Cary Whitaker led his men across the Potomac at the Shepherdstown Ford. In the early darkness the column passed through Sharpsburg on the far side, and camped on Maryland soil just beyond. The name of the creek that babbled near the bivouac was the Antietam.[19]

XV

WASHINGTON WOULD HAVE BEEN IN
OUR POSSESSION

Company D, wearily asleep beside Antietam's waters, mustered three officers and perhaps twenty-five enlisted men present for duty, from a total on the rolls of seventy-one.[1] The others were sick, wounded, under arrest, absent without leave, or deserted.

This dwindled group of effectives made up a company neither large nor small for the Army of Northern Virginia in 1864. In morale and efficiency it may have rated rather better than average. Consistently the inspecting officer marked "Good" for Company D in discipline, instruction, military appearance, arms, and clothing. Its personnel was made up of lean, whipcordy young men, used to labor and hunger, ready to fight or frolic at word of its officers. And those officers were its backbone and example. Cary, now leading the regiment, had been competently succeeded by his quiet brother Sim. The two junior lieutenants, Billy and George, continued to be interestingly different—one still the ready smiler, the smart-bearded admirer of ladies and maker of jokes; the other characteristically thoughtful, sensitive, and enduring. But they were alike in impressive courage and in attention to duty.

Wakening and marching in the dawn of the 7th, the companies heard distant firing from the direction of Harpers Ferry. Eastward moved Early's force, confident in enemy territory. Surely no Federal commander would know how small was this audacious threat. George Wills, picking luscious cherries with Billy, was sent by Cary to climb South Mountain with scouts and signalers. The rest of the command formed line of battle to wait.

George mounted the slopes, found no enemy, and stayed until after dark. Jack Whitaker, sent to recall him, lost his way in the wooded ravines and did not return until daybreak, to find his kinsmen worried about his absence.[2] At sunrise, the army moved through Crampton's Gap, felt itself snubbed by Unionists at Burkittsville and so experienced no twinges of conscience at seizing beef cattle and horses along the way. Rain pelted down that night as camp was made eight miles west of Frederick, and next morning the blankets made damp, heavy rolls on the shoulders of marching men.[3]

Gordon's Division was in the van, and as the sun climbed came again the sound of guns, great and small. By nine o'clock the main body was up. Rodes led his division past the town of Frederick and formed to command approaches to a bridge across a river—the Monocacy, that river was, some remembered it from the Gettysburg campaign. South of Rodes' position the divisions of Gordon, Ramseur, and Breckenridge, with cavalry under John McCausland, struck at Federal forces along the far side of the river. Gordon's men forded at a shallow spot, turned the enemy flank, and overwhelmed in turn three lines of defenses. Early, it was said, called Gordon off because he did not want to be encumbered with too many prisoners. As it was, Gordon inflicted losses of thirteen hundred. The Confederate loss was perhaps half as much. George Wills mourned these irreplaceable comrades.[4]

July 10, through hot dust, the army pressed on through Hyattstown and Clarksburg, swift as ever with Stonewall Jackson. And now men could guess pretty clearly where they were heading.

Washington!

They went into camp eighteen miles from the capital of the Union. The country looked poor to Billy Beavans. Cary noted signs of friendship along the way. Sprawled on their blankets, the skinny Confederates still wondered if they would strike at the heart and soul of the enemy's government. Up early on the 11th, even the cautious Cary Whitaker knew that the attack would be launched.

Footsore, panting in the bright heat, the men yet felt an eager thrill pass through their ranks. Jubal Early rode along the column from regiment to regiment, and walked his horse beside that of Cary Whitaker for a few moments. Cary's eyes smarted from dust and sweat as he saluted his commander.

"How are the men getting on?" inquired Early.

"They were suffering a good deal during the morning," Cary replied, "but I think they are doing better."

"Tell the men I am very sorry to march them so hard," said Early, "but now is the time. They can't stop now, but if we succeed in taking Washington they will be repaid for all their toil."

He quickened his horse's speed and moved on to the next regiment. Elated, Cary passed the general's words back along his column of companies. Back in answer roared the rebel yell.[5]

Through Rockville they passed, and at noon they were in the outskirts of Washington. They could see a line of massive forts.

The Forty-third stopped near a handsome brick house, the home of Postmaster General Montgomery P. Blair.[6] It stood open, and plainly had been hastily evacuated.

The men, resting in ranks, gazed with thumping hearts at the defenses ahead. Strong gun emplacements were connected by sturdy breastworks, and in front of these showed deep ditches and rows of sharp stakes. Beyond could be seen the Soldiers' Home. Farther still, men fancied they picked out the government buildings, the unfinished dome of the Capitol, the White House where Abe Lincoln must be mighty tense and tight in the face just now, the treasury, the whole business. Never, not once ever, had a real fighting force of Confederates pushed itself so close.

Craning their necks in Montgomery Blair's front yard, the soldiers of Company D forgot fagged muscles and pinched bellies. Why not a whooping, racing charge over those barricades, and on into Washington beyond? George Wills was ready and anxious. Some hearts rose as Grimes' Brigade moved up behind the line of sharp-shooters and the crack of musketry and the boom of cannon were heard. Was it coming now, that attack?

But bugle and drum were silent. Afternoon became evening, and twenty-five men of the Forty-third Regiment slid out in the dusk, almost under the muzzles of the Yankee guns. Sim Whitaker, commanding the detail, was exhausted from the march, and George groped forward to replace him.[7]

Jubal Early, never timid but never utterly foolhardy, had heard that part of the Federal ant-swarm around Richmond had been hurried to Washington. The VI Corps, in itself outnumbering Early's whole force, had reached the capital's defenses almost as Early had approached. During the night, Early heard reports of still more reinforcements arriving to face him, and in the sweet dawn of the 13th observers with field glasses could see the battlements opposite heavily occupied by infantry. And more bluecoats were surely rushing into Maryland to cut off the invaders.

Still Early held his position north of the fortifications. The Forty-third relaxed in a pleasant orchard near the Blair house. Billy Beavans replaced George on picket duty. A few shells sang ineffectually over the regiment, and two men were wounded by musket balls. Around 6 o'clock the shelling grew heavy, and then the Federals came over their defenses and advanced.

The Forty-fifth North Carolina, at the left of the Forty-third, gave way. Cary Whitaker, out in front, was withdrawing his sharpshooters. Then up came the Forty-third through the gray of evening, spoiling for a fight. Over a fence leaped Cary, and his men followed. Federals fired from behind a burning house. Cary ordered a charge, drove away the snipers, and found himself with but four of his companies. D was one of them, biting cartridges and ramming them down. Yankees sent a whickering rain of bullets at them.

Cary hopped back to find the rest of his regiment and brought it up. The battle continued fiercely as the night closed down upon it. Red flashes ripped the darkness, until the Federal sortie backed toward its forts. Then came the order to fall back.

The Forty-third carried out five dead and fifteen wounded, but Company D rejoiced over no casualties in its ranks. Rodes' Division covered the rear as Jubal Early marched off in tarry blackness. Glancing back, the Confederates saw red banners of flame above Montgomery Blair's house. Nobody knew who had set it afire.[8]

Early kept them marching all night. He had frightened the garrison at Washington, he had relieved pressure on Lee's entrenched army by siphoning off crack divisions of Federals to defend the capital. In so doing, as he confessed, some of his own command had been "scared as blue as hell's brimstone." [9] Staunch spirits like George Wills felt that Washington could have been taken on the 11th. It was too late for that now.

On they marched as the sun rose and climbed, through the constant heat and dust. At noon they rested. Behind them, at Rockville, cavalry skirmished. At dusk the infantrymen headed for the Potomac. Short of rations again, they snatched handfuls of ripe dewberries from the roadside. The night found them still marching, with occasional pauses to rest or chop down telegraph poles. A Georgia infantryman tried to steal Cary Whitaker's horse, and Sim found it and led it back.

At White's Ford, wide and shallow, they waded the Potomac on the 14th. It was a hurried crossing, for great masses of enemy were following. Back in Virginia, the Confederates rejoiced. Early camped his divisions three miles below the river, and nobody paid much attention to shelling from the Maryland side. Fine weather on the 15th, with more rest. George and Billy invited Jack Whitaker to go dewberrying with them.[10]

On the 16th, Early led them westward. Behind came Yankees, the whole VI Corps, stubborn marchers and fighters. Union cavalry cut off several wagons at Snicker's Gap. Nobody in Company D liked that. George and Billy snarled over the news, and Cary decided: "Somebody to blame for this misfortune." One circumstance pleased Cary, however: "Some of our wagons had contained Quartermasters plunder. Hoop skirts calicoes and such things—don't care if all such were burned even if it had to be done by Yankees."

Sunday, July 17, they forded the Shenandoah at Snicker's Ford beyond the pass, approached Charlestown and camped near a church. Billy watched, as usual, for pretty girls coming to hear the sermon; but for once he did not succeed with them. "They are not strong secesh enough for me in these parts," he wrote in his faithful diary. "Green backs too much in demand."

George had time to write home, and achieved a long letter to sister Mary. He described the march along the Valley, the capture of Harpers Ferry, adventures in Maryland, and the beauty of the country near Frederick:

> One of the prettiest countries I ever looked at, it was not so grand as at Harpers-Ferry, but for miles there were groves, wheat fields, beautiful residences and several other things intermixed, besides in the distance a little town to be seen, which all together was certainly beautiful. I wished at the time, that you all could be with me for a few minutes, just to look for yourselves.

About the approach to Washington:

> . . . it is candidly believed that if we had charged right then, the Forts would have capitulated, and Washington would have been in our possession; but prudence dictated otherwise and after remaining there until late in the night of the 12th, we withdrew, after a pretty sharp fight. . . . I can't tell what damage we did the enemy as we withdrew in the night, but expect we left a good many of them there.

He finished by saying that he weighed one hundred and forty pounds without his coat.

Cannon boomed somewhere while the men rested, as Federals tried doggedly to force their way through Snicker's Gap and encountered opposition. The main body remained near Charlestown and still rested on the morning of the 18th, despite occasional distant thunder of guns.

No veteran there was so disdainful of the remote bombardment as Smiling Billy Beavans. However, there seemed to be a certain sobriety about him. He was observed to read the Bible; this may have pleased his more godly relatives, who frequently had wished that Billy would profess religion publicly. He wrote some letters home, too, stopping at noon when orders came to be ready for some sort of action.

The Federals were pushing through the gap, and gunfire boomed louder and faster and closer. The regiments fell in. With General Grimes absent sick, Colonel William Owens assumed command of the brigade. Brave since Bethel days, Owens was somewhat confused as he led the regiments forward. He himself was but lately returned from hospital.[11]

Billy Beavans, with Company D, produced his diary. In his neat, easy script he penciled part of an entry:

> Monday July 18th 1864
> Remained very quietly in camp, writing letters until about noon; when orders came to be ready to move; about five o'clock we moved

Back into his pocket he slid the little book. He could finish the account later in the day. Perhaps something of interest would happen.

They headed toward the firing, and the regiments formed line of battle with practiced ease. Through woods they advanced, and into a field beyond. Just ahead of the Forty-third, the Forty-fifth had spread into open order, firing at the Federals as they came across the river.

The whole brigade went forward, ready to close with the enemy, but Colonel Owens ordered a halt. Cary chafed. Just ahead of him the ground sloped downward, to where hostile infantrymen had reached a stone fence. A charge now might disrupt them.

At last bugles rang out, thrillingly staccato in the summer air. The quavering Southern battle yell echoed them. The brigades charged.

Deadly-fierce elation possessed the charging gray infantry. In front of them the enemy lines seemed to reel and recede. The whole Forty-third pressed to within point-blank range, was ready to ram itself home against blue shirt fronts. Then Owens sent another order—halt in place.

Cary was fuming by now. He stopped his line perforce, and ordered "Commence firing." Opposite them, Federals with their backs to the river took cover behind the stone fence and made their own fire fight.

Two flags fluttered above the stone rampart—that meant two regiments directly in front. Still Cary wanted to charge, but Owens would not allow it. Musket balls from behind the fence reaped men along Cary's line. In Company D, Eli Lewis and Andrew Parks were dead. William Ball and John Winfrey fell wounded. Billy Beavans, directing the fire, felt a sudden smashing blow against his right leg, as though a giant had smashed it with a hammer. The ground flew up to meet him. He floundered, half-stunned and helpless.

At last the advance resumed. As the Forty-third approached the fence, the Federals dropped away and made for the ford. Some of them stepped into deep water and sank. Cary found a wounded colonel of Union artillery and sent him to the rear.

The Forty-third had lost seventeen killed, and carried from the field thirty-nine wounded. Four or five others were reported missing. Now, in the dark, the regiment made camp among the trees.

George had borne his part of the battle coolly and intelligently. As soon as the battle was over, he found Wash and hurried him away to find and care for the wounded Billy. Cary waited only long enough to count his losses and post pickets. Then he, too, headed three miles away to where Rodes' Division had set up its hospital in an open space among the trees.[12]

He was appalled by what he found. Scores of wounded

men, some of them suffering intensely, lay without care on blankets spread hastily on the grass. Moving his feet carefully in the darkness to avoid stepping on prone bodies, he found Chaplain Thompson and Wash, who said that Billy was nearby but asleep.

Then a voice called Cary's name in the gloom, a voice weakened but recognizable. Cary found Billy lying on his blanket, gamely striving to be cheerful. Billy's right leg was broken below the knee, and even in that poor light Cary could see that amputation must follow. The captain said what he could for comfort's sake, and he must have known that it was not much. Then he returned to his regiment, burning with indignation at the seemingly unconcerned doctors and medical attendants.[13]

Sometime in the small, pain-racked hours, Billy fumbled out his diary from the pocket into which he had thrust it before the battle. He was almost fainting from shock, agony, and loss of blood, but in a shaky scrawl he completed the entry for July 18, 1864:

> a great many wounded my right leg was broken at the calf by mu[sket] Bal remained at the Division all [night?] nothing done to me[14]

He may have slept after that, or perhaps he simply lost consciousness. Blacker than the night was the shadow of death that brooded over Billy Beavans, down on his back in its grassy Valley.

He maketh me to lie down in green pastures. . . .

XVI

NEVER YET DID I SEE FELLOWS RUN
AS THEY DID

But next morning something was done to Billy.

The dilatory surgeons examined his shattered leg and, as Cary had foreseen, ordered amputation. As with thousands of other operations in the medicine-starved Confederacy, there was no anaesthetic for the wounded man. Possibly Billy had a stiff drink of brandy or whisky to nerve him to the pain and shock of knife and bone-saw; certainly nothing else. But friends were at hand. Wash watched, and Jack Whitaker, whose wounded arm had begun to trouble him again and who had been told to report to the doctors for further treatment.

Naturally enough, both Wash and Jack were troubled because they could only watch. But they saw that Billy endured the amputation with courage and even with good humor.[1] Later, when the stump was dressed and Billy lifted into an ambulance, Cary's black servant George arrived. He and Jack rode with Billy in the ambulance to Winchester, while Wash rejoined Company D.

Put to bed in York Hospital, Billy was able to say comfortingly to the shaken Jack, "I have good cause to be thankful that it was no worse." Then he asked for his diary and a pencil. At the top of the page he achieved a slow, clumsy figure for the date:

> 19
> I went to Winchester as soon as my leg was amputated Jack and George went with me.
> Very rough no drug suffered enormous the ladies were very kind——[2]

Feebly, dreamily, his pencil slid away, and off the page. Billy looked into the faces of the Winchester ladies, so very kind, who came to help him in whatever way possible. One face was winsome, lovely, tender, the sort of face Billy had always smiled to see as he swaggered along a turnpike or halted in a village. Miss Kate Shepherd,[3] that was her name.

Back to the camp at Snicker's Ford, where the Forty-third North Carolina Regiment counted six new bullet holes in its battle flag, came word of the loss of Billy's leg. George Wills grieved deeply, and so did Sim and Cary. ". . . very sorry to hear of this," noted Cary in his own journal, "so hard for a gay fine looking young man in the bloom of youth, to be mutilated in this way . . ." Grimly practical, Cary added, "one consolation is that it might have been worse, that he is now out of the war, the loss of a leg may be the saving of his life." [4]

Those still whole and healthy had the war to wage, and at nightfall Early moved his forces westward to Berryville. The cooking details worked late, boiling great chunks of beef to ration the regiments for more travel and combat. At four o'clock the morning of the 20th, the camp rose. Cary Whitaker went to a sunrise funeral— Colonel Owens, troublesomely cautious in the fighting two days earlier, had died from a bullet through the belly at Snicker's Ford. Then on southward marched the brigade, through the little village of White Post, and once again guns were yelping, off toward the north and west.

Ramseur's Division, feeling its way about Winchester, had run into superior Federal forces and was being badly thrashed. Rodes led his own division toward the guns, but stopped when news came that the battle was over and Ramseur in retreat. Winchester, so often taken and re-taken, had fallen yet again to Northern soldiers. Jack Whitaker had scampered out of York Hospital and off to find and rejoin his company, but poor Billy, helpless on his cot, was a prisoner. Ramseur's killed and wounded numbered about two hundred, and he had lost more than two hundred and fifty prisoners and four guns.[5]

The Forty-third camped at Middletown, eight miles south of the scene of this disaster. It marched with the rest of Early's command the next day, and heard of enemy close at hand but found none. Major Walter Boggan arrived from Richmond, not particularly welcome to Cary or George. With him Boggan brought a story that Grant had been killed by a fragment of shell. Richmond papers told the same story.

"We are all rejoiced to hear it," pronounced George, "hope if it is so, that this campaign and probably the war will end soon, for no one else is so long winded as he." [6]

Long-winded. . . . a premature but deserved epitaph for Ulysses S. Grant, still alive and still stubbornly smashing at Lee. Grant was utterly different from showy but short-winded Union commanders of previous invasions, timid McClellan, self-praising Pope, Burnside out-generaled and outfought at Fredericksburg, Hooker over-whelmed at Chancellorsville. And with Grant, or sent by him to the Valley, were war-seasoned troops pretty long in the wind themselves.

July 23 was a Sunday. The army rested among hills near Strasburg, where the Forty-third found water in which to bathe. Cary, still commanding the regiment despite Boggan's presence, wrote to Billy's parents of their son's wound. George also sent the news to Lucy at home, expressing his sorrow and concern for Billy:

> . . . you can't imagine my feelings, first at the wound and then at his being in the enemy's hands, I think it was the hardest struggle for me of this war. I was becoming more attached to him every day, and in fact he seemed most like a brother to me. . . . there is one consolation to us, and should be to all his friends, that is, he will be clear of the war; and that is a consideration, since men's lives are not now insured from one day to another, and he tho. with one leg, is probably better off than any of us with two. . . .

As he wrote, George may have felt that this was dangerously close to a confession of poor spirit. Therefore, he restated his own sober resolution at the end:

> I reckon never since this war commenced, has there been a harder Campaign than the one this Corps is, and has been experiencing for the last month and a half, we are getting very anxious to be once more comfortably situated in a pleasant camp, but provided it will end the war, I am willing to keep on.

Well for George that he felt willing. Next day, Early spun the army around and northward toward Winchester again. Breckenridge led a division toward a flank of the enemy at Kernstown. That flank gave way. As other Confederate divisions advanced, the Federals retreated, then turned and fled in disorder.

Sharpshooters of the Forty-third, out in front of the main line of their regiment, were able to score on the slowest fugitives with Minié balls. George Wills and his comrades began to walk briskly to overtake their adversaries. Then, as the Union infantry quickened its pace to a gallop, the Confederates ran too in headlong pursuit.

George, his sword drawn, felt his heart leap in fierce exultation. Along the Valley Pike the two armies raced northward, the Federals disorganized and routed, the Southerners whooping and firing.

Past Winchester tore the enemy's disintegrated rear guard, with Rodes' Division pressing it. Cary shook Jack loose to hurry into town and get news of Billy. On beyond the town the race continued, and did not halt until, at sundown, the Confederates were forced to pause below Bunker Hill. Twenty-five miles they had driven their foe. Nearly five hundred prisoners had fallen into Early's hands. Even some of Ramseur's men, captured on the 20th, had been rescued and returned to their regiments. It had been a victory to even that Yankee score of the 20th.[7]

Drenching rain at dawn the next day, but bugles started the Confederates north again. They trudged out from under the damp clouds, and could not overtake the retiring Federals again. To either side of the Valley Pike were flung the scorched wrecks of wagons, burned by Union soldiers who could not save them. When camp had been made above Bunker Hill, George begged the loan of Uncle Cary's horse and rode into Winchester. At York Hospital he found Billy, surprisingly strong and in fine spirits.

The recapture of Winchester had roused the wounded man to an almost dangerous ecstasy of joy. As the fight had moved past and the Union garrison abandoned the town, Billy had almost collapsed. But now he felt better. Most earnestly he vowed that he was certain of recovering. Happily George rode back to camp with this news, and Jack again went to York Hospital to doctor his own slow-healing arm and to look after Billy.[8]

On the 26th, George felt positively cheerful as his regiment helped drive Federals from Martinsburg. On the following day, details of the army ripped up tracks of the Baltimore and Ohio Railroad, which supplied the enemy. George and another lieutenant commanded a picket of fifty men from the Forty-third, while Cary, slightly ill in camp, wondered about conflicting reports of a battle between Hood and Sherman in Tennessee. The Richmond papers credited Hood with a victory; those from Baltimore said that Sherman had won. "Someone has made false statements," summed up Cary.

Lounging on picket post, with no danger in view, George wrote to his mother. Victory sat upon his pencil as he described the fighting on the 24th:

> . . . it became the most utter rout I have ever witnessed, we walked very brisk and double quicked, together 4 or 5 miles; never yet did I see fellows run as they did . . . the Yankee loss is said to be very heavy, I don't know how many, but several hundred prisoners, and great many killed and wounded, including 2 Genl officers.
> Our loss was comparatively small.

He added, with hopeful optimism, the news about Billy's apparent progress toward recovery. And then, with his usual deep affection:

> I know my dear Mother the anxiety of you all has been very great since we left Richmond, and often very often do I think when I go to lie down after a hard day's tramp, that then, if only I could whisper to you we are all well, I would be perfectly satisfied. . . .

His mother would love to read that, of course. George added something else, that most surely would intrigue the home folks who so often had chided his delicate eating habits:

> I have something to tell you, which will surprise you. Guess what it is, can you guess? I have gotten to love beef splendid, when well cooked can eat as much of it as any-

body. Did you think I ever would get at that? Necessity
causes a great many things! [9]

Back home, North Carolina was holding an election,
and on July 27 Early's camp felt secure enough to call
on North Carolinian troops to vote for a governor in their
state. George marked a ballot for the first time in his life,
voting to re-elect Zebulon Vance, once colonel of the
Twenty-sixth Regiment, now a vigorous if highly individ-
ualistic supporter of states' rights and the war effort.
There outside of Martinsburg, Vance received more than
1800 of the 2000 votes cast by Tarheels in Early's command. His opponent, the Raleigh editor W. W. Holden,
who had changed from Unionist to secessionist and
lately to a preacher of defeat and submission, was given
fewer than 150. In the Forty-third, 164 were for Vance
and only 9 for Holden, none of the latter in Company D.
George rejoiced at the final count, and so did Cary.[10]

Afterward, Early prepared once more to approach the
Potomac. George, his health splendid, was ready. But
Wash, patient and enduring for so long, had taken sick,
too sick to follow his master with the cooking pots and
bags of food. George told him to go home to Brinkleyville
and get well, and Wash found a chance to drive a southbound supply wagon.

Before they separated, the two comrades sat down and
talked together, the tall white lieutenant and the ailing
brown servitor. George, his handsome uniform dulled and
shabby from campaigning, the sobering memory of battle
from Lynchburg to Washington and back ever with him,
the thought of Billy's crippling wound oppressing him,
found himself speaking from deep in his heart. After all,
Wash was his closest confidant, his most understanding
friend in all the army.

George confessed to Wash with sober frankness that he
faced every clash with the Federals strong in the realiza-

tion that he might not survive. True, he had lived
through desperate dangers. It must be the prayers of
those at home, of his family and his friends, and undoubtedly of the girl he held so dear, that had saved him
thus far. But he was in the hands of God, he told Wash.
Live or die, he felt happy to be so.

Finally: "Tell Mother, if I fall, she need have no fears
for my future." [11]

Those words rang in Wash's ears as he drove away.

Wash stopped in Winchester, to look in at York Hospital. Jack Whitaker wrote, at Billy's dictation, a letter of
reassurance to be carried to Mr. Beavans at Centerville
Plantation:

> . . . William requested me to write you a note, saying
> that he did not wish you to try to come up here to see him
> as he thought the journey was entirely too long & tedious
> for you, he says too, that he is better & as soon as he is able
> he will be transferred to Staunton & from there to Rich-
> mond. The surgeon says his wound is doing right well,
> but his bowels are out of order, & he has a good deal of
> fever. He has had one chill too since I've been with him,
> and is quite weak. I am in hopes he will improve very
> fast so that he can be removed to Staunton. The Ladies are
> very attentive to him. . . .
>
> My love to all
> Your aff. Jack[12]

Meanwhile, the army had reached the Potomac at noon
of the 29th. Across the river was Williamsport. Cary
bathed in the shallow river, hoping there would not be
another crossing, another bitter battle against long odds
on enemy soil. Commissary details waded over to buy
Maryland molasses for the troops. Whisky, too, was secured by some officers and men.[13]

Next morning, the army fell back from the river, to
very little expressed disappointment. Word came to the

Forty-third that Billy's condition had taken a frightening turn for the worse. As the army went into camp near Martinsburg once more, Cary rode to the headquarters of General Rodes to plead for permission to go to Winchester and see his wounded cousin.

Under a shady tree, Rodes' servant had set up a table. Several officers of high rank sat around that table with Rodes, and the division commander was pouring a round of drinks. Cary reined in his horse, stated his errand, and waited thirstily.

Rodes told him no. The situation, with enemy reportedly approaching, made it unwise that the commander of the Forty-third be absent. Tomorrow, perhaps. But not now. That was all, Captain Whitaker.

Cary jogged back to his regiment. Bleakly Rodes had made him realize that, whatever his temporary post at the head of the Forty-third, he was still a captain and no more. Further, Cary felt dry in his bearded mouth. Disappointedly he resorted to his diary:

> Gen R. . . . . was just in the act of mixing and taking a drink no doubt made of the best liquor while the balance of us, that is we poor subordinates and soldiers, can hardly ever see a drop of mean whiskey, even when wounds and sickness require such stimulants— I sat on my horse at a respectful distance and wished I had a good drink too, but the General didn't think proper to ask me to indulge so I had to forego that pleasure.[14]

The next day and the next, the Forty-third did picket duty, straining its eyes for the approach of the Federal forces predicted by Rodes. Early's cavalry was nearly all gone; it headed up through Maryland into Pennsylvania. Early had issued the harshest of orders—burn a Yankee town up there. Let the enemy's civilians have a taste of what had been happening to peaceful Valley towns and farms at the hands of the Federals.

Relieved of picket duty at last, the Forty-third camped near Bunker Hill. Again Rodes declined to let Cary visit Billy at the hospital in Winchester. George wrote home, camp news and about the election, and his continued hope that Billy would recover. Also, since his clothing was in bad shape again:

> Get Wash or Ed. to go down and see Mrs. Bradley, if she won't furnish the wool and also make the cloth. . . . I have a first-rate overcoat now, so want nine yards, to make a suit, have it dark Grey, woven three or four treaddle Jeans as Mother thinks best. I wish you to as early as possible as I shall need it if I live to see this Campaign over.[15]

If he lived; campaigns like the one George was seeing could destroy men as well as clothes. A man might not even last until cold weather made him put on his first-rate overcoat.

XVII

UPON THE VERGE OF TIME I STAND

In the hot, quiet air of York Hospital, Billy Beavans lay dying.

When Wash had looked in there on his way home to Halifax County, Billy had spoken weakly but with stubborn cheerfulness and with sense. But then, after Wash had driven away with the encouraging note for the Beavanses at Centerville Plantation, Jack had watched Billy's head sink down upon the pillow, had heard Billy mutter deliriously.

That was July 29, a bad day for Billy. The next day he seemed to recover somewhat, and he insisted that he felt little pain. But fever flushed his skin; typhoid fever, a doctor told Jack.

On July 31, Sunday, the church bells rang in Winchester. Kate Shepherd came to the hospital and sat down by Billy's cot. Jack quit his vigil and stepped away somewhere, perhaps to leave these two young people together for private talk. No doubt but that Billy mustered for Miss Kate a smile, or that she very readily smiled back. Smiling Billy Beavans had come to mean a lot to lovely Kate Shepherd.

She found a fan, and stirred the hot air around Billy's wasted, bearded face. She talked to him, said such pleasant inconsequential things as wise nurses say to the seriously ill. She was going to be gone from Winchester the next day, she told him, and then hastily promised to come and see him as soon as she returned.

"I'll not see you again," replied Billy, gently but definitely.

Kate must have stared in horrified protest.

"I am almost gone," continued Billy. "I am not afraid to die."

The girl knew suddenly that Billy spoke the exact, unshakable truth, with no dramatics. She sought for something to do, she must appear calm. With her she had brought some jelly. She dipped a spoonful of it into a glass of water, stirred it up, and held the glass so that Billy could sip the sweet mixture.

"I would like to get well for the sake of my parents," he said, and his voice was beginning to break feebly. "I would love to see them—but I will not on earth."[1]

His eyes were on Miss Kate's sweet face.

"Thank you," he said, "thank you for all you have done for me."

Had he been only a trifle stronger, he might have spoken to make her feel cheerful. He might even have recited for her some scrap of his own verse, such as he used to scribble for pretty girls:

> I would soon feel as if I had forgot
> Every thing both of trouble and pleasure,
> But of thee and the very spot
> Where I last saw you and your treasure. . . .

Jack had returned, with another lady, Mrs. Eggerson. Miss Kate left. She had to leave, even if that trip away from town had not been calling her. Billy saw her and her treasure of gentle care and sympathy no more.

Mrs. Eggerson and Jack watched. They saw that Billy had lapsed into delirium again, forgetting trouble and pleasure.

Perhaps fragments of the past came into his wandering mind; home, and dance parties with laughing young ladies . . . sweet, very sweet, was the sound of the violin . . . fox-hunting, choir-singing . . . Brother Johnny, sister Maggie, Father and Mother, the little boys Ab and Walter at Centerville . . . school, church . . . sermons preached by George's father, the Reverend Mr. Wills, or by George's brother Richard, or by a chaplain over in the Forty-fourth Regiment by the name of Harding. . . . *I walk in the valley of the shadow of death.* . . . The Valley, the Shenandoah Valley and the Shenandoah River, and Snicker's Ford across . . . and Yankees, Yankees, Yankees, scurrying in hordes like ants, but big ants, deadly-faced, in blue uniforms, firing muskets, sending leg-shattering bullets. . . .

Yes, once he had written verses. War, the most workaday and demanding of professions, had taken from him the wish and the will to keep rhyming. But once he had rhymed it, had foreseen it without knowing he foresaw:

> Upon the verge of time I stand
> With my mind wandering from place to place . . .

His mind wandering, Smiling Billy Beavans poised precariously, one-legged, upon the verge of time. Beyond that verge waited timelessness, silence, mystery, for him to enter in among them as among dark trees.

At five o'clock on the hot 31st of July, a doctor examined the limp, silent form on the cot, and told Jack Whitaker that his cousin was dead.

Jack hurried off a note to camp above town. Then he borrowed scissors and clipped locks from Billy's temple and jaw. His diary, too—those relics would be prized at Centerville. Billy's clothing? Someone had taken it away to be washed, and now it was lost, maybe stolen. Well, then, to find a coffin. One must be found, though coffins were scarcer than corpses in the Valley around Winchester. Jack went out to look.

Mr. Samuel Jones, a citizen of the town, offered a place in his private graveyard where Billy's coffin might lie until it could be shipped home. But then Kate Shepherd was back, and she said no. Billy Beavans must lie nowhere but in the Shepherd burial plot in Winchester Cemetery.[2]

The Forty-third came off picket duty on August 1 to find Jack's news waiting. Cary wrote in his diary:

> Poor Billy how I grieved to hear this; so young, so manly, so endeared to and beloved by his friends, it seems hard that he should thus be snatched away in the bloom of youth. Only 24 years of age. Oh what a sad blow it will be to his family and friends at home, how many hearts will grow sad when the news comes home that he is no more.

Cary handed the note to George, who was in the midst of his letter asking for the new uniform. George finished:

> Since I wrote the above, the Capt. has rec'd a letter from Jack at Winchester, announcing the sad, sad intelligence of Billy's death. . . . Oh! if it could have been otherwise how happy I would have been. Poor Billy, tho. I have hopes for him (I mean beyond the grave). . . .

He begged that Lucy go to Centerville and comfort the Beavanses.

Jack did his best, on August 2, in a sympathetic letter to Billy's father:

I am pained to inform you that William is no more. After an illness of thirteen days, an Allwise Providence saw fit to call him from earth. During his confinement I have been with him (excepting four days) and did all in my power to make him comfortable. Every attention was paid him by the ladies of this place. . . . Up to the time of his death he never would allow me to write for you, but always said that the journey was too tedious for you, that he was doing very well, and hoped to be able soon to be removed to Staunton. . . . Accept my sympathy, for yourself & family, for the loss of your *gallant* & *noble* son.

Finishing the necessary details of Billy's burial, Jack sought to be returned to Company D. Despite his troublesome wounded arm, he wanted to spend no more time at the hospital.

Later on, Cary wrote his condolences to Mr. Beavans:

. . . His joyous spirit and generous nature made many friends here who deeply deplore his loss—at Brigade headquarters where he served so long, in his company, in his Regiment and indeed wherever he was known, is his loss felt and lamented.

But no where outside of his own immediate family is he so much missed or his loss so deeply deplored as in that little social circle which constitutes our mess. . . . Others may forget, but we never can, and while life lasts will we remember the gallant and generous youth, who while bravely cheering on his men, gave his life to his country and her cause on the banks of the beautiful Shenandoah. . . .

William, as you know, laid no claims to being religious, but he had deep religious feelings; when speaking of marrying he always expressed a determination to marry none but a lady of piety who would help him to be a better man—previous to his being wounded, he read his bible a good deal, much more than he had formerly done, he spent a good part of the morning of the day in which he received his wound in reading the Scriptures. Latterly he seemed to have a more subdued spirit and I am confident thought more upon his latter end.[3]

That was all comrades could say; and, of course, they knew, even as they said it, that it was not enough.

Camped around Bunker Hill, Early's soldiers heard of the battle of the Crater outside Petersburg, where Federals blew up a salient in the Confederate line of forts and launched a surprise attack which was turned bloodily against the surprisers. There was life in the old land yet, decided men who were weary with mourning their own dead.

On August 4, Early moved north again. At ten o'clock on the morning of August 5, the head of his column came yet again to the Potomac. Men of the Forty-third shucked off their worn shoes and tattered pants to wade across. Cary Whitaker was able to chuckle something about "the Highland garb of Scotland," and the men with muskets hooted scornful insults at the regimental band, which never helped to fight. On the Maryland side they maneuvered against Federals, smiled at girls beside the road, and camped that night near St. James College.

Cary found a hospitable German Dunkard, who invited him to take supper. It was a good supper, too, with handsome girls to pass plates to the North Carolina captain. George, without Wash to cook for him, diced some broiled beef, heated it in water, and thickened it with meal and seasoned it well. He enjoyed this mess, and so did others, who asked for George's recipe.[4]

Next day they went back across the river into Virginia. The brief invasion of Maryland had been undertaken only to confuse the Federals, and notably it had succeeded. Jack Whitaker returned to Company D on the 7th,[5] and on August 10, General Grimes got back from sick leave and was welcomed by his brigade with cheers and a serenade by a band.[6]

Then Early ordered the army to march again on the 11th, and to form line of battle as so many times before. The Federals were gathering to meet them, two army corps and a strong force of cavalry, under young Major General Phil Sheridan.[7]

Let them come, said the stoutest hearts. Early's ranks did not lack men who felt ready for action, lots of action. These promised each other to get a Yankee apiece. That was a bleak and simple ambition. Here and there in Company D perhaps someone swore to get another Yankee beside the one for himself, another Yankee to open up the Golden Door of heaven for Lieutenant Billy Beav ans, dead and buried at Winchester.

XVIII

I AM TIRED OF THIS FIGHTING

Sheridan had 40,000 infantry and cavalry, Early perhaps 12,000; [1] but Early moved with all assurance toward a fight to settle the mastery of the Valley.

He began with another series of confusing movements, sudden disappearances and appearances, which succeeded in convincing Sheridan that a large and pugnacious force opposed him. [2] Cautiously the young Federal commander approached Cedar Creek below Winchester, and on August 13, Early occupied the advantageously high crest of Fisher's Hill. Skirmishing followed, but nothing serious in the way of fighting between the main bodies. The Forty-third threw up breastworks on the heights. "If the enemy attack us in this position we will have greatly the advantage of him," decided Cary; but the enemy did not attack. [3]

George, gazing across the bank of earth toward where the enemy deployed afar, was in a mood both fierce and eager. He had heard that Grant's whole army was on the way to the Valley, with Lee out of the Richmond defenses to pursue. If these things were so, felt George, the decisive battle of the war would be found right there around

Winchester, and undoubtedly would end with the South finally triumphant. High time, too, for he was dubious about the reverses near Atlanta. "I never feel anxiety about Gen'l Lee and his army," George wrote to Mary, "but that Southern Army does bother me some, I can't think they fight as our troops in Va. do."

Wash, as George knew, was at home and probably feeling better. Wash would be fortifying his health with watermelon, peaches, and milk. George asked that his servant be congratulated on such excellent convalescent fare, but again he boasted of his own cooking.

Both armies were glad for a Sunday of rest on August 14. Chaplain Thompson conducted the first of three religious services that morning. George listened to the sermon with his usual devout attention, and wrote home to his mother again:

> . . . I know, during the day, the thought has occurred to you, if only I had our dear boy with us, how much more pleasant it would be; but thank the Lord that tho. he is not with you, yet, there is still a high privilege given unto us, beside this, and to-day I am spared and blessed with the health & opportunity of enjoying it; & then the thought seems, if we are separated, we certainly have been highly favored. The Lord make me and us truly thankful for this kindness and blessing, is my constant prayer.

Dutiful and affectionate and pious, such sentiments; but might they bring tears to a mother's anxious eyes? George made an effort toward a brighter mood:

> What have you for dinner today? It is most time for us to begin to prepare ours, we have something extra, bought some corn and in addition to our usual soup, have corn to go in it, tomatoes would make it (if we had them) truly a *number-one* dinner, first-rate as it is . . .

Jack Whitaker strolled past his lieutenant and paused to quote a letter from Lucy Wills. Lucy had told Jack to say to her brother that, should he come home to man-starved Brinkleyville he could easily find a sweetheart. George had his own ready comment on such a suggestion, and included it at once at the close of his letter:

> . . . I however must acknowledge, I reckon, at last, that I have already one that has been on hand some time, must say positively, but it does seem that it is hard to forget her, I am compelled to own it. ha! ha!

Perhaps Mother would join in his laughter. She approved of Miss Lulu, as never of Miss Fannie.

The last of Chaplain Thompson's three services was conducted by bright summer moonlight above the earth-works on Fisher's Hill.[4]

For two days more they dallied on that strong height. Then on the 17th they moved again, back to cover the approaches to Winchester. Early had reinforcements again—two divisions from the First Corps, and some efficient cavalry under Fitzhugh Lee. Sheridan retired northward along the Valley Pike, still cautious about Early's seemingly large numbers. Early caught up, captured some prisoners from the fringe of Sheridan's army, and camped his regiments ready deployed in line of battle.[5]

Into Winchester they marched on the 18th. Along the street moved the Forty-third, company behind company. Jack Whitaker, marching in the ranks of Company D, suddenly turned and craned his neck to stare at someone sitting on a porch. Swiftly he hurried ahead of his comrades to where Cary rode, hailed him, and pointed toward the porch. That was she, Jack told Cary, Miss Kate Shepherd who had been so solicitous in her care for Billy.

Cary's eye, ever sharply appreciative of feminine beauty, had already spied out the lady on the porch. He reined

aside, let the regiment pass on its way, and rode back
to the Shepherd house. Bowing from the saddle, he
introduced himself and offered gallantly phrased thanks
for Miss Kate's exertions on Billy's behalf. She replied
courteously, even cordially; there was something about
Captain Cary rather like an older Billy. Miss Kate suggested that he call when he had time.

The troops camped just outside of town on the Berryville Road. Cary promptly sought and obtained leave to
return and see Miss Shepherd.

Return he did; but, maddeningly, two young Winchester sparks had come before him. They sat with Miss Kate
on the Shepherd porch. With grave, glum self-control,
Cary listened to the bantering conversation of these
swains, and finally had to excuse himself and report
back to camp. "Could get no private conversation with
her," he complained in his diary.[6] "One of the young men
evidently thought himself exceedingly smart, but I
thought him anything but smart and was completely
bored out with him."

At the same time, in camp by the roadside, George
also had spare moments. As was his custom, he availed
himself of the chance to write home:

> The Yankees, as usual, are bragging about their great
> superior numbers, but notwithstanding that it seems as if
> they don't care much about fighting, and are easily
> whipped. The Yankees are meaner, and commit more
> depredations every time they come into the Valley, than
> the preceding time. . . . Gen'l Early was very mad when
> he found it out, and will I think, no doubt, retaliate, he is
> certainly the wrong man to fool with, they will find him
> so. . . .

More happily, he thought about the good things at
home.

I am afraid you will not raise turkeys enough to have
more than a Christmas dinner.[7]

Two days, then, of pursuing Sheridan's rear guard,
with cavalry skirmishes just beyond sight and reach of the
main body of Early's infantry. After that, as Sheridan
turned in the direction of Harpers Ferry, Early pressed
him close. Now the gray sharpshooters exchanged shots
with the Federals, and word came back of an advance
by Sheridan to reinforce his skirmish line. Rodes, at the
front of the column, ordered Grimes to send a regiment
into action, and Grimes passed the order along to the
Forty-third.

That hard-bitten outfit responded at once, and arrived
at the point of contact to find the enemy in force and
advancing. Cary, rising in his stirrups, commanded his
men to deploy at the double-quick. The Forty-third
obeyed, stretching its line and opening fire. The Federals,
with some advantage of numbers and position, poured a
volley into the Forty-third, which began to give back.

Some of the officers had begged Cary to dismount, as
on horseback he made a shining mark. He swung out of
the saddle, just as his regiment started to retire. On foot
he rushed among the men, shouting for them to rally.
As he reached the line, a bullet struck his ankle and
knocked him flat.

He lay at full length, conscious but aware of stabbing
pain. So, he reflected, this was what it was like to be
wounded. Often he had wondered. Now he knew. Jack
Whitaker, still unhandy with a musket but present on the
firing line, came to Cary's side and raised him. The more
resolute of the regiment rallied and formed again.
Under cover of their volleys, Cary was borne from the
field.

More of both main bodies came forward and the
skirmishing grew heavy, but Early avoided a decisive

grapple with the enemy. As night fell, Sheridan retired again, through Charlestown. Early followed him confidently, perhaps overconfidently.

At the field hospital, surgeons examined Cary's wound. The bullet had penetrated between the bones of his lower leg above the ankle, carrying a fold of his heavy sock into the flesh with it. Chloroform was at hand for once, and Cary was treated with it before the sock was gouged out of the bloody hole. The bullet came away, caught in the tough knitted fabric. It was by no means as bad a leg wound as had befallen Billy Beavans a month earlier. Cary was sent to Winchester with other wounded, and subsequently was transferred to a base hospital at Staunton.[8]

George, with Sim, fought on with the army. Early continued to feel his way along Sheridan's line, then headed toward the Potomac as though to cross yet again. The Forty-third missed Cary. Still Boggan was not permitted to assume regimental command; he had been placed in arrest and threatened with court-martial, and Captain Wiley J. Cobb of Company E took Cary's place with less than Cary's efficiency.

In camp on the 24th, near Charlestown on the way to the Potomac, George found time to write to "Pa." George had heard that Wash was much improved in health and might return to the Valley soon. George would be glad to see his friend and servant again. And George was concerned for Uncle Cary's wound:

> . . . if it doesn't do as a great many have done, prove more serious than we at first suppose he will do well and have a good furlough home the expiration of which will nigh bring on winter. . . .

Captain Cobb, though doing his best for the Forty-third, was a disappointment:

. . . The Reg't will miss [Cary] very much, as there are, with it, no competent commanders, but if he does well, I must confess, I will not be any much grieved for his wound, for really to tell the truth, I am glad for one of my dear friends to get out of this, with not much hurt to him, provided he does it right; our army is losing its discipline which is costing the life & limbs of a many good man, because they have to expose themselves to get the sorry ones to do any part of their duty . . . not more than ⅓ of the men, in my opinion, does the execution, the remainder poke their heads as close to the ground as possible, and from there is not much chance of moving them.[9]

In spite of such arrantly groveling companions, George helped force the Federals to retire from Shepherdstown on the 25th and nag them to the very lip of the Potomac. The Confederates took a few prisoners among the slowest to negotiate the fords of the river, though exhaustion caused pursuing infantrymen to fall fainting in the ranks. Then they returned to camp at Shepherdstown. George, for once, found diversion in feminine companionship and conversation—that night he met "many secesh ladies." [10] On Saturday, August 27 the army was back at Bunker Hill once more.

George was happy to have his uniform laundered, and looked to a restful Sunday. Another word from home told him that Wash was still sick at Brinkleyville. George missed Wash's services and companionship.

The marching and countermarching continued. On the last day of the month, Rodes' Division surprised Federal cavalry regiments mending that railway at Martinsburg. After a brief, hot fight, the division drove them from the field. Infantry chasing cavalry—George thought it unusual, even amusing. He helped capture welcome plunder of pork, corn, and oats, with clothing of various kinds; such prizes no longer roused his disdain, for he was hungry. A civilian, just come to Martinsburg from Hagerstown in Maryland, told George that the Northern Democrats had nominated McClellan, once the Union commander in Virginia, now a peace candidate, for the presidency of the United States.

"I am rather afraid of him," wrote George to Lucy on the quiet day following, "tho the prisoners we take say he will certainly stop the war if elected . . . my spirits have been very high for the past few weeks, concerning the termination of the war, yet am very much afraid, we shall have them to try another year or so, or perhaps more."

George found opportunity to weigh himself, too. A hundred and fifty-four pounds—a gain of nearly twenty pounds since, ailing but determined, he had left Richmond two and a half months before. It was all live weight, too, good bone and muscle. George had never felt better in his life.

On September 3, Atlanta in Georgia prepared to surrender to Sherman, the grinding siege of Petersburg ground on, and John Hunt Morgan, a prince of Southern cavalry raiders, rode toward his death in Tennessee. But in the Valley, Rodes again fought and drove mounted regiments of enemy. Other divisions battled successfully east of Bunker Hill, near the fords of the Shenandoah. Rain soaked both armies, but not enough to halt action of ensuing days. By September 7, the sun shone to warm the earth and the heart of George Wills.

He felt some comfort in the news from Staunton. Uncle Sim had heard from Uncle Cary. The wounded captain was getting better, really getting better, and soon could be moved home to Enfield. He did not face a tragic death like that of Billy Beavans, not just yet anyway. George wrote to sister Lucy, his most frequent correspondent at home, and he turned almost lyrical:

> . . . this is a beautiful lovely autumn day, the sun arose and is still shining brightly, and everything is as calm and quiet as it was in the days of yore, when honest and quiet avocations supplied the place of disturbance & war. Yesterday & the two or three preceeding days, was cloudy, raining and drizzly and in fact had every element in them to make a chicken-hearted & sour-tempered man sad and lonely. I however spent the day very well, reading & making & drinking beef soup . . .

He added a message for Ed, to be forwarded to the boy's regiment at Weldon. This word, from one soldier to another, took on a tinge of sad meditation:

> Ed, I am tired of this fighting, it is getting too common for me, we will be lieing about camp, everything quiet, receive orders very suddenly to move, and in less than two hours will be fighting. . . .
>
> Do you ever go to Raleigh? If so, won't you go out and call on my *sweetheart,* as I must acknowledge she lives not very far from there. The more I think of her, the more I am compelled to think of her; ha! ha! what do you think of that? [11]

At the last George tried to laugh, but being compelled to think of Lulu wasn't as funny as he made out, not by a long shot with a bush in the way. Other elements than rainy and drizzly weather made a war-weary man sad and lonely.

To look forward to someone you could call wife, in some future time when honest and quiet avocations would supply the place of disturbance and war; but George had nobody in camp to talk to about his real yearning for Lulu. Johnny, his boyhood comrade, was still home on wound leave. Uncle Cary was absent, and Uncle Sim, for all his quiet sympathy, was a matter-of-fact old bachelor, every year of thirty-four. If Billy were at Bunker Hill

—Billy had become most like a brother to George, Billy was a poet and a romantic, would understand; but Billy wasn't there. Billy was gone where the woodbine twineth, where, the Bible told you, there was no marrying or giving in marriage.

It was hard, hard to be a good man, to do your duty as you now stood, when the fighting got too common for you and lost the thrill of novelty it had possessed at Big Bethel. The fighting had become too common for near about everyone, even for men who had faced unshaken the terrible cannonades of Gettysburg, the hurricanes of lead in the Wilderness. Nowadays two thirds of them poked their heads close to the ground when they saw those Yankee ant-armies, and the other third got itself all shot to pieces in the fighting that was too common, too common.

Did everybody feel that way? Was the fighting become too common for hard-faced Grimes at the head of the brigade, blond-mustached Rodes at the head of the division? Too common for Early, too common for Lee back at Petersburg? How about the Yankees, and Grant and Sheridan and their other generals? How common was the fighting in their estimation?

You didn't really dare to think long and sweetly of Miss Lulu, the girl with the refined manners and the good disposition, on whose plantation you had fallen in love. Because Miss Lulu was far away on that plantation near Raleigh, and you were here, right here in the Valley of the Shadow of Death. And death's shadow hung behind your shoulder, no matter how bright the September sun shone down on you after the rain. Any moment you might receive orders very suddenly to move.

Ed, I am tired of this fighting. . . . won't you go out and call on my sweetheart? The more I think of her, the more I am compelled to think of her. . . .

XIX

TELL MOTHER, IF I FALL

Paymasters arrived in the Valley with big cashboxes full of paper money, and the army was given its pay for several months' service. In Rodes' Division, still camped near Bunker Hill, soldiers wondered what to do with so much Confederate scrip that would buy, after all, so little. On September 9, George heard the shouts and laughter as someone auctioned off a razor. He himself did not bid—he had carried a razor all through the war. Sheaf of bills in hand, he strolled through the regiment and settled accounts with friends from whom he had borrowed money.[1]

Adjutant John Lacy returned from wound leave, and Sim Whitaker and George invited him to join their reduced mess. Food was plain and coarse, the simple rations of beef and flour from the commissary, with apples from nearby orchards. But George, at least, enjoyed the fare, or said he did. Lacy had a fine singing voice too, and George liked to listen to him sing.[2]

Sheridan's cavalry was on the prowl again. On September 10, Early's infantry drove enemy scouting patrols from Darksville, and again on the 13th they fought Yankee cavalry in force along Opequon Creek, with artillery chiming in from both sides. George watched with military disdain the swift giving way of the enemy horse, and was scornful to see fighting men of Sheridan's regiments pause in mid-action to carry away their fallen comrades. It was better to wound a foreman than to kill him, he decided; for several others would drop out of the line to bear back the wounded man.[3]

By September 14 the reinforcement from the First Corps was called away to help against Grant's increasing pressure on Petersburg. At about the same time Johnny Beavans returned to Company D.[4] Brotherly, he and George greeted each other. Johnny had missed all the fatiguing miles afoot since June, and he was in fine spirits and helped lift the morale of his cousin and of the company. The troops rested at the old campground near Bunker Hill. George wrote a long letter to his father, concerning recent skirmishes and thoughts of home:

> . . . It would have been so pleasant for me, to have been able to enjoy those nice vegetables & nice fruit you wrote me about, besides being at *home that* would have been a great pleasure; but still, I have been very fortunate in that respect this Summer & Fall; tho I haven't had a single bait of vegetables since I left home, yet this Valley abounds in apples of the nicest quality, and we have had them most of the time, without them hardly know how the absence of vegetable matter could have been dispensed with.
>
> I suppose at this time you are making syrup, guess you will make a good-deal of it, would be much pleased to be there now also, as have been anxious, and am longing for some recently, but suppose can do very well without it as long as I can get beef-soup and apples.

Even as George's mouth watered for that homemade Brinkleyville syrup, the bugle blew assembly. The regiments formed for dress parade. The Forty-third fell in under Captain Cobb. Major Boggan faced a court-martial, and some of the company officers had asked him outright to resign and avoid further embarrassment. General Grimes was ready to arrange withdrawal of charges if Boggan would leave the service.[5] George hoped for that; then Cary, when he came back, might get his colonelcy.

Rest and peace on September 15 and 16. Not even distant cannon fire. On the 17th, George resumed his letter where he had left off. That September sunlight was brilliant as he picked up his pen; but a cloud crawled over the blue sky, and scattering raindrops blotted George's ink. Again George wrote about home affairs, worrying over brother Richard's poor health, and:

> You probably hear from Uncle Cary through those at home, as I suppose he writes them. *We* here however never hear anything at all from him, except occasionally a man coming to the command sees him and tells us of him, am afraid he is not doing so well as we could wish, tho they represent otherwise . . . John B. seems quite cheerful and I am very happy to say, is a much better boy than he used to be, he is such a general favorite, were he to become pious, would be approaching perfection. . . .
>
> We are all very well, in fact the health of the army was never better. My love to all.
>
> The Lord be our refuge & protector and cause a speedy termination of this war, upon liberty and independence, is the constant prayer of
>
> Your very affectionate son
G. Whitaker Wills

Sim Whitaker reported sick at about the time George finished writing, and headed for the hospital in Winchester.[6] George may have handed his uncle the letter to mail.

That same afternoon Early alerted his divisions. Rodes

moved close to the camp of Gordon and the artillery battalion of Lieutenant Colonel Carter Braxton. Yankees were back at their old job of mending the railroad near Martinsburg. Gordon's men helped drive them out on the 18th, while Rodes shifted southward to Stephenson's Depot. The Martinsburg expedition brought back news; Grant had made a journey from the Petersburg trenches to confer with Sheridan, and Sheridan prepared to attack in force.

Early had little more than twelve thousand of all arms against nearly four times that many with Sheridan, but Sheridan did not know his own heavy odds. The headlong maneuvering back and forth had made Early's command seem much larger, much more formidable. But now Sheridan had word of the return of Confederate troops to Lee, and he himself had received more cavalry.

That September 18, George Wills stropped his razor and carefully shaved his square, lean jaws. His young beard was sparse and slow-sprouting, that shave would keep his face clean for a day or so to come. Perhaps George dreamed pleasantly that night, or perhaps he did not dream at all. Bugles wakened him in the dawn of the 19th, and he ate breakfast and fell in with Company D. Off somewhere south and east rang shots.

Sheridan was crossing the Opequon and driving in the pickets on the Berryville Road. Early had sent for Rodes and Gordon to come from their camps near Stephenson's Depot, and he had ridden forward in person to where Ramseur's Division was already engaged in open country east of Winchester. Ramseur's skirmish line exchanged volleys with a powerful advance of Federals. Breckenridge, too, faced enemy several miles to the north, and Early's cavalry moved, ready to screen the flanks of the army as it came into position.

Three miles away from Ramseur's battle, Rodes made

ready to move. George Wills had a decent uniform that day, perhaps the one he had ordered made in Brinkley-ville nearly two months before. Carefully he buttoned up the snug jacket, and into his breast pocket put his well-thumbed New Testament.[7] The army was full of stories about pocket testaments turning bullets. Once or twice, laughed the godless, decks of cards had similarly saved their unregenerate owners.

As Rodes' regiments formed column for the march, Captain Cobb made a swift, anxious survey of the Forty-third. The recent campaigns had left him pitifully short of officers. Company B, for instance, fell in without captain or lieutenant, and it needed resolute leadership in the fighting that surely was upon the army. Where could Cobb find a good man to command B?

No other company had officers to spare. Company D, for instance, had only Second Lieutenant George Wills present for duty; but D was a tried and sturdy little unit, with good noncoms. Let Sergeant Johnny Beavans take over there, said Cobb, while George led B. Obediently George moved away to assume his new command.[8]

It was made up of men from Union and Mecklenburg counties and, in so small a regiment, those men knew George Wills. He had been a good sergeant at Gettysburg. More recently, he had been a good lieutenant outside Washington, at Snicker's Ford, up and down the Valley. You could follow a long, tall, self-respecting young officer like Lieutenant Wills. Off the infantry moved, Rodes coming up behind Gordon, toward the right flank of the enemy advance as it pressed Ramseur.

Nearly 35,000 Federal infantry were on the field there, the VI and XIX Corps, crack veterans of the Army of the Potomac and toughened by months of summer marching and skirmishing. Against this overwhelming threat, Ramseur could bring the fire of but 1,700 muskets. Rodes and Gordon had between them perhaps 5,000 more. Breckenridge was heavily engaged miles away. The little cavalry force dismounted to help. Nobody seemed to quail today.

It was 10 o'clock in the morning when Gordon deployed well to Ramseur's left. Rodes hastily formed to support Gordon's right and fill the gap. The terrain was somewhat uneven, but fairly clear of trees between Winchester and Opequon Creek. Through murky clouds of smoke and dust each army saw the other plain. The Federals shifted part of their fire toward the division opposing their right.[9]

Artillery bombardment grew heavy. A shell fragment tore Rodes out of his saddle, and he fell dying under the hoofs of his big black horse. No time for standing aghast and sorrowful; Gordon instantly assumed command of Rodes' troops as well as his own, and ordered both divisions forward. Johnny Beavans, shepherding Company D, told several unarmed men to go to the rear. That order included Jack Whitaker, still unable to load and fire a musket because of his injured arm.[10] Pushing toward the enemy flank, the two divisions planted themselves stubbornly and began to fire at close range.

The fainthearted of the regiments, the cowering men for whom the fighting had become too unbearably, perilously common, began as usual to drift back out of formation. Several, indeed, turned and made for the rear. Staff officers at the rear of the two divisions sought to rally these. Chaplain John Paris of the Fifty-fourth North Carolina, who found himself just behind Grimes' Brigade, helped to stop timid retreaters and head them toward the firing again. Like Chaplain Yates at Camp Ellis in 1861, Paris was ready to fight as well as pray.

But he felt his heart sink to see the whole brigade of Grimes suddenly turn its back on the enemy and start toward him, as though retreating in a body. He gaped in horror—those splendid troops in panic? Then, almost the next moment, he saw that his guess was both wrong and ungrateful. The brigade sought a better position, that was all. Without losing formation, it retired, halted, and faced about once more. Paris watched. His young friend George Wills, son of Paris' colleague in the Methodist ministry, was directing the fire of Company B point blank at the enemy, about 150 yards away, just there.

The ear-smashing thunder of artillery, stitched through and across by volleys of musketry, staggered the earth and rent the sky. The North Carolinians, reinforced by the stragglers shamed back by Paris and others, were reaping lives in the formation opposite them. Every Confederate shot seemed to count.[11]

George, carrying in his hand the sword Uncle Cary had given him in the camp at Cold Harbor, walked up and down Company B's firing line. He was seen to smile, he was heard to laugh. That was to encourage these men he led, for long ago George had ceased to find anything laughable in combat. He felt no assurance of living through the tempest of bullets, and no terror. "Tell mother, if I fall, she need have no fears for my future," he had directed Wash, and he had meant it. But, if he was undisturbed about himself, he must worry about Company B. The new position it now held was awkwardly exposed. If he could shift the men, just a little way, to where the cover was better . . .

Yonder he saw Adjutant Lacy, he who sang sweetly in the bivouacs. George would ask permission of him, then complete the movement. He paced quickly toward the adjutant, still smiling.

A shell exploded at his very side as he hurried. The long, swift body of Lieutenant George Whitaker Wills tumbled full-sprawl on the grass. A sergeant of Company

B, dashing to his side, thought that George looked quiet, calm, as though he had fallen asleep.

Lacy, too, reached George, leaned down, and saw that he was dead. Had the bursting shell killed George by a tremendous shock? But blood had sprung redly out on that neatly buttoned gray jacket. A musket ball had drilled George through the body, and it had killed him instantly.[12]

Lacy hurriedly caught up George's fallen sword, and the sergeant raced back to command Company B, again left officerless. The gap where the lieutenant had dropped must be filled up, every musket must be aimed forward and kept firing, again, again. The mighty flank of blue opposite the divisions of Rodes and Gordon had begun to waver, to sway. Then it moved—backward. Sheridan's crushingly superior numbers were on the point of retreating.

Early, watching, gloried in the success of his flanking movement. It looked like victory, perhaps greater victory than any since Chancellorsville. The ground at the right of the Federal line was strewn with dead and wounded. If Early had but a single fresh division to send in—but he had none. He was using every man. As the sun, close to its autumnal equinox, reached the top of the sky, Early stretched his line thinly from Abraham's Creek on the south to Red Bud Creek on the north. Before him loomed the Federals, checked but not yet crushed.

Both lines whanged away at each other, into the afternoon. Johnny Beavans reeled and almost went down as a bit of shrapnel gashed his head. Stanching the flow of blood, he tottered back out of the fight, and was sent with other walking wounded toward Winchester.[13]

Still they hoped to win, Early's outnumbered, tired men. But from their left appeared new danger. The Federals had driven back Breckenridge to the north, and came, a whole new corps pointed by galloping cavalry, right down the Martinsburg Road toward Winchester's northern outskirts.

Early's line gave. It had to. Back it fell, back from where George Wills lay as though sleeping in the midst of the country where, fifteen months ago on the way to Gettysburg, he had wished to have been born. Early made a stand again, behind some sketchy defenses built just outside Winchester in 1861, but the pressure was too great. The din of bombardment sounded like the whole world exploding into dust.

Flanked once again, Early's outnumbered little army backed into the town. Grimes, in a black rage at seeing his brigade start to break, rode in among his men and threatened to blow out the brains of the first who left his post. Then he drew his sword and struck at fleeing infantry of other commands. Somehow he and other officers kept the fight going as their brigades fell back along the streets.

Ammunition and commissary wagons, hastily hitched ambulances with sick and wounded, careened away south toward Fisher's Hill. Sim Whitaker, still miserably sick and weak, managed to crawl from his cot and run with the others. So did Johnny Beavans, able to keep his feet but groggily hearing, as if in a terrible dream, the news of George's death. Jack Whitaker, too, escaped capture. The fighting divisions, keeping some order but dangerously close to panic, abandoned Winchester and in the dusk of evening rallied four miles south of town.

Sheridan pressed them no further. They marched twenty miles more that night, to Fisher's Hill. On the high ground once approved for defense by Cary Whitaker, Early reorganized to meet any Federal move that might follow. Then he counted his casualties.

He had lost forty per cent of his force—3,600 from the

infantry had been killed, wounded, or captured, and perhaps 1,000 from the cavalry. Some of his best officers had fallen. Rodes, brave and brilliant at the head of his division since it had headed for Gettysburg, would be missed the most sorely. A splendid brigadier, A. C. Godwin of Ramseur's Division, also had been killed. Fitz Lee was wounded. Regimental commanders were dead or captured, and would be hard to replace.[14]

In Company D they mourned for George Wills, also hard to replace, slain in the moment when victory had seemed certain, his body left on the field captured by the enemy.

XX

LET US NOT MOURN AS THOSE WHO HAVE NO HOPE

Miss Lulu was back at Elba Academy in Brinkleyville by late September. When someone shouted outside that George had been killed, she slid to the classroom floor in a swoon.[1]

Almost as stunned by helpless grief was the Reverend Mr. William H. Wills. He reread the long letter George had written on September 14 and 17, with its news, its hopes, its affectionate messages, its invocation of God's help for the Confederacy. He wrote a note to attach:

> This is the last letter ever received from my dear Boy. He was killed on the Battlefield near Winchester Va two days after the date of the supplement viz: 19th Sept. 1864. George was a noble youth and I think a Christian. No more letters from him! O God! help me to be resigned to thy will and may I meet him in thy kingdom.[2]

The news that George's body had not been rescued was only a lesser sorrow. By lifelong custom, the minister thought rather of the soul, and George's soul, he told himself, was safe in heaven.[3] The boy had convinced him of that with his letters of the recent months, after the troublesome period when George had confessed something of boredom with religious matters.

"Why should George have been so long and so strangely preserved, and *now* fall?" Mr. Wills said to his wife.

He may have meant the question rhetorically, but the mother and sister of soldiers did not so take it.

"Because he was not quite ready," she replied, comforting her husband and herself.

Other letters arrived in Brinkleyville:

> *Camp of Grimes' Brigade*
> *Near Strasburg Va Sept. 20th 1864*

Dear Mr. Wills——

   . . . On the engagement yesterday with the enemy near Winchester, your noble and gallant son, George fell, a victim to this cruel war. About 11 o'clock A. M. the Division was formed in line of battle & moved rapidly to meet the enemy who were advancing in strong force towards Winchester. A few moments only elapsed before the Div. was hotly engaged with the enemy at very close quarters. . . . George fell, supposed to have been shocked to death by the explosion of a shell. A shell was seen to explode right at him & at the same time he fell to rise no more. A Serg'nt of the company which he commanded told me that he looked as if he was a sleep. Late in the evening the cavalry having given way on our left, the Infantry was forced to retire leaving George's body with many of the wounded in the hands of the enemy. His sword was taken out by Adj. Lacy and will be sent home the first opportunity. . . .

   But "let us not mourn as those who have no hope," for by his upright walk and Godly conversation, we are assured that he is now at ease with his God in heaven.

> I remain very affectionately yours
> J. R. Whitaker

Strasburg, Va. Tuesday 20th Sept 1864

My Dear Brother Wills

. . . On Yesterday he [George] fell at his post, in command of Company B, 43rd Regt. . . . Lieut. Whitaker was not in the battle. He was sick in the hospital, but has been reported to me as able to get off with the army somehow. John Bivens is wounded in the head severely, though I hope not dangerously. . . .

Respectfully yours
John Paris

Gen'l Hospital Staunton Va
September 22nd 1864

Mr Wills
Sir

. . . Monday about 10 A. M. Rodes' Div'n charged the Enemy and was under very heavy fire for one hour. Geo's Com'y "B" being very much exposed Geo started up the line to have it removed & just before reaching Adj. Lacy a minnie ball passed through his boddy from the effects of which he fell to the ground and quietly passed from Earth to Eternity. . . . No one excepting his parents and sisters can or will mourn his loss more than I. I loved him as a brother & can hardly relize his death. It seems like a mere dream, *God grant* it was a dream.

Your affec' friend
John Beavans, Jr.

These condolences Mr. Wills stowed carefully away among the family's chief treasures. On September 29 he wrote to Richard: "I believe God has been preparing him for this." [4]

Wash had been on his way back to the Valley when, somewhere on the road, he heard the news.[5] He hurried on to find the camp of the Forty-third, and to learn what he could of his master's death. It had been instantaneous; that, at least, was a sort of comfort to Wash. For he had not been needed. He could not have helped in any way had he been there. Drowned in misery, he found his way back home to Brinkleyville. To Richard Wills he wrote, honestly and movingly:

Dear Master Richard

I will now try to give you an account of my feelings toward my young master who is now dead. I hope and trust he is saved. I have reason to believe so by the light which he gave me. . . . It seems all fear had been banished from him through all. I am glad to tell you his coat was buttoned up in the prettiest style of uniform and in his breast pocket was his little Testament. Master Richard, I say to you it is good to be religious . . .

We talked over everything, trouble sorrow and sickness, we talked that while I was sick, the evening before I left for home, and that it was better for a man to be in another world. He said he never went in any battle with the expectation of coming out safe, he seemed then to give himself up into the hands of Providence, he would review over his life and seemed to be thankful that he had been spared through so many battles. . . .

When I look over the troubles of men nowadays especially of the poor soldier in the army, I feel this morning that I am glad to tell you he is not there, he is in a better world than this. Master Richard, I believe it as much as I ever believed anything in my life, that he is at rest, my heart believes it. I say it seriously, your brother loved you dearly, you were a great light in his eye, he is now where you will have to give him no more advices, but we must try to meet him in heaven. I tell you my experience as a servant, it is great in raising children. A child when he becomes a man either regrets or praises the way he was raised. I desire to be a better christian I want to get to heaven . . .

I am at home I don't know for how long. Master Eddie says he wants me to go with him, I will go and do the best

I can for him. I am willing to do anything I can to help
out our struggling country. I desire to see you and talk
with you, have a long talk about one thing and another.
If we ever be so fortunate as to be able to do it so it will
afford me a great consolation certainly Master Richard
I know something about trouble

> Your faithful servant
> Wash[6]

Johnny Beavans, his head wound becoming troublesome, was sent home to Enfield from the hospital at
Staunton, but Sim Whitaker was back with Company D
about October 1.[7] He must have listened with more than
his habitual quiet gravity to the tale of how Sheridan's victorious host, pressing south out of Winchester, had driven
Early from Fisher's Hill on September 22. He found
the little army reorganized. Breckenridge and his troops
had been transferred, and a division under Kershaw had
replaced this force. Ramseur had been shifted to the
command of Rodes' Division, while John Peagram headed
that of Ramseur. A few more cavalry had joined Early,
too, giving him a total of perhaps fourteen thousand
with which to fight the great Federal host he had succeeded in drawing away from the siege of Richmond and
Petersburg.[8]

Sheridan, full of elation after twice overwhelming his
feeble adversary, was devastating the northern end of the
Valley. He burned corn shocks, mills, barns, tanneries,
houses, granaries, and sheds. With manifest pride in this
accomplishment, he declared that the Valley contained
nothing to nourish man or beast.[9] After him came Early
once again, stubbornly offering battle.

Early's military policy had the logic of desperation. The
odds against him were tremendous, but with bleak realism
he told himself that they would never become less. He
had to keep Sheridan from sending back the troops that

Grant needed. That meant fight, and fight was what Early did.[10]

On October 18, with gingerly stealth, Early approached the position of the Federals without alarming their scouts or pickets. Three army corps lay camped across the Valley just below Middletown, at Cedar Creek. Early sent Gordon, with his own division and those of Ramseur and Peagram, behind the north fork of the Shenandoah. The remainder of the infantry, divided under Kershaw and Gabriel Wharton, waited at Strasburg to strike at the fortunate moment. In the small hours before dawn of October 19, Gordon splashed across the river at Bowman's Ford, scattered unwary enemy pickets, and charged into the camp of one Union corps, then another.[11]

Routed from their blankets, the Yankees fled in confusion. But a third camp—the resolute VI Corps—was not reached. Those troops rose quickly, formed for action in the foggy morning, and presented a ready front, bristling with musket muzzles.

The Confederates did not strike at once. Early, said Gordon and others later, ordered a pause while he waited for the VI Corps to retreat. Early was to claim that his men stopped to loot the captured camps.[12] Whatever the reason, precious time was wasted while Sheridan, who had been absent on a flying visit to Grant's headquarters in the Richmond area, heard of the battle as he reached Winchester. Back he galloped twenty miles, heartened and rallied his shaken army, and counterattacked.

Worse than at Winchester a month before was the Confederate rout at Cedar Creek. What had looked like sure victory was turned again into defeat. Only demoniac artillery fire covered the rush rearward of the demoralized infantry and saved Early from utter destruction. The army had to run all the way to New Market.

Ramseur had been killed. Other valuable officers were

dead or wounded. Most of Early's artillery had been captured. The brigades were terribly punished.[13] And Sim Whitaker was wounded in the arm, but had escaped capture again and went back to the hospital.

Thus the army crouched at almost midpoint of the Valley it had left Richmond to defend, and clamor against Early rose throughout all the Confederacy. Three times in a row he had been badly beaten by Sheridan. But he had inflicted upon Sheridan's command some fifteen thousand casualties, as many as his own army had ever numbered at the largest. He had saved the crops of the Valley in early summer. He had kept fully forty per cent of Grant's army occupied, well away from the beleaguered Confederate capital.

And still he sought to do more. When Cary Whitaker returned to duty in November,[14] he found the army camped at New Market, having fought half a dozen small engagements with Sheridan's cavalry while the main body of the enemy fortified near Winchester. The little force had been whittled down again. Kershaw's Division had gone back to Richmond. Brigadier General Grimes was temporarily assigned to command the division in front of which Rodes and Ramseur had been shot away, and Colonel D. G. Cowand of the Thirty-second led the brigade.

In the Forty-third, Major Boggan had at last resigned.[15] Cary was heartily welcomed, as capable of leading his regiment. But he received no promotion. His command numbered few more than had the Enfield Blues in 1861.

But Cary betrayed neither disappointment for himself nor despair for the army. He had been away, nursing his wounded leg, while his comrades had suffered those three devastating reverses at Sheridan's hands. Men could talk about such things, but to Cary Whitaker, late county attorney for Halifax, what they said was no more than

hearsay evidence. He himself had never been driven.
Even at Gettysburg, the Forty-third had withdrawn in
orderly fashion. And Grimes strove energetically to improve the division by drill and better organization.

But if Cary's certainty of final triumph over the Federals continued unswerving, he stared with amazement
and horror at the plight of his men. It was cold around the
camp at New Market—snow had covered the mountaintops
on November 6, the day that Boggan had left—and bare-
foot soldiers, with scarcely rags to cover themselves,
hunched their shoulders and chattered their teeth as they
mustered for duty. Cary frowned to see men with their
trouser legs worn away to the very hips, and some wearing
only underclothes. The folks at home in Enfield never
would believe it.[16]

Food, too, was scarce. North of where Early's camps
lay, the Shenandoah Valley had been robbed of rations
for men, forage for horses. Unground corn was issued to
some regiments, and the hungry troops either parched it
whole or milled it in coarse makeshift fashion and cooked
it into grubby pones and dodgers.

But, cold and hungry though they were, they marched
on November 10 to demonstrate against Sheridan's positions. The enemy retired into fortified strong points, and
Early dropped back to New Market. More snow fell on
November 23, while Grimes led his division to meet
and turn back four thousand Federal cavalry. On the
next day, the thermometer stood at twenty degrees. The
whole army, from generals to privates, yearned for permission to build warm winter quarters.[17]

By the first week in December, Sim and Johnny returned to what poor cheer Company D could afford
them.[18] They missed George Wills in Company D, in the
entire regiment.[19] Joylessly, the mess ate scanty rations
and thought of gaieties dead and vanished.

Still no orders to build those huts against the winter winds and snows. Instead, on December 9, Lee sent for the divisions of Gordon and Pegram to head back to the Petersburg trenches. Snow fell heavily on the camp of Early's remainder, two inches of it whitening the ground to make shoeless men miserable. On December 13, Grimes was ordered to follow the rest of the Second Corps.[20]

The division reached Richmond on December 15, riding flat-wheeled cars behind wheezy engines over the almost outworn rails of the Southside. It went into camp on Swift Creek, three miles north of Petersburg and two miles west of a string of fortifications that looked toward the Federals along the James River.[21] Below Petersburg were more entrenchments, and eastward were still more, a great system of defenses, soggy and dismal.

For miles they extended, those works, in curves and angles and long stretches, bracketing Petersburg. Batteries crowned high points, and everywhere were soldiers, like the brigades of Grimes, in reserve. Within the defending ditches, Lee's Army held itself ready to defend the Confederate capital.

On the foggy mornings and chill evenings Southern infantrymen looked bitterly across to other breastworks and strong points and batteries, the ring of Grant's fortifications that contained and threatened the ring of Lee's. Only here and there did gaps show in this double system—at the James and the Appomattox rivers, and where stubborn gray guardians still kept open the South-side Railroad. Other lines of communication and supply were cut off. That included the Petersburg and Weldon, which would lead no more to Enfield in Halifax County, North Carolina.

Few more than 50,000 Confederates held those ramparts and supporting positions. Outside waited 120,000 Federals. The bitter cold that lay on the muddy land discouraged major conflict, but sharpshooters of both armies crept back and forth in the precariously debatable territory between the lines, sending bullets at any hostile head that showed above the parapets. And off there beyond, the whole South was direly beset.

Sherman closed in on Savannah at the end of his march to the sea. In Tennessee, John B. Hood had lost the battle of Franklin and was about to lose the battle of Nashville. Fort Fisher, on the North Carolina coast, frantically staved off attackers to keep Wilmington the last open port of the Confederacy. It looked like the end of things, or very close to it, to all but a few unconvincibles like Cary Whitaker, senior captain and commander of the Forty-third North Carolina Regiment.

On the shores of Swift Creek, men of the division botched together hovels or dug caves for shelter from the frost. Camp Rodes, they called their bivouac, after the brave general they had lost on the same day they lost George Wills. Cary assigned Jack Whitaker as a clerk at regimental headquarters.[22] Sim, the only officer left with Company D, and Johnny, the senior sergeant, were leaders enough for the decimated outfit. It needed no more officers and noncoms than it had. What it needed, what the whole Army of Northern Virginia needed, was more privates.

XXI

WE CAN STILL WEATHER THIS STORM

Christmas was upon the army, with little cheer for heart or belly. The farms around Richmond and Petersburg had been stripped of the last ear of corn, the last mouthful of meat. Boxes of delicacies came from home no more; if a shipment did survive the threat of Yankee capture, almost invariably it was stolen by hungry railroad employees.

And things were thin and rough at home too. Soldiers returned from furlough with doleful tales of family privations, of civilian talk in terms of despondency and despair and wish for surrender and peace, any kind of peace, under the conqueror. When at holiday time the ladies of Richmond could provide for dinner only a few scraps of ham, turkey, and beef, with a scattering of biscuits, it seemed to destroy what morale was left. Snow and sleet buffeted the camps and the trenches. Across from Yankee parapets came shouts, not unfriendly, about plenty of food and fuel. By January, Lee's army was reduced by desertion as by sickness and wounds.[1]

John B. Gordon, as senior division commander, headed the Second Corps at Petersburg while Early remained in the Valley with almost no troops and almost no reputation. Lee liked and trusted Gordon, whose fame grew, though his corps had no more than eight thousand six hundred effectives at the beginning of 1865.[2]

Cary Whitaker, a lawyer once, frequently was assigned to court-martial details.[3] Still at Camp Rodes on Swift Creek, he wrote home to his brother, G. A. T. Whitaker on February 6 of how he felt concerning the plight of the South in general and of the Army of Northern Virginia in particular:

> . . . I think the people as well as the Government ought to make extra efforts to feed and clothe the soldiers, for if our soldiers were well clothed and fed I don't believe there would be one tenth of the desertions then. If the Yankees were fed and clothed as we are they wouldn't have an army a month, while if our army received their treatment, we would seldom have a deserter. Though I have a pretty good character for veracity at home, my friends would hardly believe me if I were to tell of the destitution and suffering I have seen in the army—when in the Valley of Va, the snow on the ground, I have seen soldiers with their pants worn off up to their hips, and nothing but an old pair of drawers on, worn out and exposing the person in many places—and still were I to go to Halifax and point out this in the most glowing colors I would hardly get a dozen pairs of pants for the very army which is now keeping the enemy from their homes and firesides. . . .

Fighting men could not help but feel depressed, argued Cary, when their families wrote and spoke so hopelessly:

> It is almost impossible for a soldier to go home on furlow without coming back somewhat demoralized and despondent for the gloom that seems to pervade the people at home . . . and their insane desire for peace on any terms which seems to have taken possession of many of them.

> I cannot but think that this is the crisis of our govern-
> ment and our cause but if our army is sustained I believe
> we can still weather this storm and bring peace and hap-
> piness to our stricken country. . . .

Cary had heard that Bryan Grimes, who had led the
division ever since late October, would soon get his commission as major general. Though Grimes impressed Cary
as "brave and a good disciplinarion," still Cary doubted
his general's ability to shine at a rank higher than that of
brigadier. Rodes, who once had declined to offer Cary a
drink, was the captain's ideal of a commander. Cary continued:

> . . . If Genl Grimes is promoted I don't know who will
> be our Brigade commander but whoever it may be it will
> not be the equal of Gen Daniel. . . . Col. Cowand of the
> 32nd is in command of the Brigade and if Gen Grimes is
> promoted I think he is looking forward to promotion as
> our Brigadier. He is a very clever gentleman and I like
> him but I am with him as with Gen G., I don't think he has
> too much mental capacity, but Brigades are not much
> more than regiments should be.

It was the same everywhere in the army, had Cary but
stopped to think. The best had been killed in battle—
Jackson, Stuart, Rodes, Daniel—or languished like Ewell,
or were discredited like Early. Gordon himself had never
been a professional soldier. Leaders of the other two
divisions in the corps were brigadiers like Grimes, and
colonels commanded most of the brigades. Elsewhere,
command was shot to pieces. Of all the old chieftains who
had begun the war, only Lee and Longstreet seemed the
same.

Cary finished by asking his brother a favor:

> I wish you would try to have me a pair of shoes made.
> If you can get them made on reasonable terms that is,
> without taking almost a year's pay to pay for them.

To his sister Mary Whitaker Wills, too, on February 11, Cary complained of the despair with which home folks infected the troops.

At that, the Forty-third and the division to which it belonged had been spared the full ordeal of battle so far in the winter. Muddy roads around the defenses had slowed up Grant's assaults. But spring was on the way, moving up from the southward, and with it would come death for many.

On February 15, Grimes received his commission as major general, with, almost in the same hour, orders to make ready for battle.[4] On February 24 the division moved westward from its cabins on Swift Creek to where the extreme right of the defenses touched Sutherland's Station on the Southside Railroad just below the Appomattox River.[5] "We have moved from winter quarters for good," wrote Cary to Mrs. Wills, "and I think the campaign has pretty well commenced with us." [6] However, Sutherland's Station was located opposite a dense forest of pine, swarming with the scouting parties of both armies but hard for artillery to travel. The gray brigades remained stuck in the mud, and so did the blue ones.[7] The month of February ended and March began, with only sporadic exchanges of gunfire at that point of the lines.

On March 13, Grimes' Division replaced that of Bushrod Johnson in the trenches below Petersburg. By midnight his brigades took their positions, thinning their line to cover a wide segment of the defenses. Pickets scrambled over the parapets and sneaked forward. By dawn they found themselves looking almost into the faces of Federals opposite.[8] Beyond the open formation of enemy pickets they could see the solid works of Grant's massive main line.

Chilly, rain-lashed, were the days and nights of March,

and constantly the bitter air echoed with the shots exchanged by pickets. Cary Whitaker, his court-martial
duties finished, still kept his young cousin Jack at headquarters for paper work. Sim and Johnny stayed in the
trenches with their company, wallowing in mud to the
ankles and sometimes to the knees.[9] Like every company
in the entire army, D was too small, too thinly clad, too
hungry, for the job it was given to do.

Still Cary refused to join the ranks of the despairful.
Over yonder, with Grant's divisions, other troops felt
themselves impossibly ill-used. Federal deserters sneaked
across no man's land and into the earthworks of the
Forty-third, to surrender. "I don't know but what they
have as many [deserters] as we do," wrote Cary to Mrs.
Wills on March 22.

On that day, not too far below Enfield, Joe Johnston's
army finished a bloody and valiant delaying action against
Sherman's inexorable marauders. In that fight and others,
young Ed Wills had shown himself as brave as his brother
George had been. Ed's young companions in arms, awed
by three days of what Armageddon must be like, had
forsaken their showy habits of cursing for prayer.[10]

March 25 was black before the dawn, and Gordon
shifted his command and carried the fight to the foe.

It was to be a surprise, launched against the massive
ramparts of Fort Stedman near the left of the fortified
crescent around Petersburg. At that point the Federal
works were just 150 yards away. Gordon selected three
hundred men and organized them in three columns to
lead the attack, and told off the strongest to carry axes
to chop through the fabric of beams and sharp stakes that
lay on the glacis of the fort. After these advance parties
would charge the rest of the Second Corps. Once inside
Fort Stedman—who could tell? Maybe a smash clear

through the rear defenses of Grant, a hole in the Union position that would break it up like a breached dam in a freshet.

At four o'clock, Gordon spoke solemnly and encouragingly to the sharpshooters who would open the fight. Then, at his word, someone fired a musket as a signal. Forward went the Confederates, headlong in the darkness. The axmen frantically chopped the way clear for the charge. A final leaping rush, and they were inside Fort Stedman.

The breakthrough seemed completely successful. Drowsy Federals were struck down or brushed aside, Gordon's men charged both ways behind the ramparts. Cannon were captured, battery after battery. Artillery details who had accompanied the charge quickly formed into crews to swing these pieces around and fire them at the men driven from the fort.

But other Yankees came to their senses and their feet. To left and right and on beyond, more distant batteries of guns fired into the captured segment of trenches. From the rear Fort Stedman and adjacent defenses were partially open. Gordon's men found themselves exposed to withering fire in the dawn.

They had to abandon the guns they had captured, under a whole skyful of shells and bullets. The surprise had almost succeeded, but not quite. At eight o'clock, Gordon had to retreat.

The retreating was the worst of it. The 150 yards of open space between the lines was swept by the guns of the Federals, over and over, as a barley field is reaped bare by relays of sickles. Only the bravest of Gordon's men dared attempt the flight to shelter, and of those only the luckiest survived. Many stayed where they were, completely cowed, surrendering to the Federal counterattack. The price of the brief occupation of Fort Stedman was three thousand five hundred officers and men, more than half of them left prisoners in the enemy's hands.

But Cary Whitaker had come back safely, and Sim Whitaker, and Johnny Beavans.

After advance and retreat in the early morning, frantic defense at noon and in the evening. The Union commanders took note of the large force that had assaulted Fort Stedman—that meant the works had been stripped elsewhere. Charges against the outer ramparts of Petersburg inflicted more casualties. Perhaps as many as five thousand were killed, wounded, or captured between predawn and sunset of March 25, a staggering body blow to Lee's dwindling army. And equally as damaging, perhaps, was the sapping of the spirit of proud fighting men who had reached but could not hold their objective.

Grimes' Division shifted back to its old position at the center of the line. It had suffered heavily, 478 killed and wounded and missing. Grimes himself, tamelessly brave, wished that day for the dawn of peace.[11]

But there was no peace. Three and a half miles of clammy, muddy trenches were assigned for the division to hold. At the right, near the still-raw gash where the Crater had been blasted the previous July, Grimes stationed what survived of Ramseur's old brigade, under Colonel W. R. Cox. Next came a scratch brigade, of Virginia Junior Reserves, three battalions under Lieutenant Colonel F. H. Archer. To the left of that, at the center of the division, Cowand marshaled his brigade that included the Forty-third. To Cowand's left were the Alabamians of Edwin W. Hobson, and beyond Hobson the Georgians of E. A. Nash.

All together, those five brigades numbered perhaps two thousand two hundred effectives, to occupy and hold more than six thousand yards of front. That meant there would be no rest for anyone. A full third of the men, directed Grimes, must occupy the pits that were strung in front of the breastworks as a picket line. Another third must remain alert, day and night, in the main trenches, while the remaining third, though permitted to cook and sleep, could never lay aside arms or accouterments, must be ready to form and fight on an instant's notice. The closest formation Grimes could hope for would see his soldiers spaced fully eight feet apart. He held his share of Petersburg's works with no more than a string of skirmishers.

On April 1, off to the west and beyond the trenches, disaster swept upon unwary Pickett at Five Forks. That afternoon Sheridan's audacious cavalry rush cut off ten thousand Confederates, killing and capturing many. Only heart-sinking rumors of this reverse came back to Lee's main army.

If the rank and file of Grimes' brigades mourned Pickett's debacle, they soon had worries of their own. Their thin line was undergoing a bombardment that, instead of slackening with the fall of night, grew progressively hotter. At ten o'clock the volleys from cannon and mortars rose to a slaughtering peak, forcing the infantry to hug its shelter. Then just before midnight a charge from across the way drove Grimes' pickets from their holes.

The main line, tensely ready, responded by pouring a blistering fire into the dark. The Federals retired, while the pickets crept back. It was a recovery, but only a brief one. At daybreak another smashing charge drove in the pickets as before, and this time the enemy advance reached the main works and chased back Nash's Georgians at the left.

Cowand's North Carolinians and Archer's young Virginians rushed across to this threatened point. It was somewhat like a reversal of the situation a week ago at

Fort Stedman; the Federals had snatched a strong point, Fort Mahone, and were reaching out both ways for more. The Confederates slashed at them from either side, driving them out of traverses and ditches. But they kept their grip on Fort Mahone.[12]

Into the thick of the battle Cary Whitaker led the hundred-odd of the Forty-third. Cary's beard bristled, his eyes glared at the stubborn enemy in those captured ditches. Every shot was needed against Fort Mahone. Dropping his handsome sword, Cary stopped and possessed himself of the musket of a wounded soldier, then straightened to his full height of six feet, brought the weapon to his shoulder, and aimed.

His action caught the eye of a Union marksman inside the captured redoubt. Before Cary could touch trigger, the bullet from the Federal's musket struck the gun barrel, sang along it, and plowed through Cary's left hand, then his right.[13] He did not go down but staggered back, helpless, while Captain Cobb hastily took command of the regiment.

A final rush by details from the Forty-third and another unit recaptured Fort Mahone and rounded up prisoners inside. Grimes made good his re-established line. Now, if he but had a few reinforcements, only five hundred——

But there were no reinforcements. Not in all the army.

All Grimes could do was hold on as best he could, as other commanders were doing, until dark. After that he need hold on no more.

For Lee was pulling his army out of its trenches. He was abandoning Richmond and Petersburg, he would head away west and south. Somewhere down that way Joe Johnston was still intact, facing Sherman. If Lee could join Johnston, the combined forces surely would defeat Sherman, destroy him utterly, and then turn around to dispose of Grant.

The firing slackened, and Grimes' men fell back from their defenses without mishap. They marched quickly north, crossed the Appomattox, then off west along the Hickory Road and toward Goode's Bridge. There they could cross again, beyond the trenches of both armies, and get away. Lee would head thirty miles to Amelia Court House. A railroad ran through that little settlement, there would be food and ammunition and supplies.

The Forty-third had brought out Cary Whitaker, his wounds roughly bandaged. Friends suggested to him that he was unable to travel, but he gestured that opinion away with a lint-swaddled hand. He swore that he would not remain behind for Grant's advancing troops to capture. He'd get well and fight Grant again. Into an ambulance he scrambled, and rolled away with other wounded toward Burkeville. There they would be loaded aboard a train and sent to the hospital at Danville.

The army took its own road in the early hours of April 3.[14] Behind, Richmond was fallen, after so many Federal assaults.

XXII

BLOW, GABRIEL, BLOW!

The Second Corps was the rear guard. Badly handled as it had been on April 2, it still was in better shape than the First, which had been weakened by the near-obliteration of Pickett, or the Third, which during the day had been battered and driven, and had lost A. P. Hill from its head. Ewell followed from Richmond, with what was left of the capital's defenders. President Davis and his family and cabinet, with a hastily organized bodyguard, were already gone ahead of everyone.

Between the Second Corps and the rest of the army rolled the artillery and the wagon train—ramshackle wagons, those were, with shambling, scrawny teams, like the wagons and teams of shiftless farmers. The troops of the rear guard plodded, halted, and plodded again. They welcomed the pauses to let guns and wagons move forward. Months of trench warfare had worn them, months of starvation diet had enfeebled them. And the enemy was not catching up as yet, the withdrawal had been ably handled. That was a comfort, that and the sense that they were marching. By marching they had done their wonders in the past, with Jackson, with Ewell, with Early. Now and then they ate, such of them as had managed to bring rations in their haversacks.[1]

Lieutenant Sim Whitaker led Company D, and Sergeant Johnny Beavans kept it closed up. Those were no great problems for either of them, for D numbered only a score or so. But it was part of an army not utterly downhearted. Somewhere lurked a hope of ultimate victory. And just now the move was toward Danville, by way of the promised rations and cartridges at Amelia Court House. Captain Cary ought to be at Danville by now, maybe getting better, maybe recovering to lead the Forty-third again.[2]

The Second Corps camped on the road that night, marched all day of April 4, and had the heart and throat to raise the rebel yell as Lee rode past it on Traveller.[3] At dark it camped again, five miles from Amelia Court House. Next morning, while slow rain pattered, it marched into the little town. Now for something to eat . . .

But there wasn't anything to eat.

The expected supplies had not arrived, nobody seemed to know why.[4] Foraging parties combed the surrounding country with little or no success; that part of Virginia had given up its food months ago to rebels or Yankees. The pause and the fruitless search lost Lee his head start. That day the pursuing Federals came up, baring their teeth at the lean, hungry flanks of the fugitive Army of Northern Virginia.

The retreat started again, at one o'clock in the afternoon. Last to depart from Amelia Court House was Grimes' Division, just as dark came down. After the muddy nightmare of the trenches, the muddy nightmare of the roads, black hours of marching, marching, faint and hungry. And in the morning, with heavy masses of

Union infantry approaching from the north and east, they had to fight as they fled.

Hastily Grimes strung Cowand's and Cox's brigades across the rear, and half a mile farther along he drew up the other three brigades in similar battle array. At this bold defiance the Federals paused, deployed, and sent out skirmishers. Promptly Cowand and Cox retreated in formation and filtered through the other line of brigades, which in turn presented its show of fight. All day Grimes moved thus to cover the army, opposing the enemy with one line of battle, then the other.[5]

Ahead of these of the rear guard moved the wagon trains. Gordon led the Second Corps after them as they turned northwest from the main road, not knowing that the rest of the army had continued straight on while the wagons changed direction. At four o'clock, where Saylor's Creek flowed northward across the road to join the Appomattox River, the creaky wheels mired down, the feeble teams could not drag them free. Word came from Lee to stand and give battle.

Purposefully, insistently, the outnumbering Federal infantry approached Grimes' rear guard, while cavalry again prodded Lee's left flank. Almost five thousand of Lee's men were cut off and made prisoner, with Lieutenant Generals Ewell and Anderson and the commander's son, Major General Custis Lee. Fourteen miles north of this disastrous loss, Gordon and Grimes savagely refused to accept a similar fate.

Standing on the banks of Saylor's Creek, they fought with a spirit and deadliness that would have kindled the eyes of Jackson, while the toiling wagons managed to cross the muddy ford and crawl on beyond. Still covering, the infantry staved off assault. The outnumbering Federals spread wide to attack both flanks at once. At last Gordon's men had to cross the creek after the wagons, but on the far side they rallied and held.[6] Then, momentarily free of envelopment, they marched again and on into the new night, wounded, weary, hungry, desperate.

It was cold as well as dark. Four days of flight were too much for hundreds of worn-out foot-soldiers. Many of these fell out, utterly wrecked in body and spirit, unable to go further. The Federal advance rounded them up. Those who still kept their feet reformed in their regiment-sized divisions, their company-sized regiments. They were joined by the broken remnants of the commands of Ewell and Anderson, such as had escaped the smashing elsewhere on the wide battlefield of April 6. And words of hope drifted through the thinned, staggering ranks. Food waited at Farmville—it would really be there this time, it wasn't just a rumor. The Second Corps shielded the wagon train as it crossed the Appomattox, and still tried to get away from a hundred thousand pursuers, still held itself ready to do battle if overtaken.

At Farmville, a thrice-welcome pause, and grateful reception of two days' rations of corn meal and bacon. What tin plates and battered skillets had survived the retreat from Richmond were set over campfires. Meal and water were mixed for bread, sliced meat crackled appetizingly. Then, in the midst of the joy over cooking, the sound of shouts, the braying of bugles. Here came the Yankees again.

Grimes' men gulped half-fried mouthfuls and tumbled into line of battle.[7] As the Second Corps established its position, Robert E. Lee himself rode to the front, as though to lead.

"No, no!" squalled bony-faced, tense North Carolinians of the Fifty-fourth Regiment. "But if you will retire, we will do the work!" [8]

Lee retired, obedient to these common soldiers. Fierce

pride burned in the hearts under filthy, shredded jackets.
The division of William Mahone, driven back by the
inexorable Union infantry, was forced to abandon some
guns. A countercharge by Grimes' whole division, a
whooping, racing charge like the charges of the great
glory-bright days of the Confederacy's rise, repulsed the
enemy and recaptured the guns and took prisoners. Lee
himself, banished from the point of dangerous contact
by his men, sent personal compliments to Grimes.[9] Again
the army was able to retire in order, going northward
now, toward Lynchburg. From there it would still seek
to join Johnston.

All along the way men collapsed, lay by the roadside
while the army passed along, and were captured by the
pursuing enemy. Some, close to giving up but not quite
there, managed to stay with their companies by throwing
away blankets, muskets, haversacks, dragging along only
their starved, half-conscious bodies. Others straggled, then
found somewhere the will and energy to catch up again.
Such men, with their aching feet still under them—maybe
ten thousand effectives remained to Lee—clung to the
shreds of hope.

Lynchburg, that was the word they spoke to each other.
Once in Lynchburg, with the mountains at hand to rampart them, they could fight off their overwhelming, harry-
ing foemen and get away. Menwhile, other carloads of
food had been ordered, to a point about twenty-five
miles away. That place—what was it called, asked some,
as on the night of June 30, 1863, they had asked about
the town beyond Heidlesburg in Pennsylvania. And others answered them. It was Appomattox. A bleack-sound-
ing name, that, like the click of a musket hammer
thumbed back.

April 8, Saturday, found the marchers sweating, wheezing, their feet and their knees unsteady. But no enemy appeared, not all day. Grimes, still at the rear of the Second Corps, reined in his splendid horse Warran to watch as, in the afternoon, his men waded across a clear, dancing stream of water. That was the Appomattox River, just below its source, and on its banks hereabouts was the town of Appomattox. Just ahead of Grimes to the westward, among groves and thickets, other divisions of the Second Corps were camping. Grimes called a halt. His men, tired to the bones that stared through their stringy flesh, dropped down among trees and fields. Most of them were asleep by sundown.[10]

If any remained wakeful in Company D, in the Forty-third North Carolina Regiment, in the brigade led by Cowand or the division led by Grimes, they must have seen that darkness did not fall utterly. Beyond the army to the west, the evening sky glowed red. That meant camps, the watchfires of a hundred circling camps.

Part of Grant's army had pushed ahead of them, was blocking the escape of Lynchburg.

Then guns, those eternally barking and booming guns, from where the fires burned. Grimes hopped to his feet, ordered couriers and aides to waken the brigade commanders, to rouse the men. At nine o'clock he had formed his division and marched it through a little crossroads cluster of brick houses—Appomattox Court House—and caught up with the other divisions of Gordon. Skirmishers were out, and Grimes made his way to where Gordon conferred with Fitz Lee of the cavalry.

The generals talked anxiously and wondered and wished for light enough to see by. Gordon's Second Corps, even counting the addition of survivors from other commands after the Saylor's Creek fight, could bring into action no more than sixteen hundred armed men. Nobody knew how many times these forces were outnumbered, there to the west. The dawn of Palm Sunday, April 9, was approaching.

By the first gray streaks Gordon and Lee could see along the Lynchburg Road. Across it, about a mile away, a smaller road ran northwest. The fields to either side of the crossroads point were slashed with hastily erected banks of earth, Union breastworks daring Lee to pass.

Grimes, impulsively brave, said that he would attack and drive back the holders of those defenses.

"Well, drive them off," said Gordon, perhaps sharply, perhaps gratefully.

Grimes was well aware that his own effectives numbered but a few hundred. "I cannot do it with my division alone," he told Gordon, "but require assistance."

"You can take the other two divisions of the corps," granted Gordon.

While they spoke, the light grew stronger and brighter, from dark gray to pale gray. Grimes saluted and ordered his advance.[11]

His own division was toward the center of the formation, between James A. Walker's and that of Clement A. Evans. Out in front Grimes sent the Forty-fifth North Carolina as skirmishers.[12] Fitz Lee circled off to approach the Federal flank, and shells began to arrive from guns behind those works at the crossroads.

Forward in the dawn charged the line of little regiments. In the hands of the men in Grimes' Division were some 750 muskets—say 150 to a brigade, four to a company like D in the Forty-third. Johnny Beavans had a musket that day. In Lieutenant Sim Whitaker's hand gleamed a sword. Over all fluttered the bullet-pierced flags. Hairy throats raised once more the rebel yell, wild and shrill and tremulous—*Yieee-heee!*

Before they knew it, almost, they were at those make-

shift breastworks, hurdling over them and at the defenders. Clubbed muskets flourished aloft. Not fifty bayonets remained in the whole division of Grimes, but
bayonets were not needed. The enemy was running
again, turning blue backs as at Big Bethel, as twice at
Manassas, as up in the Valley before the gray backs had
been forced to turn. *Yieee-heee! I see your back, Yankee!*
. . . And dead were abandoned on the field. Leaping
over these, the victors could see that the fallen bodies
wore short waist-length jackets, knee boots. They were
dismounted cavalry of Sheridan's column. These quiet
ones, at least, would never stand in anybody's way again.

The breastworks were swept clean of defenders. Two
guns fell into the gaunt hands of Grimes' men. There
beyond, the routed Federal troopers were scrambling into
their saddles to get away.

Gordon, riding forward, took command. He wheeled the
divisions to face leftward, a line south of the road. That
road was open now. Let word be sent to Lee, let the army
go on past while the Second Corps held that position,
and Lynchburg was no more than twenty miles or so
west.

Grimes questioned prisoners snatched up at the breastworks. They pointed away toward the right of his line.
They had friends there, they said, lots of friends. And
up came more blue hordes, infantry this time. Against
them, and against others hurrying toward the crossroads
from in front and from the other flank, Gordon directed
the fire of his muskets and artillery.

It was eight o'clock now, and still the rebels fought
there across the line of works they had charged and
taken. Sim Whitaker encouraged his handful. Johnny
Beavans worked a musket, ramming down charges and
firing to his front, to his right and left—thank the God of
battles, there was plenty of ammunition this morning.

Nobody seemed terrified. There was no time for that, no time for anything but to stand and fire and fire again.

Then, abruptly, the order to fall back. The Forty-fifth's skirmish line strung out to cover the withdrawal. As the Confederates retired toward the river once again, a sustained deep shout of triumph rose from the Federals. Out of some trees to the south burst a charging column. One more volley, from Cox's North Carolina brigade, halted this advance, beat it back to the trees from which it came.[13]

The men pulled well back, and paused. This time, no enemy offered to counterattack. Sweet spring morning was bright around the regiments. They waited, wondering and asking questions and offering theories.

From somewhere, at last, came word that a white flag had gone forward, borne by a mounted officer, to the Federal lines.

Bryan Grimes, off to one side, was in furious argument with Gordon. This meant that Lee was giving up, surrendering the army. Why hadn't Gordon told Grimes so before? All right then, Grimes would call on whatever men were still game and would break through the lines and away. He turned to ride toward his division. Spurring after Grimes, Gordon caught him by the shoulder, earnestly reminding him that such an action would amount to desertion, repudiation of Lee, disgrace for Grimes.

The North Carolinian accepted this, and went on to join his men. He wanted to keep the news from them as long as he could; indeed, he did not quite know how to break it. But as he walked his war horse in among them, they could see by his face, habitually fierce to indomitability, that calamity was upon them.

Several pressed close. One of them dared speak.

"Has General Lee surrendered?" he asked.

"I fear it is a fact," Grimes was forced to reply.

The soldiers stared at him, momentarily mute with disbelief.

Few of them, if any, had thought much about other Confederate armies still in the field. Those other armies, even Johnston's command which they had hoped to reach, were distant, shadowy, heard about, but never seen. This, here on the banks of the Appomattox, was the army they knew. It was the Army of Northern Virginia. It had always won its battles. It had just finished winning a sort of a battle. Surrender? What did the word mean?

Anyone with the will to surrender had done that thing already as an individual, straggling from the march, or slipping away to meet a patrol of Sheridan's cavalry and hold up his hands, or just sitting down and waiting for Yankees to come and gather him in. These men of Palm Sunday had risen above fatigue and hunger and fate to come so far. They were the defiant clattering bones of Dixie's last stand.

Surrender was a strange military term, out of some esoteric drill manual, that must be defined and explained and learned. That was the way it had been, far, far back yonder at Camp Ellis, before ever the fighting started at Big Bethel. They had had to learn new orders and execute them. Attention. Shoulder arms. By the right flank, march. Handle cartridge. Charge bayonet. Now—surrender.

The man who had questioned Grimes hurled his musket away. It bounced on the spring grass. He flung his hands up toward the sky.

"Blow, Gabriel, blow!" he choked out. "My God, let him blow, I am ready to die!" [14]

XXIII

VALOR AND DEVOTION COULD ACCOMPLISH NOTHING

The cry, "Blow, Gabriel, blow!"—anguished, apocalyptic —was a dying word for the Army of Northern Virginia.

For it was Judgment Day. The end of the Confederacy was the end of the world and of the life these men had known. Let Gabriel blow his trumpet, the last trumpet anybody would ever hear. They were ready to die, to become nothingness, along with their lost nation.

Sitting his horse, Grimes managed an order. The handfuls that had been regiments formed column and fell back again, back past Appomattox Court House and across the dancing little river. They came to a halt in a broad, shallow depression where other troops had already gathered. A second order, passed along by regimental commanders, and they stacked arms and fell out.

But they stayed in groups as units, from habit and from the misery that needs the presence of friends. The few survivors of Company D huddled together, with Sim and Jack Whitaker and Johnny Beavans as a sort of family entity within it. They felt the aching holes in the ranks where once the bravest had held place, Cary Whitaker

and Smiling Billy Beavans and George Wills, and Thomas
Baker and Jimmy Whitehead and all those others who
perhaps rejoiced, wherever they were, because they need
not say they had surrendered.

The valley where they waited was a pleasant place.
Over to the westward showed lumpy knolls from which
trickled down creeks, to form the headwaters of the
Appomattox River. The grass was green and the oak
trees were in April tassel. April . . . it had been April
in 1861 when the Enfield Blues waved good-by to wives
and mothers and sweethearts and answered the sound of
the drum; April again when the Forty-third North Carolina Regiment chose its field officers, soldierly Kenan and
gallant Lewis and uninspired Boggan; another April
when they besieged the garrison of Old Washington on
the coast; and yet again April, in 1864, when they received the surrender of Plymouth, before heading into
Virginia and the Wilderness and the Valley of the Shadow
of Death.

The sun climbed behind the clouds. It was noon. Exhaustion unstrung them, without relaxing them. They
had strength left for nothing but wretched sorrow. Men
who could march and fight no longer could still weep.
Tears were jewel-bright on sunburnt hairy faces.[1]

Hours wore themselves slowly away. From overhead
the sun slid halfway down its course to the western
horizon. Then, from wherever he had ridden to the
tragedy he must bring upon them all, Robert E. Lee
came back into their sight, the gray man on the gray horse.

Faithful scarecrows surged toward him from right and
left. They pressed close to him, touching his coat, his
boots, the skirts of his saddle, the flanks and withers of
Traveller.

Lee, the cosmically self-contained, had tears in his eyes.
When he spoke, his voice shook:

"Men, we have fought through the war together—I have done the best for you that I could——"

A hubbub of cries drowned out his words.

"General! We'll fight 'em yet!"

It was all they had left to offer him. Not to win, not to rout or crush Grant's mighty encircling hundred thousand; only to fight once more, one last time, for Robert E. Lee, and die fighting.

"General, say the word, and we'll go in and fight 'em yet!"

But Lee did not say the word. His heart was too full to say anything more. He rode on, and they let him go, and watched from a distance as he slowly dismounted under a tree. Couriers and aides formed a cordon around him. His brokenhearted soldiers returned to their little groups.[2] Time resumed its inexorable crawl past them. Evening grew dim upon their squatting-places.

Finally, surprisingly, wagons came rolling from the southward, Federal commissary wagons. There was food, quickly parceled out and distributed. The men lined up to take the rations that their conquerors supplied them. It was a profusion almost embarrassing—nearly a pound of bacon apiece, and great fistfuls of hardtack. When had they eaten hardtack last? And real coffee, and sugar to stir into it. Many of the Confederates ate the bacon raw, great rashers spread on the big tooth-defying crackers. It was more than enough for stomachs shrunk to fit scatterings of parched corn.[3] Coffee they brewed over fires, in cups or cans or whatever utensils they still had, and their numb, sick hearts rose ever so little. They squatted or sprawled, and between mouthfuls of bacon and gulps of coffee they talked.

Even after Judgment Day there was some sort of future. It could not be wholly empty. Surrender might mean prison, or a humiliating march before hooting crowds in Northern cities, to grace the triumph of Grant. But that wouldn't last forever. Sometime they would get home. If the nation had fallen, the land was still there.

Most of the men were farmers; Sim Whitaker could look away to his acres at Strawberry Hill, Johnny Beavans' parents still kept Centerville's fields. If they were home now, they might plant crops for food and money. April wasn't too late to put in corn and vegetables.

Those who talked about planting were the most cheerful. Their comrades from the cities, who had been lawyers or clerks or artisans or merchants, also felt the stir of hope reviving. There would be work for them, too, rebuilding and reorganizing, standing up again.[4]

The sun set and fires were bright, in this valley for the Confederates, on neighboring slopes and heights for the Yankees. They slept, both armies, to waken in rain on Monday morning.

There was more food from the wagons of the victors, and a huddling under what shelter could be found. As the weather cleared, came news of what surrender meant. It was not as bad as some had feared. They must give up their arms and flags, swear to fight no longer. Then they could go home.

That made them almost happy. Again they began to talk, plan, hope. Bitterness had somewhat departed from them, and despair. In drifted some of the stragglers that had been missing for the last few days. These eagerly accepted the bountiful charity of the Federal quartermasters. Munching, they looked at the lean-ribbed horses from artillery and transport teams in search of grass or weeds along the valley. Men talked of the war that had been.

Twelve of the surrendered army looked back to Big

Bethel and the victory of four years ago. These, all comrades once in that first regiment under D. H. Hill, were
scattered through the various corps.

Sim and Johnny, in Company D, with one other Old
Bethel, Captain J. Marshall Williams of the Fifty-
fourth, had been in the final charge with Grimes. They
could say, if they wished, that they were first at Bethel,
last at Appomattox, and make of it a boast, but not an
idle one, for all time to come. Williams had been with
Company H, the swaggering Fayetteville Independents.
Six other old Independents were present at Appomattox,
but had not participated in the charge. They were Major
E. J. Hale, assistant adjutant general of James H. Lane's
Brigade: D. M. Graham, assistant surgeon of the Thirty-
seventh Regiment; Charles M. Steadman, major of the
Forty-fourth; Lieutenant W. E. Kyle and Adjutant John
H. Robinson of the Fifty-second; and J. A. McCay, a
gunner with William's Battery. Walter B. Taylor, once
with the boy-soldiers of the Charlotte Grays, captained
Company A of the Eleventh Regiment that still carried
the Bethel banner, and Cousin Spier Whitaker was adjutant for the Thirty-third.[5] James Lane commanded his
brigade.

On the 11th, another order to fall in. They formed
single file, company by company, to receive smudgily
printed slips, each filled in with name and company and
regiment, and signed at the bottom by the regimental
commander. These were melancholy certificates of grad-
uation from the most brutal and heartbreaking of schools:

APPOMATTOX COURT HOUSE, VA.
April 10th, 1865
THE BEARER, *1st Lieut. J. S. Whitaker,* of Co. *"D,"
43rd N. C.* Regt. of *N. Carolina,* a Paroled Prisoner of the
Army of Northern Virginia, has permission to go to his
home and there remain undisturbed . . .

On Wednesday, April 12, they mustered for their last parade under arms.

Gordon's Second Corps led the way. At the head of his column, Gordon marshaled the surviving scrap of that brigade which, long ago with Jackson at First Manassas, had stood like a stone wall. The others took their places behind this one. In Grimes' old brigade, 164 men answered roll call for the Forty-third North Carolina Regiment, and Company D, with two couriers added to its ranks, counted 25 under Lieutenant Sim Whitaker.[6]

"Attention. . . . Shoulder arms. . . . Right face. . . . Forward. . . . March!"

Above each shrunken regiment floated its battle flag, a starry cross on red. So close together were these flags in the decimated ranks that they seemed like a walking garden of bright flowers. Silently the column moved, without music, south and west along the road, toward where a solid rank of men in blue stood waiting.

A quick word of command passed back from officer to officer. The men shifted their muskets from the shoulder to the carry, the infantry marching salute. Glancing ahead, they saw the reason. The generous and sympathetic Union commander had brought his own force to the carry. Thus, at salute, the blue stood and the gray approached.[7]

Brigade by brigade they halted, faced into line, fixed such bayonets as remained to them. Once more: "Stack arms!"

Into little pyramids they built the muskets they had carried so long and to such deadly purpose, then took a pace backward from them. The color sergeants folded or rolled the flags and laid them on top of the stacks. The Eleventh North Carolina delivered up only a staff— Captain E. R. Outlaw had ripped from its fastenings the banner that bore the proud word *Bethel* and had burned it, all but a morsel that he could carry home for a souvenir.

All these things happened in heavy silence. Nobody spoke. Nobody glanced at his agony-dulled comrades.[8] Then Gordon rode close to the front of the formation.

"Soldiers of the Second Army Corps!" he began, fighting to keep his voice steady. "No mathematician can compute the odds against which you have contended. . . ."

More tears channeled bearded cheeks as Gordon spoke with earnest affection, praising the courage of his men, exhorting them to maintain patience and dignity in the face of hard times to come. "The blood of the martyrs is the seed of the church," he made an end.[9]

Weaponless, they trudged back to their camps.

Drawn up beside the little remains of their personal baggage, the soldiers of the Forty-third heard an adjutant read aloud the last order Lee would ever give his men:

"After four long years of arduous service, marked by unsurpassed courage and fortitude, the Army of Northern Virginia has been compelled to yield to overwhelming numbers and resources . . ."

There it was at last, and a man was bound to believe it. Lee had said it.

"I need not tell the brave survivors of so many hard-fought battles, who have remained steadfast to the last, that I have consented to this result from no distrust of them; but feeling that valor and devotion could accomplish nothing that could compensate for the loss that must have attended the continuance of the contest, I determined to avoid the useless sacrifice of those whose past services have endeared them to their countrymen . . ."

Oh, but he had needed to tell them that, so that they could know he understood. And if Robert E. Lee understood, the rest of the world could go hang.

"You will take with you the satisfaction that proceeds

from the consciousness of duty faithfully performed; and I earnestly pray that a Merciful God will extend to you His blessing and protection . . ."

If George Wills had only lived to hear this—George had always thrilled to the words of his chiefs.

"With an unceasing admiration of your constancy and devotion to your Country, and a grateful remembrance of your kind and generous consideration, I bid you all an affectionate farewell." [10]

That was all.

"Dismissed!"

Now they could go.

A final visit from the Federal wagons, a final bestowal of two days' rations apiece. Grimes appeared among the men, blinking back tears from his fierce eyes. He shook hands with several he knew personally.

"Good-by, General; God bless you," sobbed a gaunt, tattered private soldier. "We will go home, make three crops, and then try them again."

Grimes could not control his own voice. It broke as he replied:

"Go home, boys, and act like men, as you have always done during the war." [11]

Slowly, dully, those who had fought and lost began to trail off, singly or in little groups. They sought roads and trails toward wherever home was. The Enfielders of Company D set a course east by south. It was almost exactly a hundred miles, as a crow would fly, to Enfield in Halifax County.

Sergeant Johnny Beavans turned away from Appomattox River and from Appomattox Court House. Into his mind's eye stole a sweet face, intent and hopeful and smiling, the face of Miss Laura Gunter.

Miss Laura would be in Enfield when Johnny arrived. with his parole in his pocket. Once, back in 1861, she had said that she would marry him when the war was over. Well, it was over for Johnny Beavans.

His heart rose like a sudden soaring bird. He straightened his ragged shoulders. He lifted his feet with the old energy, for the long, last march home, the journey that would end in a lovers' meeting.[12]

AFTERWORD

Sim Whitaker and Johnny Beavans reached Enfield at last, weary and hungry from their long journey on foot but otherwise in good health, and were affectionately greeted. Cary Whitaker, his ripped hands gangrened, died in the army hospital at Danville on April 20, perhaps before his surviving comrades reached home. Some thought that Cary's insistence on being borne from the field was fatal—Union surgeons, better equipped than Confederates to care for serious wounds, might have saved his life. His body was brought to Strawberry Hill and was buried in the churchyard at Whitaker's Chapel.

On April 26, Johnston surrendered to Sherman near Greensboro, North Carolina. Ed Wills trudged home from there, accompanied by the unflinchingly devoted Wash, to glad welcome at Brinkleyville.

Miss Laura Gunter, true to her promise, married Johnny. Several years later, the quiet but assured Sim courted and won Miss Susan Waldo. Both these veterans prospered as planters, and survived into the twentieth century. Their descendants live in the Enfield community today.

The body of Billy Beavans remains in the grave offered by Kate Shepherd, last of many lovely girls to be drawn by his ready smile and brave spirit. Nobody has ever found out where George Wills sleeps forever.

NOTES

I

1 Enfield, North Carolina, was the first town established in Halifax County, early in the eighteenth century. It grew from a crossroads trad ing hamlet to a center for cotton growing and shipping, and for a while was the county seat. In 1860 it had less than 400 inhabitants. Today, with a population of 2500, it retains provincial charm and individuality.

2 The Enfield Blues, as organized in 1859, were something of a society company. Enfield's ladies presented a United States flag on June 5, 1860. Miss Fannie Whitfield spoke in typical antebellum periods of the bravery all took for granted in the local militiamen. When, early in 1861, the company voted to change flags, Miss Whitfield cut up a blue silk dress to piece out the red and white from the discarded banner, which also furnished gold fringe and tassels. This flag is preserved in the Hall of History at Raleigh, North Carolina. For a fuller history of the company's organization, see Miss Katie Riddick, "The Enfield Blues" (hereafter cited as *Miss Riddick*) in *Prize Essays Presented by the North Carolina United Daughters of the Confederacy* (hereafter cited as *Prize Essays*), pp. 105–107.

3 Governor John W. Ellis, seriously ill when he defied the Federal government, undoubtedly hastened his death on July 7, 1861, by his exertions. See Samuel A'Court Ashe and Stephen B. Weeks, eds., *Biographical History of North Carolina From Colonial Times to the Present*, Vol. VII, p. 101. Governor Ellis' correspondence with the Secretary of War in Washington is in the Fayetteville, N.C., *Observer*, April 18, 1861, p. 3, col. 3.

4 The daily drill sessions in the spring of 1861 are mentioned in *Miss Riddick* in *Prize Essays*, p. 107, and in another company history by the senior second lieutenant of the Blues, Francis Marion Parker, in a newspaper clipping of uncertain place and date (hereafter cited as *Parker*).

5 Cary Whitaker was born on January 1, 1832, and received the best education of all the children of Dr. Cary Whitaker of Strawberry Hill. He became county attorney of Halifax in 1859. His career is outlined in a penciled memorial by his brother and war comrade, John Simmons Whitaker (hereafter cited as *Cary Whitaker Memorial*), now in possession of John Simmons Whitaker's descendants, who also have preserved their Uncle Cary's sword and glittering dress epaulets.

6 John Simmons Whitaker's prewar career was described to me by his son, Waldo Whitaker, and his daughter, Miss Susie Whitaker, of Strawberry Hill Plantation, Enfield, N.C. Sim and Cary Whitaker were original in wearing beards before the war. Most Enfield Blues joined the colors with smooth-shaven faces.

7 Entries in William Beavans' two war diaries (hereafter cited as *I* and *II William Beavans*) are brief but vivid and often self-revealing. Early entries in *I William Beavans* are about work in the store at Hamilton.

8 John Beavans' age in 1861 is from the muster roll of Company I, First North Carolina Volunteer Regiment, in the National Archives, Washington, D.C. Centerville, the Beavans plantation home, stands two miles east of Enfield and is now occupied by Mrs. Stanley Whitaker, daughter of Walter Beavans and niece of William and John.

9 George Whitaker Wills' character is splendidly set forth in more than one hundred letters to his family, included in the great mass of family correspondence (hereafter cited as *Wills Papers*) deposited in the Southern Historical Collection at the University of North Carolina, Chapel Hill, N.C., by his nephew and namesake, Professor George S. Wills of Westminster, Maryland, and by the children of his sister, Mrs. Lucy Wills Hunter, Arcola, N.C. Save when otherwise specifically noted, all George Wills' letters referred to are from *Wills Papers*.

10 There is some dispute concerning the date of the Enfield Blues' departure for the camp of instruction. I follow *Parker*, which says: "It [the company] boarded the train . . . on April 26, and reported at headquarters on the 27th." *Miss Riddick*, in *Prize Essays*, p. 107, says: "On April 27, 1861, the Enfield Blues entrained for Raleigh, going via Goldsboro." W. C. Allen's *History of Halifax County*, p. 108, dates the departure April 17. Parker, who was very much there at the time, undoubtedly was surest of the date.

11 William Beavans did not keep a sustained diary of his soldiering. His first journal book has printed dates on the various pages. Some of these, without entry, are filled with fugitive verses and other jottings. The lines about the violin and the drum are on a page of *I William Beavans* headed March 26, 1861, and would seem to have been written in a thoughtful moment at the beginning of his military career.

II

ALL THE BOYS WELL IN CAMP

1 George Wills' appearance and behavior have been reconstructed through a study of two photographs, muster rolls of his regiments, and his own home letters.

2 Two photographs of William Beavans show a decidedly handsome, intelligent and good-humored face and a well-set-up figure of the sort once called elegant. His height and age in the spring of 1861 are from company muster rolls. His success with the ladies, at home and throughout his war wanderings, are today a lively tradition in Enfield. His journals refer frequently to parties, dances, chance meetings and tender exchanges. Neither in wish nor in practice was he a cruel heartbreaker, but he liked pretty girls.

3 George Wills, to his sister Lucy, April 30, 1861, says: "We started from Enfield Saturday at twelve, reached Goldsboro at three." *I William Beavans,* entry of April 27, 1861, identifies members of the party: "I took the cars with Mr. Page and George Wills; we reached Goldsboro before night."

4 Jesse Page had a brilliant postwar career as a minister. For appearance and character, I use family reminiscence, *Wills Papers,* and Burton J. Hendrick, *The Training of an American; The Earlier Life and Letters of Walter H. Page, 1855–1913,* p. 35.

5 The mothers of William Beavans and George Wills were respectively Mrs. Peggy Whitaker Beavans and Mrs. Anna Maria Whitaker Wills. This and other genealogical information is from a Whitaker family tree in the possession of the Strawberry Hill descendants.

6 Wash, the Negro servant, is frequently and affectionately mentioned in George Wills' home letters and in the writings of George Wills' comrades. Wash did not long survive the war, and for a description of him I am indebted to Professor George S. Wills.

7 Goldsboro was founded in 1847, an important stop on the Wilmington and Weldon Railroad. Photographs taken in mid-century show two lines of track along the principal street. This unusual and awkward state of affairs was remedied in 1926, when citizens arbitrarily tore up the rails. George may have been less pleased with Goldsboro than was William Beavans. To his sister Lucy, April 30, 1861, George wrote rather dully: ". . . had to stay there [Goldsboro] until one O clock next day." *I William Beavans,* entries of April 27 and 28, 1861, speak more cheerfully of seeking lodging and strolling through the town.

8 William Beavans wrote several times in his diaries of drinking whisky, brandy, beer or wine, though there is no indication that he overindulged. Jesse Page, as a Methodist minister, was a teetotaler. So, by family training and by evidence of his home letters, was George Wills.

9 Except in certain acrostics, William Beavans did not name the ladies

to whom he addressed verses. The lines quoted are from *I William Beavans*, on page dated March 26, 1861.

10 Surviving members of the Whitaker-Wills relationship are inclined to avoid telling the full name of George Wills' sweetheart. She most emphatically was not Miss Fannie Whitfield, maker of the Enfield Blues flag.

11 Leah remained as housekeeper for the Wills family for many years after emancipation and Appomattox.

12 William Beavans' library is catalogued as "List of Books" in *I William Beavans*, on page headed June 30, 1861. In *ibid.*, on page headed July 27, 1861, he wrote:

"Books Wanted
Major Jones Courtship
Byron Poetical Works"

13 *I William Beavans*, entry of April 28, 1861, says: "This morning we walked over Goldsboro, went to church came back took dinner and left for Raleigh." The journals show that he attended church often, but his hesitation at publicly professing religion sometimes concerned his more devout comrades.

14 The state fair grounds at Raleigh in 1861 were located and described for me by Herbert Paschal of Greenville, N.C., from a study he made as part of his work toward a graduate degree in history at the University of North Carolina.

15 George Wills' satisfaction at his camp quarters is expressed in his letter to Lucy, April 30, 1861: ". . . but we fair a little better than the rest and are living in the house inside to exhibit the things brought to the fair. . . . A fiddle and bower are going all day by some one. . . ."

III

UNTIL WE ARE PREPARED FOR IT

1 Professor George S. Wills, speaking from boyhood memories and family traditions, called the Wills home atmosphere one of "understanding Christian affection." Everything gleaned from other sources bears out this estimate. The career of W. H. Wills is sketched in an anonymous pamphlet, *Memorial of Reverend William H. Wills*, published after his death in 1883. Professor Wills supplied dates of birth and other material on the Wills sons and daughters.

2 No less than fifty references to food, enjoyed or otherwise, appear in George Wills' home letters. His bouts of dysentery and bronchial trouble suggest some sort of allergy.

3 Evidence of the affection in which the good servant Wash was held by his master's family is a note from Richard Wills to his father, May 30, 1861, with *Wills Papers*: ". . . tell them [George and Wash] my prayers are made for them. O my God, our loving heavenly Father be a shield

unto them to protect them from the darts of the enemy & above all keep their souls unto life eternal." The comradeship of George and Wash is like that of master and slave in dozens of sentimental Southern novels.

4 Regimental muster rolls, various letters and family reminiscences tell ages, appearance, behavior and character of many of the Enfield Blues. Montgomery T. and Theodore Lucien Whitaker were brothers, first cousins of Sim and Cary Whitaker and therefore first cousins, once removed, of George Wills and the Beavans brothers. Cary Whitaker emerges clearly from photographs, letters and in particular the two volumes of his war diary (hereafter cited as *I* and *II Cary Whitaker*).

5 The Halifax Light Infantry's brief stay at Camp Ellis is referred to in *Southern Historical Society Papers* (hereafter cited as *SHSP*), Vol. XIX, p. 214.

6 For the brief, bloodless prewar exploit of the Edgecombe Guards, see John A. Sloan, *North Carolina in the War Between the States* (hereafter cited as *Sloan*), pp. 81 and vii, note B.

7 How the Charlotte Grays acquitted themselves at war is readably told in Louis Leon, *Diary of a Tar Heel Confederate Soldier* (hereafter cited as *Leon*). Entry of April 25, 1861, p. 1, describes quarters at Camp Ellis: ". . . lo and behold! horse stables with straw for bedding is what we got. I know we all thought it a disgrace for us to sleep in such places with our fine uniforms—not even a washstand, or any place to hang our clothes on. They didn't even give us a looking-glass." Probably such entries were revised in later years, but they carry conviction.

8 These and other companies at Camp Ellis at the time are listed in *XIX SHSP*, pp. 214, 217.

9 Spier Whitaker was a distant relative of Cary, Sim, George Wills, and the Beavanses, but they always greeted him as "cousin."

10 Major William Gilham, *Manual of Instruction for Volunteers and Militia of the United States* (hereafter cited as *Gilham*), was the militiaman's standard drill book North and South in the spring of 1861. Orders and execution of them for forming a company are detailed on pp. 141–142, and would refer only to recruit drill. Gilham adds, in a sage footnote to p. 142: "When the company is in good discipline, the files may be formed in ranks at once, each man having his proper number in the company depending on his height, and being able to take his appropriate place without creating confusion." So, undoubtedly, it was with the Blues before they left Camp Ellis.

11 Boy students at the North Carolina Military Institute were eager for war from secession's first rumblings. To keep them from playing truant to join volunteer companies anywhere and everywhere, Governor Ellis ordered them to Camp Ellis as drillmasters. See Walter L. Clark, ed., *History of the Several Regiments and Battalions From North Carolina in the Great War, 1861–65* (hereafter cited as *N.C. Regts.*) Vol. V, pp. 654–56.

12 First order to form a North Carolina regiment was dated April 19, but apparently was not immediately made public. George Wills wrote to Lucy, April 30, 1861: "The companies were read out yesterday who were to form the first regiment, some of the companies got mad because they were not in it."

13 North Carolina captured a large stock of fine rifled muskets at the Fayetteville arsenal, which was promptly sent to Virginia. The smoothbores issued at Camp Ellis were not effective at long range, as is pointed out in *Parker*. The rather tedious succession of orders to accomplish loading is from *Gilham*, pp. 112–15. It irritated many young men who handled arms with skill.

14 A good description of D. H. Hill in 1861 is in Douglas Southall Freeman, *Lee's Lieutenants*, Vol. I, pp. 19–21.

15 Copies of Hill's delightfully biased textbooks are painfully rare today. Quotation here is from brief passages included in the sketch of Hill in E. A. Pollard, *The Early Life, Public Services and Campaigns of General Robert E. Lee and His Companions in Arms*, p. 450.

16 Hoke's order of April 20, 1861, couched in purple language characteristic of the time's public documents, is in *XIX SHSP*, p. 213.

17 George Wills' letter to Lucy, April 30, 1861, several times quoted already, may have been his first message home. His reference to the overnight stay in Goldsboro suggests this. He wrote to various members of his family, but intended each letter to be read by all.

IV

LESS FEAR IN EACH PASSING DAY

1 George Wills thus commented on the health situation to Lucy, May 11, 1861: "There has been a good deal of sickness in the camp since I came, most every one has been sick in some way. I felt a little unwell for several days but feel quite well now . . . Mother always told me I was too particular about eating and I find it so. I haven't eaten anything from the table in over a week; Mr. Wilbert Page brought me two boxes, these together with the one from home have been what I have eaten; (*I have eaten enough tho*) . . ."

2 Hinted family disapproval of George's romance with Miss Fannie can be detected in various items of *Wills Papers*. George's parents may have thought him too young for serious courting.

3 No parental obstacles were offered to the courtship of Laura Gunter by Johnny Beavans. They had been childhood sweethearts. Miss Gunter's attractions were recognized by no less a critical expert than Johnny's brother Billy, who wrote verses for her (*I William Beavans*, page headed August 20, 1861). This was not serious fraternal rivalry; Smiling Billy rhymed for many young ladies.

4 Billy's "Camp Life" rhyme is in *I William Beavans*, page headed August 2, 1861. Apparently they were written early in the service.

5 The new organization of the First North Carolina Regiment is in *XIX SHSP*, p. 214.

6 George Wills, to Lucy, May 11, 1861, tells of his own unrest and of the shooting in "one of the western companies." Names of the wounded officer and the mutinous private have not been found. "He [the soldier] probably would have killed him [the captain] had not some one knocked his hand down."

7 Orders for the departure of companies to form a new regiment are in *XIX SHSP*, p. 214; George Wills mentions the move to Lucy, May 11, 1861.

8 Official return of the election for field officers of the First North Carolina is in *XIX SHSP*, pp. 215–16.

9 No word of what befell the mutinous soldier can be found in regimental or court-martial records: "It is the opinion of some he will be shot," wrote George Wills.

10 An account of Hudson's death at Camp Ellis, with the claim that he was the first Confederate soldier to die in service, is in *V N.C. Regts.*, p. 578.

11 Turner was a slave of Sim Whitaker, and, after emancipation, a family retainer for many years. His character and war adventures are remembered today at Strawberry Hill.

12 "Written in a very independent way," George Wills later described Miss Fannie's correspondence to Mary, September 17, 1861.

13 Wash returned to Camp Ellis on May 17. George Wills wrote to "Pa," May 17, 1861: ". . . was very glad to see Wash with the comers this morning." That Sim Whitaker was also in Enfield is plain from a phrase in the same letter: ". . . told Uncle Sim to be sure and tell you to exercise your own judgment about sending him [Wash]."

14 Formal enlistment of the Blues apparently was a company ceremony. *I William Beavans*, entry of May 13, 1861, says: "Today . . . we were sworn into the service of the state for six months." Original muster roll for the company bears that date of enlistment for all officers and men.

15 The final order of companies in the First North Carolina is clarified in an order of May 15, 1861, in *XIX SHSP*, p. 217. Substitution of the Fayetteville Independent Light Infantry for the Randalsburg Rifles is recorded in *ibid.*, p. 216. Portraits of officers in the elaborate uniform of the Independents are in *I N.C. Regts.*, facing p. 69.

16 Regimental staff appointments are in John W. Moore, *Roster of North Carolina Troops in the War Between the States* (hereafter cited as *Moore's Roster*), Vol. I, p. 427. Chaplain Yates' words, from *XIX SHSP*, p. 221, are changed from indirect quotation to direct by substituting first person for third.

17 The regimental flag, now crumbling tatters, is in the Hall of History

at Raleigh, N.C. Like the flag of the Enfield Blues, it was made to the pattern of the Confederate flag, with eight stars instead of seven.

18 The order for rationing and transferring the three companies to Richmond, in *XIX SHSP*, p. 217, was known in advance throughout the regiment. George Wills, to "Pa," May 17, 1861: "I think it very probable from what I learn here, that we will stay here only a few days longer, & understand that Colonel Hill will leave tomorrow with three companies, and the rest will leave soon."

19 Something of relaxation after Hill left is hinted in *I William Beavans*, entry of May 20, 1861: "This day has been very pretty, the boys enjoying themselves. In the evening the State voted herself out of the Union; several rounds of cannon were fired."

20 Details of the departure of the bulk of the regiment for Richmond are from the *Western Democrat*, May 28, 1861, quoted in *XIX SHSP*, p. 218.

21 George Wills' letter to "Pa," written on the eve of the move to Richmond (May 17, 1861), is full of assurance and affection. It concludes: "Tell the Negroes Howdy, and tell them they must do right. Good by. Affectionately your son G. W. Wills."

22 Arrival at Petersburg is from a continuation of the *Western Democrat* article, in *XIX SHSP*, pp. 218–19. Apparently the dispatch is from a Charlotte soldier.

23 Fatigue after reaching Richmond is mentioned in several war reminiscences. Exact time of reaching camp is hard to establish, but it was late. *I William Beavans*, entry of May 22, 1861, says: "This morning about 1 o'clock we reached Richmond." George Wills wrote to "Mother," May 31, 1861: ". . . Wednesday morning [May 22] about two o'clock." The lateness of the hour, his bruised heel, and the final march to camp "nearly used me up."

24 Howard's Grove has been located through the help of George Scheer of Chapel Hill, N.C. The journey from Petersburg to Richmond undoubtedly was made on the Richmond and Petersburg Railroad, which crossed the James River north of the Danville and Richmond bridge, passed the Virginia Steel and Iron Works to the east and came to its depot at Eighth and Byrd streets. Howard's Grove was then undeveloped property north of town, enclosed in a triangle formed by the Mechanicsville Turnpike, the Nine Mile Road, and the Creighton Road.

25 Hill's decision to drill his regiment may have been inspired by the visit of Richmond elite to Howard's Grove. The account is from *Parker*. Any temptation to identify the lethargic young soldier as George Wills must be resisted. *Parker* says of the man, years after the war: "I am glad to report him 'present for duty' and in robust health today." And George Wills had been dead since 1864.

26 George Wills took the guard assignment unhappily, though he was not one to complain to superior officers. In his letter to "Mother," May 31, 1861, he added to his description of the arduous journey to Howard's Grove: ". . . and what was worse than that, we had to stand guard the

day we got to Richmond." Billy Beavans, without a stone bruise, wrote
simply (*I William Beavans*, entry of May 22, 1861): "At 9 we had to go
on guard."

27 The view from Howard's Grove looked beautiful to a soldier whose
letter, signed "Southron," is in *XIX SHSP*, p. 219. "Southron," however,
was free from guard duty and other details.

28 George asked "Pa," in his letter of May 17 from Camp Ellis, to buy
oilcloth ground sheets for him and Jesse Page. To "Mother," May 31,
1861, he wrote: "Tell Pa we have the oil cloth; got it in Richmond."

29 Discomforts of the voyage to Yorktown are wryly remembered by James
C. McRae, in *Our Living and Our Dead*, September, 1874, p. 36.

30 Sadler's death was mentioned as important news in two letters, one from
"Southron" and the other signed with the initial "R," quoted in *XIX
SHSP*, pp. 219–21.

31 ". . . we reached [Yorktown] in the night," says *I William Beavans*,
entry of May 24, 1861. The following day's entry tells of tent-pitching
and exhaustion.

32 On this confident note, "Southron" concludes his letter quoted in *XIX
SHSP*, p. 219.

V

THE GOD OF BATTLES IS ON OUR SIDE

1 The first Sunday at Yorktown is described by "Southron" in *XIX SHSP*,
p. 220. "There are many servants of God in our camp," says the letter.
"Can such a regiment be conquered? Never!" George Wills, writing to
"Pa," on June 16, 1861, expresses similar sentiments: "All our field
officers, Adjutant, and Colonel's Aid, are pious Christians, so our success
can be but sure."

2 Few of the Enfield Blues seem to have admired or liked Magruder ex-
cessively. His appearance and character are described in *I Lee's Lieutenants*, pp. 14–17.

3 Cornwallis never used his preparations to blow up storming Con-
tinentals; Washington forced Yorktown's surrender by bombardment
and cutting off of supplies. George Wills did not mention his survey of
the old works until he wrote to "Pa" on June 16, 1861.

4 George describes the false alarms of May 26 and 29 to "Mother," May
31, 1861. Indirect quotation of Colonel Hill and Wash are made direct
by substitution of first person for third. George habitually responded
to earnest exhortations of his officers.

5 "Today it is drill, drill, drill all the time," grumbles an anonymous
correspondent in the Fayetteville *Observer*, June 3, 1861, p. 3, col. 1.
"Yesterday it was spade, spade, spade." The account tells of volunteer
work on new ramparts, and says that the regiment slept several nights
without removing uniforms or shoes.

6 George expresses his disappointment at staying in camp while others marched to possible action, in his May 31 letter to "Mother." The anticlimactic result of the march on Hampton, with work orders for June 1 and regimental organization for battle, are from the Fayetteville *Observer*, June 6, 1861, p. 3, col. 1.

7 Many military doctors of the time recommending growing of beards to ward off throat ailments. Billy Beavans began the war smooth-shaven, but a picture taken early in 1862 shows a heavy beard. George seems to have tried whiskers, briefly and unsuccessfully, late in 1861.

8 Lawrence Whitaker writes to his brother Cary on May 31, 1861: ". . . I hav been trying to hav your company clothing mad as fast as posible but hav not succeeded in get on as fast as could be desired." The letter has been preserved by the present-day Whitakers of Strawberry Hill. M. T. Whitaker, to his brother Ferdinand, August 15, 1861 (correspondence in the Southern Historical Collection) speaks of having advanced $174 for supplies for the company.

9 "This morning to our unhappy feeling we got orders for a march," says *I William Beavans*, entry of June 6, 1861. "We prepared two or three days rations and marched of. We reached Bethel sometime in the night —(15m) Though wet and Rainy we had to sleep out on the ground for the first time." *Leon*, p. 3, misstates the date as June 3, ". . . when we marched fifteen miles and halted at Bethel Church . . ."

10 Descriptions of Big Bethel Church and the terrain are found in *I N.C. Regts.*, p. 84. A map of the region, in *ibid.*, facing p. 92, was drawn by William Gaston Lewis, then a lieutenant with the Edgecombe Guards.

11 Some improvement in morale is indicated by the close of the entry for June 8, 1861, in *I William Beavans*: "This morning we still feel bad; have no coffee scarcely no bread; nothing but Ship Biscuits. Some were working; and some went scouting, which fretted the Yankees no little!"

12 Home letters treated this minor engagement like a decisive battle. See *XIX SHSP*, pp. 23–24, 239–40.

13 *Leon*, p. 3, tells entertainingly several foraging adventures.

14 "We had a bad time on guard I tell you," says *I William Beavans*, entry of June 9, 1861. "Nothing scarcely to eat!" George Wills saved his complaints for a letter to "Pa," June 16, 1861.

15 *I William Beavans*, entry of June 10, 1861, begins: "This morning at 3 o'clock the bugle sounded, and we had to march 3 miles and back." *Leon*, p. 3, says: "At 3 o'clock this morning [June 10] the long roll woke us up. We fell in line, marched about five miles, then counter-marched, as the Yankees were advancing on us." This entry may have been revised, or written wholly from memory, in later years. Billy Beavans' on-the-spot mention of a bugle is probably accurate. Hill's battle report in *War of the Rebellion: Official Records of the Union and Confederate Armies, First Series* (hereafter cited as *OR*), Vol. II, p. 94, says of the advance and retirement: "We learned that the foe in large force was within a few hundred yards of us." The old lady who warned Hill was

not named in dispatches, but officers of the regiment made her a present of money.

16 Bell was absent from the battle. Montgomery Whitaker may have been at Big Bethel, but did not serve with his company. Hill's report, *II OR*, p. 96, says that "Lieutenant Whittaker" commanded the Blues, but other evidence indicates that Parker was senior officer.

17 Battle positions of all companies of the First North Carolina and attached units are shown on Lewis' map in *I N.C. Regts.*, facing p. 92.

18 W. G. Lewis' letter to his fiancée, Miss Mittie Pender, June 12, 1861 (with Southern Historical Collection), describes Hill's behavior as the battle began. A lively account of the bombardment and feelings it evoked are in *XIX SHSP*, p. 224.

19 The story of Jesse Page's prayer and attendant circumstances is from *Parker*.

20 Most of the battle details are from Hill's report, *II OR*, pp. 94-96. Action close to the defenses on all sides would have been visible from where the Blues held their position.

21 A good description of the field after the battle is in *XIX SHSP*, pp. 225-26.

22 Henry Lawson Wyatt, first Confederate soldier to be killed in action, was a good and intelligent infantryman. Some personal history, and the manner of his death in action, are told in *I N.C. Regts.*, pp. 100-101, and in James C. Birdsong, *Brief Sketches of the North Carolina State Troops in the War Between the States*, pp. 196-98. Magruder's report, *II OR*, p. 92, praises Wyatt. After the battle Wyatt was buried at Richmond with military honors. A statue of him stands in front of the State House at Raleigh.

23 Lucien Whitaker's granddaughter, Miss Kate Riddick, tells in a typescript biography of her grandfather of the Federal straggler's capture, adding that some consider him the first Union prisoner of the war. However, as told elsewhere, a prisoner was brought in the day before the main battle. Six Federal soldiers were captured during the battle itself.

24 *I William Beavans*, entry of June 10, 1861, concludes: "After the fight was over the Lou. Regt came." George Wills describes the Zouaves in his letter to "Pa," June 16, 1861. The other reference quoted is from *XIX SHSP*, p. 226.

25 "Colonel Hill . . ." continued George Wills to "Pa," "closed by saying that not to us, but to a higher Being, was all the praise, and to whom all should be given." And George agreed.

26 The first page of George's letter to Mary concerning the battle has been lost. A second page, undated but marked in pencil "to Mary Wills," is with *Wills Papers*.

VI

1 The verse, "War," is in *I William Beavans,* on page headed July 30, 1861.

2 Home letters of seventeen-year-old James A. Whitehead, covering his Yorktown experience from June 12 to August 1, 1861, a lively, though originally spelled, record of recruit life, are in the manuscript division of Duke University Library, Durham, N.C. Quotations are from his first three letters: to "Father," June 12, 1861, to "Sister," June 16, 1861, and again to "Father," undated but apparently written shortly after June 16. His first mention of food is to "Sister": "We boys have a plenty to eat such as it is rye bread and western meat and rice at time molases sugar &c."

3 He wrote to "Sister," June 16, 1861, with grieved concern for his deranged cousin. George Wills, to Mary, June 15, 1861, wrote more circumstantially and coolly, but he, too, felt a sense of tragedy. The body of B. F. Britt was sent to Enfield for burial, under escort of Sergeant Lucien Whitaker. Robert Whitehead, discharged as insane, recovered his reason at home.

4 Magruder's speech to the troops is included in George's letter to Mary, June 15, 1861, following the account of Robert Whitehead's violent outbreak. George quoted Magruder indirectly, but placed the remarks within quotes. Quotation is made direct by substituting first person for third.

5 George, to "Pa," June 16, 1861, describes the review as staged so that Magruder might feel safe in reprimanding the Louisianans. Without complaining directly, George hinted dislike of Magruder's cautious method.

6 The Whitakers admired James A. Whitehead's preacher-father. Young James, in an undated home letter, says: "They is a Whitaker here that used to be a debity sheriff . . . told me the other day if I ever made such a man as you it would be good enough. he said you was a mity good man." Probably the "debity sheriff" was Sergeant William E. Whitaker, who before the war held several political offices. James may have felt ready for action because food arrived from home. To "Sister," July 4, 1861, he writes appreciatively of "that cake."

7 Wash was still in Yorktown on June 16, as he asked George to include greetings to the family in a letter to "Pa" of that date. But George's letter to "Mother," June 30, 1861, shows that both Wash and Jesse Page were at Brinkleyville: "I reckon Mr Page and Wash think this the shortest week they ever saw, it seems to them as only a day; I have no doubt but the table had justice done to it while he was there. . . ."

8 The rhymed address to the victors of Big Bethel ran six verses in the Raleigh *Standard,* quoted in *XIX SHSP,* pp. 230–31.

9 James A. Whitehead's letter to "Sister," dated July, 1861, without day of the month, tells of seeing friends in the Fifth North Carolina. Undoubtedly he boasted to them of his own regiment.

10 Jesse Page was a jokester of sorts. George Wills, to Lucy, July 3, 1861, says that Page and Wash arrived on July 2 ". . . and seemed to be as lively as you please, Mr. P. was bowing and scraping as he generally does when he wants to have fun, and told his fine tales in abundance." George continues, maddeningly obscure: "Tell Mother, Wash told her a tale; I never thought of such a thing, and hope she will not say anything about it; I would rather for her to let it alone, I have no notion of doing it myself, for I have no cause whatever to think of such a thing; tell her please let it drop where it is." Of John Hammill, George comments: "I reckon his conscience reproached him so much that he couldn't stay away any longer." Hammill fought bravely until severe wounds crippled him in 1864.

11 Not only brandy pleased James A. Whitehead. To "Sister," July 22, 1861, he mentions ham, biscuits, butter and coffee. Montgomery Whitaker, to his brother Ferdinand, August 15, 1861, says with plain satisfaction: "Our boys are getting whiskey rations now which will be a benefit if properly used."

12 George Wills mentions First Manassas, calling it "Bull's Run," to Lucy, July 21, 1861, showing that news of the victory arrived at Yorktown within hours. His request for new pants shows despair of military supply: "It seems that the Government or State either is not going to give us any clothes, so I must have a pair of pants made."

13 Promotions of Sim Whitaker and George Wills to corporalcies are noted on the company muster roll for August 31, 1861. Apparently these promotions took place in July, though exact dates cannot be set.

14 Blues who died late in July were Marcus Aulsbrook, John Coker, Samuel Arrington, and William Whitaker (not "Major"). James A. Whitehead lists them in order of their dying, to "Sister," August 1, 1861. George Wills, to Lucy, July 28, 1861, says: "We buried three of our company in so many days . . . measles." As he wrote, his kinsman William Whitaker lay dying.

15 Cary Whitaker esteemed his nephew George. To W. H. Wills, August 5, 1861, with *Wills Papers,* he says: "Truly do we hope that he may be spared for us for he is a good and obedient boy and one who promises to be a useful and worthy member of society."

16 Date of James A. Whitehead's death from sickness is noted on the company's muster roll for August 31, 1861. W. H. Wills, to "Dear Wife," August 10, 1861, with *Wills Papers,* says: "I performed Burial services this evening, over the son of Laurence Whitehead the Baptist preacher near Dawson Roads."

17 George's impatience at being absent from prospective battle, for sickness or any other cause, here expressed to "Mother," September 3, 1861, was characteristic of him throughout the war.

18 George's September 3 letter continues: "Did you know our Reg't had left York[town]? Such is the case, it has gone down the river about ten miles, at a place called Ship's Point, I suppose it is both for the health of the Reg't and to keep the Yankees from landing there." To "Pa," he writes, Sept. 6, 1861, from Cocklestown: "I returned to Camp (Ships Point) Wednesday night and staied there until yesterday when we had to commence march for this place six miles off." A Fayetteville soldier, quoted in *XIX SHSP*, p. 241, compared sheepshead caught at Ship's Point favorably with "our finest shad" from the Cape Fear River.

19 George Wills, to Lucy, September 10, 1861, calls Camp Fayetteville "The prettiest place we ever camped at, it is a beautiful grove, which if it was cleared up properly, would make a splendid place for a dwelling." George repeatedly expressed delight in trees around his quarters. He continues with a chuckling account of the flag presentation, which is also described in *XIX SHSP*, pp. 242–44, 246, with considerable quotation from John W. Baker's muddled speech.

20 George expresses wrath over the election of officers in the same letter. Montgomery Whitaker expected Parker to defeat him. He writes to his brother Ferdinand, August 23, 1861: "I received a letter from Capt Bell stating that he had sent in his resignation. don't know who will be elected Captain. Some think Parker will be. don't care much." Again to Ferdinand, September 18, 1861, he wrote: "If I am not popular I can't help it. . . . the duties of Capt are very arduous, it is very hard to give satisfaction to so many men. Frank makes a good officer, as good as any in the regiment."

21 George's dislike for beef was not approved at home. He describes his privations to Mary, September 17, 1861, adding: "Mother will say, it may be, that she is glad of it, so I may learn to eat beef, but tell her it is no use, for I will eat dry bread before I eat beef."

22 George continues: "I received a letter from ——, the other day, it was written in a very independent way indeed, in fact it was overbearing; the part I speak of, was about those letters that I received after I got to Raleigh; I replied to it in every way, and in so independent a manner, as to cause what you all have wished for a long time, it is also what I wanted, what do you think of that?" His avoidance of writing Miss Fannie's name is typical of letters and journals of his group. Such policy probably indicated fear that private papers might be captured by leering Federals. George then changes the subject: "Ask Mother, if I can get a *position* [i.e., a commission], will she be willing or rather won't she want me to continue in service? Don't you let it get out of the family tho, I have a notion (if pa & Mother think it proper) to try to get a position in the Confederate army, I think I would be delighted at such a thing." But he concludes with what was on his mind throughout the letter. ". . . don't you let pa see this letter, for I don't want him to see that part about ——."

23 Again Cary Whitaker wrote to Brinkleyville of George's illness, Septem-

ber 22, 1861. W. H. Wills, to "Dear Wife," from Camp Fayetteville, September 27, 1861, says that Cary Whitaker and Wash sat constantly with the ailing George. Sim Whitaker had a "bile," and could not help nurse his nephew. W. H. Wills' letters of September 30 and October 1, 1861, say that George felt better, but had stomach pains.

24 Promotions of Montgomery and Cary Whitaker are from the company's muster roll, October 31, 1861.

25 The memorial of the First North Carolina's officers is quoted in full in *I N.C. Regts.*, pp. 124–30. About this time the organization began to be called the Bethel Regiment.

26 William Beavans resumed daily entries in his diary on November 8, 1861. Entries in *I William Beavans*, November 8–16, 1861, describe the end of the six months' service and the return of the Blues to Enfield.

VII

WOUND UP IN LOVE AS BY A CLOAK

1 Cary Whitaker spent very little time in Enfield after the Blues were mustered out of service. *Cary Whitaker Memorial* says: "The 1st Regiment was enlisted for six months and wer disbanded about the 15th Nove Cap Whitaker as soon as he reached hom went to Raligh & was appointe Capt by the State Oct 6 with authority to raise a company." His new commission was contingent upon enlistment of enough men to follow their captain to war.

2 William Beavans, after the briefest of daily journal entries about the end of his service at Yorktown, wrote more fully and happily about first days at home. George Wills' visit, with calls on kinsmen and other social events, come in for fairly full description in *I William Beavans*, entry of November 22, 1861.

3 The rhyme about the awkward suitor "Wound up in love as by a cloak" is in *I William Beavans*, page headed July 15, 1861. It is written in ink, suggesting that the author composed it at home. His Yorktown diary is in pencil, as are most of his war verses.

4 Apparently Billy Beavans liked his "Upon the verge of time" verse very much indeed, for *I William Beavans* includes two versions, on pages headed May 27 and 28, 1861. The second of these, here quoted, seems to be a revision of the first. Possibly there were other polishings before it was offered to the lady who inspired it.

5 The entry of December 3, 1861, in *I William Beavans*, is kindly enough in its reference to Sim Whitaker's bachelordom. Enfield tradition indicates that Sim was a quiet but hospitable planter, admired by several ladies but not, as of 1861, eager to marry.

6 The series of holiday-season parties, saddened only by the Hunter funeral, is noticed in *I William Beavans*, entries of December 11–30, 1861. The new war-music titles are from a list in the same journal, on

page headed July 27, 1861. A later journal, *II William Beavans*, includes other titles of songs about love and war. Whether Smiling Billy played or sang cannot be established, but he liked music.

7 Today nobody knows why George and Johnny disputed with their girls at John Branch's New Year's Eve party. Billy Beavans enjoyed the business hugely. His entry in *I William Beavans*, under penciled date of January 1, 1862, is on a blank page immediately following the entry of December 31, 1861. His list of New Year's resolutions, with the final jibe at George, is on a flyleaf at the end of the book.

8 Billy wrote a practice draft of his letter on the pages dated July 6 and 7, 1861, in *I William Beavans*, and may have changed it before sending it. The lady who received these confidences seems to have been Miss Susan Waldo.

9 Priscilla Macon's valentine verse, in *I William Beavans*, page headed September 4, 1861, is one of several such acrostics addressed to several girls. The others are even less skillfully done, and none speaks so plainly a love message. Possibly Miss Priscilla was seriously courted by Billy early in 1862, though no evidence identifies her as the girl he calls "my sweetheart" in his later diary. The verse, "Soon to the war I expect to go," in *I William Beavans*, page headed September 13, 1861, is assigned to early 1862 rather than before Billy's first service with the Enfield Blues because none of his earlier writings indicate any deep tenderness for a special lady.

10 Billy penciled the date *March 5th, 1862*, in *I William Beavans*, under the printed date Tuesday, March 5, 1861.

11 In a letter to his sister Maggie, March 18, 1862, Billy tells entertainingly and comprehensively the story of his and George's trip to Camp Mangum. This letter is in the possession of Mrs. Stanley Whitaker, along with copies of the daguerrotypes taken of Billy and George in Goldsboro. George, to Lucy, March 20, 1862, indicates that he reached Camp Mangum on March 18.

12 Muster rolls of the unit as Company D, Forty-third North Carolina Regiment, are in the National Archives at Washington. Billy finished his March 18 letter to Maggie: "As I have to make out my roll tonight I will have to stop," indicating that he finished the day as orderly sergeant. George's March 20 letter to Lucy speaks of several kinsmen: "I don't know when Uncle Sim will come . . . the Capt [Cary Whitaker] has just come in and told us we are in the next Regm't. . . . as Billy is waiting for me now I will close."

13 Officers and non-commissioned officers of Company D were chosen on March 18, 1862. They are listed in the company muster roll for April 30, 1862, all of them ranking from March 12.

14 Wash was not yet at camp on March 24, 1862, when George requests "Pa": "Send those towels by Wash." Wash had arrived by April 7, as a letter of that date shows.

15 Many students and historians believe that the original Bethel Regiment continued in service as the Eleventh North Carolina. But the Bethel Regiment was disbanded in November, 1861, while the Eleventh North Carolina was organized on March 31, 1862, with many company officers from old Bethel companies, and the flag officially presented to it. However, neither of the Eleventh's brave colonels, Collett Leventhorpe and William Martin, were from the Bethel Regiment, and few of the enlisted men had been at Yorktown. Full 135 old Bethels served as Confederate officers with various organizations, including four generals, fourteen colonels, eighteen other field officers, and many excellent staff officers.

16 George Wills writes of the field officers of his new regiment to "Pa," March 24, 1862: "I am very well pleased with the result myself as the Col & Lieut Col. (I don't know anything about the Major) are as good officers as could be found." This somewhat cautious estimate of the three was borne out by their later careers. Daniel and Kenan served with gallantry and efficiency. Boggan was never competent. A sort of tactful secrecy shrouds his record. His early adventures as a bibulous lieutenant are in W. A. Smith, *The Anson Guards*, pp. 26–27.

17 "Wash tells me he didn't like it any too good about Billy Beavans being appointed 1st Serg.," writes George to Lucy, April 7, 1862, "tho it very much surprised me, and also thought at the time that it wasn't right, yet I haven't allowed it to give me a moment's dissatisfaction."

18 When Billy received his commission as second lieutenant, George was the more determined to fight down any twinge of jealousy because of loyalty to his Uncle Cary. ". . . in the first place the Capt saw fit to appt him 1st Sergt so after that he was entitled to it because of being higher in command," George elaborated to Lucy, April 23, 1862. This was in keeping with George's resentment the previous September, when juniors were voted over the heads of their erstwhile seniors in the Enfield Blues.

19 On the company muster roll for April 30, 1862, George ranks as orderly sergeant from March 12, 1862.

20 Mrs. Stanley Whitaker has preserved several delightful items of correspondence relating to the efforts of Maggie Beavans to reconcile her cousin George with her school chum Miss Fannie. George's savagely triumphant rejection of such overtures is dated April 29, 1862, after he had been reseasoned to the military life by full six weeks at Camp Mangum, most of the time as orderly sergeant. The letter continues: "I didn't see her last sunday, so have nothing to tell you about that, Lieut Sim was very anxious for me to see her, said he wanted to see what I was going to do." I have found no other writing of George Wills which expresses anything approaching such a mood of angry mockery. Quiet, mannerly and kind, he endured all hardships and disappointments save Miss Fannie's heartless coquetry.

VIII

1 Cary Whitaker found himself as a captain of infantry, and seems to have been happiest as such, though he served ably on temporary staff and court-martial details and later in the war commanded a regiment. "He was true to all the duties of life," wrote his old comrade, Francis Marion Parker, in *Parker*. The muster rolls of Company D for its three years of existence always include high marks for discipline, equipment, and appearance.

2 George's efforts to gain the adjutancy were not long or strenuous. He wrote to "Pa," March 24, 1861, that "I don't think there is much chance for me to get the place of Adj't, because I think he will be taken from among the Lieuts of the Regm't. . . . I would like very much to get some position, but if I can't will have to do without it." Lacy, who became adjutant (see *III Moore's Roster,* p. 196), was efficient and brave.

3 George probably reflected his comrade's opinions in a letter to "Mother," April 22, 1862: "The whole Regm't is dissatisfied now, Col. Daniel didn't accept, Col. Kenan was then elected Col. we all like this part of it very well, but then the other officers went up by rotation, therefore our Maj. (who to day is not able to drill a battalion) is Lieut Col. and the Capt of Comp. B who cannot and will not be able hardly to drill a squad, is to be our Maj. It is the cause of much dissatisfaction throughout the whole Regm't, as for my part if *I* couldn't beat either of them drill I would quit altogether." This, for George, was extraordinary self-praise. Captain Robert P. Waring of Company B was only briefly mentioned as a possible major for the Forty-third. Courageous but uninspired, he fought well at Gettysburg and resigned on November 30, 1863 (see *III Moore's Roster,* p. 200).

4 George's scornful ridicule of Major Boggan to Mary, April 18, 1862, may have been colored by a feeling that Cary Whitaker deserved the majority.

5 Boggan's promotion would have followed, as a matter of course, Kenan's election to the colonelcy, but undoubtedly Boggan's unsuitability was recognized by higher command. Wrote George to "Pa," April 29, 1862: ". . . the Adj Gen. decided that it was proper to have an election for Lieut Col in this Regm't, so that we are now better pleased, as that has been done and Maj Lewis of the 33rd is our Lieut. Col. It goes now Kenan Col. Lewis Lieut Col. & Boggan Maj the last will do, but don't think him to be a good officer by any means."

6 "Tell John I would give $50.00 for my part of it, if he and Jack [Whitaker, another cousin] will come," wrote George to Maggie Beavans, April 29, 1862, "for Billy is now Lieut Beavans, so is *above* me, well so it will be, no he ain't above me either, only in rank, but I imagine so . . ." Johnny enlisted May 13, 1862, as recorded in Company D's

muster roll for June 30, 1862, and ranks as fourth sergeant from that date.

7 Billy Beavans' draft verses could not have been written before the draft became an actuality in the spring of 1862, and must therefore have been his last scribbling in *I William Beavans,* where they appear on page headed September 10, 1861.

8 George's disposal of the subject of sweethearts to Maggie is dated May 11, 1862, and is in the possession of Mrs. Stanley Whitaker.

9 To Lucy, on May 9, George Wills describes the site of Camp Holmes and the nervousness of certain comrades. ". . . it is very amusing to hear some of the men talk. I believe they are scared all the time, when in fact I don't think there is anything to be frightened at."

10 In the same letter, George mentions the armament of his company. He liked the Enfield muskets. ". . . if we had enough of these we would be well armed."

11 "The camp here is very dull indeed," George writes his mother on May 28, 1862, "nothing but drill, drill, hep, hep, all the time, so I am getting tired of this sort of work."

12 George describes his daily routine as orderly sergeant in letters to both sisters. On April 18, 1862, to Mary from Camp Mangum, he outlines early roll call, morning nap, and back to drill. ". . . makes a fellow a little lazy when he has nothing to do." On May 22, 1862, to Lucy, he tells much the same story. ". . . so you see my work is regular, and for this reason haven't anything to write."

13 George continues by telling Lucy of the battalion drill. "I believe Col Kenan is the greatest man for such things I ever saw," he comments. To "Mother," May 28, 1862, he expresses a wish to be with Stonewall Jackson.

14 George maintained throughout the war a soldierly amusement at nervous comrades, but did his best to comfort such shaky ones. To Lucy, May 22, 1862, he says: "The men get to be awfully upset sometimes about some tales men bring here, but I can talk them out of that." The alarm of June 7 and the contagion of timidity he describes to Mary, June 9, 1862. ". . . one old fellow who had his wife and child down here, told them he expected to be in a fight in less than a half-hour and had them scared to death, most."

15 George describes mess arrangements to "Pa," June 4, 1862, also the purchase of quinine and his flagging interest in religion.

16 "I have just had mine today," adds George in his note to Lucy, June 9, 1862, "and it was a poor dinner, worse than it has been heretofore, because we have just gotten out of provisions of every sort most."

17 George's account of the march to Fort Johnston to Lucy, June 17, 1862, is accented with his fatigue. "I was necessarily very tired. . . . I slept as soundly as I ever did . . . and when I reached my destination . . . I was one tired boy." Yet he and his comrades were toughening. They

accomplished twenty-two miles between sundown of one day and noon of the next, with but six hours of rest.

18 The regiments of Daniel's Brigade had assembled from various training camps. The Thirty-second was organized from independent companies gathered in Virginia, the Forty-fifth came direct from Camp Mangum at Raleigh, and the Fiftieth and Fifty-third came from near Weldon at the state line. George, writing to Lucy, from "the woods near Drury's Bluff, Va.," June 28, 1862, tells of the brigade organization and General Holmes' stirring speech.

19 Continuing, George says: "The Capt is right poorly too he is with us tho." Cary Whitaker hated to miss a fight, and probably was an example to George and the others.

20 Sergeant Curys B. Watson of the Forty-fifth, in *III N.C. Regts.*, p. 39, tells frankly of his regiment's demoralization, naming several who fled. Plainly the shelling from the Federal gunboats was fierce. "This was, what has always seemed to me, a poor way to break in a raw regiment," Watson felt. "The regiment thought so, and eight companies immediately broke to the woods and 'Stood not upon the order of their going.'" Deaf General Holmes, says *Battles and Leaders of the Civil War* (hereafter cited as *B.&L.*) Vol. II, p. 390, came out of a house at the height of the bombardment, hand cupped to ear, and said, "I thought I heard firing." George writes to "Pa" on July 3, 1862: "For an hour they threw them pretty thick along the whole brigade, but as providence would have it nobody was killed in our Reg't, only one or two wounded." Four days later, to Mary, he told his amusement at less staunch Confederates: "Ha! ha! it was funny to see some of the fellows stick their heads under the side of the fence the other night when we were shelled, but the poor fellows were scared, so reckon mustn't laugh at them."

21 In his July 3 letter to "Pa," George sounds disappointed in his inactivity near Malvern Hill. ". . . never did I hear anything equal to the cracking of musketry and booming of artillery, we were drawn up again in line of battle near the same place we did the day before, we were then looking every minute for work to do, but it didn't come and we remained there all night waiting, having slept only as we could catch a chance. . . ." Holmes' Division was needed at Malvern Hill, but Holmes, for all his oratory, was dilatory and uncooperative.

22 Miss Fannie's letter, in possession of Mrs. Stanley Whitaker, is hard to read, inasmuch as part of it is written lengthwise of the page, across other script. Such measures were common with Confederates to save precious paper.

23 "If you want to make a fortune," George advises Mary, July 7, 1862, "just get a lot of chickens, vegetables, &c. and come down here to Petersburg, they don't give anything away but you certainly have to buy what you can get here." Listing prices, he adds: "So you will see that Pa's garden would bring him an independent fortune were he to have it all here and sell it all."

24 *Leon,* p. 7, entry of June 23, 1862, complains of muddy camping. "But there is a factory here, and plenty of girls to make up for the damp ground." And on July 7, 1862, *ibid.,* p. 8, after the march back from Drewry's Bluff: "We return to our factory girls again—all O. K., you bet."

25 Joe John Cowand's war letters to his cousin Winifred Cowand in Bertie County are in the manuscript division at Duke University. Though Cowand's spelling and punctuation are bad, he wrote an excellent hand, and his language is vivid and delightfully humorous. Despite his many romantic successes in Virginia, he seems to have felt most tenderly toward "Cousin Winaford," who after his death mourned deeply and never married.

26 George did not intend seeing out the war in a training camp. A lieutenancy as drill officer "might not be a permanent one," he writes home on July 13, 1862, "yet it would lead to an appointment for the war."

27 W. H. Wills' home letter from Petersburg, July 25, 1862, tells of George's severe illness. The vegetables Mr. Wills brought were welcomed by the hungry mess, and again the intelligent minister saw how such food, or its lack, could affect the health of the men. "This by the way is one cause of their sickness."

28 George's longing for return to camp is expressed to "Pa," July 28, 1862. On August 1, to "Mother," he tells a like eagerness, the more so because news comes of possible action. But some peacetime pleasures are described: "I hear a band of music down at the Hotel, it makes me feel so much like old times, I must go down."

29 George was still weak as he rejoined his regiment. To Lucy, August 8, 1862, he says that his host, Mr. McIlwaine advised him against reporting too soon. However, "I took up my knapsack (no *I* didn't Wash did), and walked." Of his dinner of fruit and fresh tomatoes: "I was pretty well filled."

30 Gaston Lewis, to his fiancée, Miss Mittie Pender, August 13, 1862, writes casually about marching and maneuvering.

31 George ascribed his gain in weight to the plentiful tomatoes that supplemented his rations. See his letter to Mary, September 10, 1862.

32 George described the Suffolk march to "pa," September 23, 1862. The march covered nearly 100 miles in "pretty stiff weather."

33 The "slice-potato pie" which George declined was described to Lucy, October 5, 1862: ". . . no, it didn't suit my fancy, it did *look* really nice tho." His new gain in weight was reported to "pa," October 17, 1862.

34 The news of Mrs. Wills' coming delighted all the Whitaker kindred, as George wrote home on October 7 and 17, 1862. Wash left around October 29. See George to Lucy of that date: "Wash . . . will be home to conference (by himself tho, I am afraid). . . ." George includes a pen-picture of camp: "It is all still and dull now, except an occasional shout from one of the men playing marbles, or the chop from Uncle Sim's ax."

35 The upright-log style of winter quarters, described to Lucy by George

on November 19, 1862, was one of several followed by the Army of Northern Virginia. Cold weather came early to that part of the world in the fall of 1862, as Lieutenant Colonel Lewis lyrically informs Miss Pender, November 8, 1862: ". . . the hues of Autumn have been changed to the snowy drapery of winter. . . . The sun is laboring hard to break through the clouds & cheer us with its beneficent rays; but it seems a hard task. Snow, mud, rain & cold wintry winds will I am afraid be our constant companions for the remainder of this winter."

36 Chaplain Eugene Thompson, criticized by George to his brother Richard, November 16, 1862, was thirty when assigned to the Forty-third, and had been a Methodist minister for eight years. He served through the war with his regiment and was considered brave, helpful, and inspiring by less critical acquaintances than the orderly sergeant of Company D. After the surrender he was a North Carolina minister until his death in 1877. "How precious his memory!" sums up A. D. Betts in a thumbnail sketch of Thompson in *IV N.C. Regts.*, p. 614.

37 George reports being vaccinated in a letter to "pa," December 12, 1862. "It looks read all around the place, so think from that it will take." Vaccination was not compulsory in Confederate ranks.

38 The brigade's uncomfortable journey from Drewry's Bluff to the chilly bivouac outside Goldsboro is traced in *Leon*, entries of December 15–21, 1862.

39 More and cheaper provisions were the only advantage George could find in the new camp, as he wrote to Mary on December 24, 1862. ". . . and you may know we eat most all the time, as there is not possable anything else to do, no books to read or nothing of the sort." The supplies did not, however, include holiday delicacies. *Leon*, p. 14, entry of December 25, 1862, is even more doleful: "This is certainly a hard Christmas for us—bitter cold, raining and snowing all the time, and we have no tents. The only shelter we have is a blanket spread over a few poles, and gather leaves and put them in that shelter for a bed."

IX

I BELONG TO GENERAL LEE'S ARMY

1 "I enjoyed myself very much indeed," George says of his Goldsboro visit to Lucy, January 4, 1863, "and wished often you had come."

2 Wash probably went home on January 15, 1863, when George wrote to Mary. Recruits arrived for training the same day.

3 It is impossible to fix the date and length of George's furlough. Probably it lasted fifteen days. A letter from camp, March 1, 1863, says he had just returned to his regiment.

4 Hill's appeal to Secretary of War James A. Seddon, in *XVIII OR*, p. 891, calls Robertson's cavalry "wonderfully inefficient," and says: "With one more brigade I could harass the enemy, detain his troops in this State,

possibly force him to send others here." The return of Daniel's Brigade is in *ibid.*, p. 888. Recruiting soon greatly increased Daniel's numbers.

5 George missed his kinsmen in Company D. To "Pa," March 1, 1862, he complains of his Uncle Cary's absence at a court-martial: "I do wish they would put that general court into session and let the Capt alone." Four days later, to Lucy: ". . . no one here but Uncle Sim (I mean my mess) and he reading about the only book we have with us. Uncle Cary is on another court-martial, John is drilling a detached company or at least a company that isn't in the Reg't, and Lt. Baker isn't any cousin to me, so am left alone. . . ."

6 Hill's address to his troops is in *XVIII OR*, pp. 894–95. George further paraphrases it to Lucy, March 5, 1863: "He says, those of us who have heard the booming of artillery at a distance shall have the pleasure of hearing it nearer; within the next 2 months, and on the way we then fight, shall depend the fate of this war, for if we whip the Yankees at every point, the war must end by July, but if they whip us, it will keep on through Lincoln's administration."

7 Cary Whitaker helped George's quest for a navy commission by a letter to Confederate Congressman W. N. H. Smith, as George tells "Pa" in his March 1 letter. Nothing came of it, as George relates in another letter, April 6, 1863.

8 "Willy will get the appointment of ord. off. if he wants, Gen. Daniel told the Capt. the other day," reports George to "Pa," March 1, 1863. This indicates that the assignment suited Billy Beavans, though later in the war he seemed to prefer service with Company D.

9 *Leon*, p. 18, entry of February 26, 1863, tells of the whipping of the deserters—thirty-nine lashes apiece.

10 The March 8 battle was at Core Creek near Kinston. Federal Colonel Richter Jones, Fifty-eighth Pennsylvania, pays soldierly tribute to the Forty-third North Carolina in his report *XVIII OR*, p. 161: "They are a different class of troops from those I have hitherto met, contesting successively every strong position and giving way only to my superior numbers."

11 George describes his pig-hunting to Mary, March 21, 1863.

12 Movements of Daniel's Brigade, with attendant discomforts, on the way to Washington are told in *Leon*, p. 20, entries of March 30–April 1.

13 George's first chance to catch a mail was April 6, 1863. He says the cold night of April 4 was "the worst evening I ever saw I think. . . . I was afraid it would make us all sick but only Uncle Sim and myself suffered from it." Lest his parents worry, he adds: "I hope you will not let my being a little sick pester you, as I am today a great deal better and will I think be well in a day or so, in fact haven't been too unwell to attend to my duty."

14 *Leon*, pp. 20–21, entry of April 2, 1863, says: "We are within hailing distance of the Yankee line of pickets. . . . Saw the place, their breastworks and camps very plainly." In his April 6 letter, George Wills describes a

similar survey of the enemy: ". . . with a glass can see what they are doing over there; it seems that they are strengthening their works on the river, also moving some guns on the other side of the town to protect themselves from Gen's Pettigrew and Garnett who are over there."

15 Shelling by gunboats was a commonplace, says Lieutenant Colonel Lewis to Miss Mittie Pender, April 13, 1863: "The sound of artillery & the whistle of shot & shell are as familiar as the whistle of a locomotive used to be."

16 *Leon,* p. 23, entry of April 15, 1863, describes the besiegers' misery in the rain. Food was again George Wills' concern. To "Mother," April 14, 1863: "If my feelings were consulted we would not long remain here, for the country is very bare of provisions and we necessarily have to live hard, nothing but meat & bread, and yet it is as costly as anything we could use."

17 "The enemy give us a pretty smart shelling before we left," George writes to Mary, April 18, 1863, "but hurt no one. I believe the boys were pretty scared as usual and I saw some fun, notwithstanding the danger."

18 Hard marching and short rations probably contributed to frequent desertions. *Leon,* p. 27, entry of May 11, 1863, tells the story of the execution without naming names.

19 George's letter mentioning Chancellorsville is undated, but probably was written before news of Jackson's death on May 10 had reached him.

20 *Leon,* p. 27, entry of May 17, 1863, describes breaking of camp and departure for Virginia. Desertion of the Edge brothers is noted on Company D's muster roll for June 30, 1863, and no record of their capture or other news of them has been found.

21 The full name of George's new sweetheart is not remembered today by any of his surviving kinsfolk. He himself never called her by name in his home letters, though in the upper left corner of a letter from Virginia, dated September 16, 1863, he wrote "Lulu." Probably he had known her before the war, and came to a romantic understanding with her during his February furlough. The whole Wills family liked her.

22 The march was a forced one. "We left Richmond Friday morning," George writes to Lucy, May 25, 1863, "with four days rations (the distance being about 65 miles) in order to give us full time in consideration of the very hot weather; but instead of taking until this evening as it was thought, Col. Lewis made a fine march of it and reached here yesterday by dinner, making about 26 miles per day. I stood up, but was very tired when I got here." George adds the observation that Lieut. Col. Lewis "acted very wrong and I am sorry to say lost the confidence of the men in a great degree," but this disapproval of Lewis soon faded. The other regiments were slower. The Fifty-third, says *Leon,* entries of May 21–25, 1863, started a day earlier than the Forty-third and arrived a day later.

23 For reorganization of Daniel's Brigade and assignment to Rodes' Division, see *III N.C. Regts.,* p. 5.

24 George wrote from the regimental bivouac at Hamilton's Crossing, near Fredericksburg. "Our Brig. is a great addition, as it is nearly, or in a great respect, as large as a division. . . ." Considerable recruiting and return of men detached for special duty had almost tripled Daniel's strength.

25 *Leon*, p. 28, entry of May 29, 1863, describes the review and the appearance of Lee, ". . . a gray-headed old man." He also sets out organization of Rodes' Division and of the Second Corps under Ewell.

26 Says *Leon*, p. 29, entry of June 4, 1863: "Got orders to cook three days rations immediately. We left our camp at 3 this morning, marched fourteen miles and halted." Apparently no sure word of where they were going had been spoken, but the spirit of invasion was in the air.

X

OUR BRIGADE WAS IN IT GOOD

1 Numbers, character, and equipment of the Army of Northern Virginia in the Gettysburg campaign are described in more than a score of standard reference works.

2 Muster rolls of the Forty-third North Carolina show that Major Boggan was detached before the northward march began. The nature of his special assignment does not appear.

3 *Leon*, p. 29, entries of June 4–10, 1863, describes this advance of the Second Corps. The Gettysburg narrative in *II William Beavans* begins with the move to Brandy Station and Billy's own delay in reaching camp.

4 Maneuvers of the Second Corps from the Rappahannock to Gettysburg are outlined in *III Lee's Lieutenants*, pp. 20–37. The Gettysburg narrative in *II William Beavans* and *Leon*, p. 30, entries of June 11–12, 1863, tell some adventures of the smaller units of the corps.

5 The capture of Berryville was effortlessly easy, as described in *Leon*, pp. 30–31, entry of June 13, 1863; in the Gettysburg narrative in *II William Beavans;* and by George Wills to his mother, June 18, 1863.

6 "It is raining very hard," says *Leon*, p. 31, entry of June 13, 1863, "and there is, of course, no shelter for us."

7 Numbers of prisoners and guns taken are from *XXVII OR*, pt. 2, p. 464. George to his mother, June 18, 1863, says "3500 prisoners," and laments that "Milroy, the commander and *outlaw*, was however fleet footed enough to escape."

8 The Gettysburg narrative in *II William Beavans* says: "We saw several pretty young ladies and got a good deal to eat" at Martinsburg. *Leon*, p. 31, entry of June 14, 1863, complains of the long march.

9 William Gaston Lewis writes to Mittie Pender, June 18, 1863, of effortless successes in the valley: "I think it equal to any of Jackson's campaigns, so don't be discouraged at his death for we have other Jacksons living yet." *Leon*, p. 31, entry of June 15, 1863, is equally elated: "Have

driven the enemy from the Rapidan to the Potomac, captured prisoners, arms, camps, quartermaster and commissary stores . . . they always ran at our appearance."

10 George's letter of June 18, 1863, tells of crossing the Potomac. The Gettysburg narrative in *II William Beavans* tells the order of divisions and brigades wading over. *Leon* calls the river "knee-deep," p. 32, entry of June 17, 1863.

11 *Leon*, p. 32, entry of June 19, 1863, calls Hagerstown "very pretty," and records camping by the Antietam.

12 Lewis writes eloquently to Miss Pender, June 28, 1863, of the beauties of the Cumberland Valley. *Leon*, p. 32–33, entries of June 22–24, 1863, records "glum looks and silence," "nary a smile." George, to Lucy on June 28, 1863, quotes indirectly the conversation between Wash and the Pennsylvania woman. Here indirect quotation is made direct by substituting first person for third.

13 Of Pennsylvanians, George writes on June 28: "They are afraid we will imitate their soldiers and destroy all their property." *Leon*, p. 33, entry of June 25, 1863: "They thought we would do as their soldiers do, burn every place we passed through, but when we told them the strict orders of General Lee they were rejoiced."

14 The story of the Thirty-second North Carolina's flag is in *II N.C. Regts.*, pp. 525–26. George wrote of the music. Several memoirs mention the general's speeches, but do not report what they said. The Gettysburg narrative in *II William Beavans* says nothing of the ceremonies, but remembers the whisky and ice water.

15 Joe John Cowand's note to "Cousin Winaford," June 28, 1863, is the final item among his war letters at Duke University.

16 General Rodes, in *XXVII OR*, pt. 2, p. 552, says he camped at Heidelsburg. The Gettysburg narrative in *II William Beavans* tells of stopping "about 7 miles off" from Gettysburg, and *Leon*, p. 34, entry of July 1, 1863, describes passing through Heidelsburg in the morning.

17 The approach beyond Heidelsburg, as it must have seemed to ordinary marchers, is well told in the Gettysburg narrative in *II William Beavans*.

18 The farmhouse where the Forty-third paused was the Forney House on the Mummasburg Road above Gettysburg. The big building in town was Stevens Hall, and the tower belonged to Pennsylvania College.

19 Rodes' battle, with a good map, is described in *III Lee's Lieutenants*, pp. 82–88, and his report, *XXVII OR*, pt. 2, pp. 552–54, is the best on this part of the Gettysburg campaign.

20 Several narratives describe the blood-won triumph of Daniel's Brigade. Daniel's report, *XXVII OR*, pt. 2, pp. 567–68, is restrained in praise of his own behavior and in criticism of Iverson. Thomas Kenan's history of the Forty-third, in *III N.C. Regts.*, pp. 5–6, speaks briefly and proudly. William Gaston Lewis, who reported for the regiment in *XXVII OR*, pt. 2, p. 573, also glories in the deeds of his men. Captain J. A. Hopkins, reporting for the Forty-fifth in *ibid.*, p. 575, tells of the recapture of the

Twentieth North Carolina's flag, a tale remembered for years by Daniel's veterans. *Leon*, pp. 34–35, entry of July 1, tells his own adventures vividly. The Gettysburg narrative in *II William Beavans* says only that Billy's comrades "drove the Yankes before them though with great loss on both sides. . . ." George Wills wrote home about the battle, but part of his letter is lost.

XI

FOUGHT WELL AND WAS COMPLIMENTED

1 *Leon*, pp. 34–35, entry of July 1, 1863, tells of helping to mop up in Gettysburg after the day's fighting.

2 Daniel noticed Cary Whitaker's courage, and Lewis noticed that of George Wills. Their written opinions are cited below.

3 Daniel's Brigade was at the extreme right of Ewell's Corps, which held the left of the line. The troops supported by Daniel were of Pender's Division. Rodes describes positions in *XXVII OR*, pt. 2, p. 555.

4 Kenan, in *III N.C. Regts.*, p. 6, remembers the Forty-third's second day at Gettysburg and the reverent salute as Lee came to the front. James Boyd, in his novel *Marching On*, includes an incident perhaps based on this actuality.

5 Twice is Lee called "our father" in *Leon*, pp. 39 and 41, entries of July 11 and 14, 1863. Leon, Jewish and foreign-born, may have expressed himself individually, but his devotion to Lee was characteristic of the Army of Northern Virginia.

6 Daniel's was one of two brigades sent by Rodes to help storm Culp's Hill on July 3 (see *XXVII OR*, pt. 2, pp. 556, 568). *Leon*, p. 35, entry of July 2, 1863, visualizes the night move: "Just at dark we were sent to the front under terrible cannonading. Still, it was certainly a beautiful sight. It being dark, we could see the cannon vomit forth fire."

7 Lewis, in *XXVII OR*, pt. 2, pp. 573–74, describes the Forty-third on the slope of Culp's Hill. The Gettysburg narrative in *II William Beavans* says drily: ". . . quite a hot place . . ." A good account of the effort to take the hill is in *III Lee's Lieutenants*, pp. 142–43, with praise for Daniel's Brigade. And, says *Leon*, pp. 36–37, entry of July 3, 1863: "You could see one with his head shot off, others cut in two, then one with his brains oozing out, one with his leg cut off, others shot through the heart. Then you could hear some friend or foe crying for water, or for 'God's sake' to kill him."

8 Says the Gettysburg narrative in *II William Beavans*: "The troops fell back and formed where they were the first day after driving in the Yankees; there we remained in the rain until night when we commenced falling back towards Hagerstown."

9 Company D's Gettysburg casualties are listed in the muster roll for August 31, 1863. George writes to Lucy, July 29, 1863: "Lt. Baker, and

7 of the men were wounded or killed there." Regimental and brigade losses are in *XXVII OR,* pt. 2, p. 342.

10 Lewis writes his sententious judgment of Gettysburg's result to Miss Pender on July 15, 1863, but supplies no details of the battle itself. He devotes most of his letter to soldierly courtship.

11 Family tradition says that Joe John Cowand was killed at Culp's Hill, and that his cousin D. G. Cowand made a brave but unsuccessful effort to rescue the body. *Leon,* p. 36, entry of July 4, 1863, dolefully lists his company's heavy losses.

12 The Gettysburg narrative in *II William Beavans,* and *Leon,* pp. 37-38, supply details of the early phases of the retreat.

13 The Gettysburg narrative in *II William Beavans* understates the rear-guard action: "The Yankees were annoying us a little in the rear." *Leon,* p. 38, entries of July 5-6, 1863, and Daniel's report, *XXVII OR,* pt. 2, p. 570, tell of lively skirmishing.

14 George mentions the capture of Kenan, Baker, "and perhaps others of your acquaintance" in a letter to his father of which only part survives with *Wills Papers.* No date shows, but it must have been written during the retreat to Virginia.

15 "I have knocked along tho," George makes light of his sickness to Lucy, July 29, 1863, "and by the kindness of Billy Beavans, who gave me a ride for several days, kept up with the Regt." *Leon,* p. 41, entry of July 14, 1863, describes officers caring for wounded and Lee's frequent appearances at the rear.

16 The Gettysburg narrative in *II William Beavans* tells of reaching Hagerstown and Billy's departure.

17 George's undated fragment to his father is one of several messages urging that brother Ed be given a good education and offering to share the expense.

18 *Leon,* p. 39, entry of July 11, 1863, says: "Orders read out today from our father, R. E. Lee, that we would fight the enemy once more on their own soil, as they were now in our front." The order is in *XXVII OR,* pt. 2, p. 301.

19 *Leon,* p. 40, entry of July 13, 1863, picturesquely recounts the crossing of the flooded Potomac. See also *III N.C. Regts.,* p. 7.

20 Distances of the daily marches are from *Leon,* p. 41, entries of July 14-16, 1863.

21 George could not disguise his pride in commanding the company. To Lucy, July 29, 1863: ". . . something I never expected to happen in our Comp'y, to be commanded by the O[rderly] S[ergeant]. . . ." His letter to his father was written from Darksville, July 19, 1863.

22 Lewis' mention of George's good conduct in action is from *XXVII OR,* pt. 2, p. 574; Daniel's praise of Cary is in *ibid.,* p. 570; and Ewell includes George in a list "honorably mentioned for gallantry" in *ibid.,* p. 451.

XII

FALLEN IN LOVE ON SOMEBODY ELSE'S PLANTATION

1 The diary, here cited as *II William Beavans,* is unpaged, and after the recipe for curing the itch appears an account of Billy's Gettysburg experience, hitherto quoted and cited. This narrative, covering several pages at the front of the book, is broken after the events of July 12, 1863, and is continued at the back of the book. Part of his Gettysburg adventures he copied on a large sheet of foolscap, now in possession of Mrs. Stanley Whitaker of Centerville, and probably sent it in a home letter.

2 Brigade mess accounts, with names of staff officers including Billy, follow the list of songs in *II William Beavans.*

3 The widespread religious revivals in the Army of Northern Virginia and in other Confederate forces are described and diagnosed in many works. George's notice of Chaplain Thompson's labors is included in a letter to "Pa," August 20, 1863. George himself had no need of conversion; any earlier doubts and complacencies had been banished by his Gettysburg experience.

4 George's wish for bacon, expressed to Lucy, July 29, 1863, may have been intended as a family joke about his eating habits.

5 The letter about Wash's return was written August 15, 1863. Some of George's views on faint-hearted neighbors sound like echoes of D. H. Hill's savage order of February 25, 1863. Lucy probably knew all about Miss Lulu, despite George's teasing.

6 Company D's numbers and efficiency are noted on the muster roll for August 31, 1863. George, to "Pa," September 2, 1863, speaks of the rumored praise of the Forty-third as having happened earlier than the August 31 inspection.

7 Sim rejoined on September 1, 1863, as indicated in George's September 2 letter. He was eager for duty—had "a fever to go back to camp," writes George to Lucy, August 15, 1863.

8 George mentions news of Baker's death in his August 20 letter. On September 2 he heard that Company D might be judged too small to need another lieutenant: ". . . if so I will hate it rather. . . ." He refers to his promotion in a letter to Mary, September 16, 1863, with a casualness perhaps studied.

9 *Leon,* p. 47, entries of September 14–15, 1863, describes the move to Morton's Ford. September 15, Jewish New Year's Day, brought Leon within plain sight of the lurking enemy.

10 Lieutenant Colonel Lewis, in a letter to Miss Pender, September 28, 1863, eloquently describes the position of the Forty-third and the surrounding country.

11 The shooting of the deserter impressed many. George, to Mary, September 16, 1863: "Today the Division must be out to witness the execution

of a deserter. . . ." Lewis, September 17, 1863: "I witnessed yesterday the most solemn scene, that ever appeared before my eyes. A military execution according to the form of War." *Leon,* too, p. 47, entry of September 16, 1863, offers one of his careful descriptions.

12 *Leon,* pp. 48–49, entries of September 19–30, 1863, is briefer than usual, but soldierly and lively.

13 It is hard to establish whether George speaks of Miss Lulu's plantation literally or figuratively. Like Miss Fannie, the lady lived near Raleigh, and may have been there on holiday from Elba Academy when George wrote.

14 Details of the Bristoe Station campaign, as seen by men in the ranks, are from George's letters to Lucy, October 17 and 20, 1863, and from *Leon,* pp. 49–51, entries of October 9–November 6, 1863.

15 Again Lewis writes colorfully to Miss Pender, November 5, 1863, of the scenery around the Kelly's Ford bivouac. The exact date of George's furlough cannot be established, but his letters suggest an approximate date.

XIII

HARD, HARD TO BE A GOOD MAN

1 George, writing to his mother on the day of his return to duty, mentions his still shaky digestion.

2 The Kelly's Ford action is described in *III Lee's Lieutenants,* pp. 265–68. *Leon,* pp. 51–52, entry of November 7, 1863, presents a sharpshooter's-eye view.

3 George to his brother Richard, December 8, 1863, says: "Justice to myself would have had me before the Board [of examiners] a week or two ago, but couldn't bear the idea of having it said that I had left on the eve of a battle, so roughed it out. . . ."

4 *III Lee's Lieutenants,* pp. 270–75, sums up the Mine Run campaign. *Leon,* pp. 52–54, entries of November 27–December 2, 1863, offers the action as it must have impressed a hard-fighting private soldier—a dubious skirmishing and scurrying through chilly woods. To the enfeebled George, as told to "Pa," December 3, 1863, it was "one of the most unpleasant weeks I have spent for a time. . . ."

5 George mentions Dr. Brewer's return in letters of December 3 and 8, 1863. From all accounts, Brewer was a gruff but competent military surgeon.

6 George's December 8 letter to Richard is full of brotherly affection and expresses the wish that the two may eat Christmas dinner together. Sympathetic, intelligent and not too much older than George, Richard exercised great influence on his brother's thought and behavior.

7 W. H. Wills, to Richard, February 26, 1864, describes George's prolonged and serious illness at home.

8 In *II William Beavans,* Billy resumes his daily journal on January 3, 1864. Entries of January 16–February 4, 1864, tell of a three-week furlough at Enfield, with news of George, Cary, and other relatives.

9 Famine's pinch upon the Confederacy is set forth in a dispassionate market survey in the Wilmington, N.C., *Daily Journal,* January 6, 1864, p. 3, col. 3. Bacon ("scarce and in demand") brought from $2.25 to $2.50 a pound; butter, $5.00 to $5.50 a pound; corn ("scarce and in demand"), $8.00 to $10.00 a bushel; corn meal ("the supply is very light, and not equal to the demand"), $10.00 a bushel; wheat flour, $90.00 to $100.00 a barrel; lard, $2.25 a pound; molasses, $15.00 to $16.00 a gallon; fresh pork, $1.25 to $1.50 a pound; salt, $13.00 to $15.00 a bushel. These prices, in a locality fairly rich in farm produce, probably were lower than throughout most of the Confederacy. Many dealers would not accept the sharply depreciated currency and sold only by barter.

10 Jack Whitaker's date of enlistment is from Company D's muster roll for February 29, 1864.

11 "My friends were all glad to see me," George tells Lucy, February 29, 1864, "and most of them expressed themselves as being surprised at my coming back and advised me to apply for another furlough. On March 11, 1864, to Mary, he says: "Uncle Sim. will leave Enfield Wednesday nest, you all will please send some provisions down for him to bring on as we do most of our living from home now."

12 George's gain in weight must have been appreciable. To Lucy, March 20, 1864, he suggests that his new uniform pants be cut to a roomier pattern.

13 "Wash is rather upset at my last decision" to refuse a furlough, says George to Mary, April 6, 1864.

14 Billy was relieved as brigade ordnance officer on March 24, and rejoined his company on April 4, 1864, after another stay in Enfield.

15 The *Albemarle* was built on the banks of the Roanoke River in Halifax County, of lumber sawed on the spot and metal ingeniously forged. This makeshift ironclad played an important part in the capture of Plymouth, and later was destroyed by recklessly brave Federal raiders.

16 George's judgment that Ed needed schooling is borne out by Ed's poor spelling and punctuation, but the boy's upbringing had been good. To "Mother," May 10, 1864, he writes: "I think this is one of the most low life company ever was nothing but the lowest class of the country except two or three. Nothing but swaring all the time or something just as bad. I dont want you to come down here unless you go over to Mr Samuels house because the men has no more respet for a lady than if she was a hog they will say any thing in the world that comes to hand."

17 The Wilderness campaign is comprehensively dealt with in *III Lee's Lieutenants,* pp. 347–514, with frequent reference to the splendid service of Daniel's Brigade. Cary Whitaker's first journal volume (hereafter cited as *I Cary Whitaker*), entries of May 7–June 3, 1864, tell of the

Forty-third's ceaseless battling, as does *II William Beavans,* entries for the same dates.

18 Relatives and acquaintances wounded are named in a letter of W. H. Wills to Richard, May 27, 1864.

19 George wrote home almost at once. To "Mother," June 5, 1864, he says that he found "the troops in the finest spirits." He tells Lucy, two days later, of being joshed about his spruce uniform, a pleasantry she would appreciate.

20 "I haven't heard from Cousin Lucien, Jack or John since I wrote to pa, so only have to surmise from the condition they were then in, that they are still improving," comments George's June 5 letter; and, in that of June 7: ". . . we are so, in this army, that if a friend is not wounded so as to injure him, we don't care much; such wounds save more severe ones or life itself frequently."

21 Billy's comparison of the enemy forces to ants is indirectly quoted in George's June 7 letter to Lucy, which also says that Cary, in his fresh uniform, "looks like a new man."

22 George tells Mary, June 10, 1864, of getting the sword from Cary, and asks for food from home.

23 The veteran's advice to Ed is from the June 10 letter.

24 Entry of June 12, 1864, in *I Cary Whitaker* tells of Chaplain Harding's sermon and the text. *II William Beavans,* entry for the same date, says simply: "Attended Church."

25 *I Cary Whitaker,* entry of June 13, 1864, says the march started at 3:00 A.M. *II William Beavans,* entry of June 12, 1864, says: "At night we received orders to be ready to move at 2 a. m. on the 13th inst." Cary, as regimental commander, probably was right.

XIV

STILL THE WILL IS HALF THE MAN

1 Numbers and organization of the Second Corps are included in Jubal Early, *Autobiographical Sketch and Narrative of the War Between the States* (hereafter cited as *Early*), p. 372.

2 *I Cary Whitaker* and *II William Beavans,* entries of June 13–15, 1864, detail the first days of the march. Cary's daily mileages are more exactly given, and are probably more correct, than those of Billy.

3 George's struggles to overcome his weakness and indirect quotation of his talk with Dr. Brewer are told to Lucy, June 16, 1864. He quotes Wash as thinking "I am doing remarkably well."

4 *I Cary Whitaker,* entry of June 16, 1864, describes the country with an appreciative farmer's eye and notes the rumors about Hunter and Sherman. *II William Beavans,* entry for same date, records similar tags of military gossip.

5 *I William Beavans,* entry of June 17, 1864, relishes the ice cream and

cherries. *I Cary Whitaker,* entry for same date, lists no refreshments but admires the scenery.

6 Entries of July 18, 1864, in both *I Cary Whitaker* and *II William Beavans* describe the railroad journey to Lynchburg.

7 *II William Beavans,* entry for July 19, 1864, quotes Valley farmers on the demoralization of Hunter, and charge pillage and destruction. *I Cary Whitaker,* entry for following day, says: "The Yankees took all horses and provisions in their route," and tells of the green-apple diet of his men.

8 Pulaski Cowper, ed., *Extracts of Letters of Maj. Gen. Bryan Grimes to His Wife* (hereafter cited as *Grimes*), p. 58, tells of the pleas for bread. *I Cary Whitaker,* entry of June 20, 1864, reports scanty rations. George, to "Pa," June 22, 1864: ". . . it was tough and the men quarrelled so much about not having anything to eat."

9 Continued pursuit of Hunter is described in *I Cary Whitaker,* entries of June 21–22, 1864. Both Cary's journal and George's letter of June 27, 1864, to his mother speak gratefully of the chance to bathe in the stream.

10 George's June 27 letter is partially indecipherable, but the nature of his assignment to prisoner guard is made clear in *I Cary Whitaker,* entry of June 24, 1864, when George returned to his unit.

11 "Saw several girls at the roadside in front of the College but none of them were pretty," complains *I Cary Whitaker,* entry of June 23, 1864.

12 George in his June 27 letter, and *I Cary Whitaker* and *II William Beavans,* entries of June 25, tell of the parade past the grave of Jackson and entertainment in Lexington. For another account, see *I N.C. Regts.,* p. 275.

13 Both Robert E. Lee and Jubal Early regretted that Hunter had not been destroyed. See *XXXVII OR,* pt. 1, p. 766.

14 "Very pleasant marching," says *II William Beavans,* entry of June 28, 1864. Entry for same date in *I Cary Whitaker* calls the march "easy," and describes fields of wheat, timothy, and clover.

15 *II William Beavans,* entry of July 2, 1864, tells of Sim's foraging for noon dinner. *I Cary Whitaker,* entry for same date, disparages the supper he and George bought.

16 *I Cary Whitaker,* entry of July 4, 1864, describes at length the Forty-third's entertainment at Charleston. *II William Beavans,* entry for same day, says: "People very liberal and kind; saw many pretty ladies." George, to Mary, July 17, 1864, includes nothing of food or fair faces, but calls Charleston "old John Brown's resting place."

17 The gay time at Harpers Ferry is described by George in his July 17 letter, and in *I Cary Whitaker* and *II William Beavans,* entries of July 5, 1864. George's mention of wine among the prizes is the only reference in all his home letters to alcoholic beverage as a possible refreshment; and quite probably he did not partake. Billy records his own indulgence in "Ale Porter Lager Beer & cider"—undoubtedly with tem-

perance. Later in his account of the day's adventure, he adds: "There was a good deal of Brandy Whiskey, Wine, vegitable, crackers & c. down at the Ferry. Some few men got wounded there." Which suggests that the casualties were plunderers.

18 "Enemy threw several shells at us, one or two of which came in close proximity to us," says *I Cary Whitaker*, entry of July 6, 1864. *II William Beavans*, entry for same day, agrees: "The Yankees shelled us."

19 The entry into Maryland may not have excited anyone. Says *I Cary Whitaker* ". . . crossed the Potomac at the Shepherdstown Ford, passed through Sharpsburg after dark . . . and camped on the banks of Antietam Creek." *II William Beavans*: ". . . crossed the Potomac; passed through Sharpsburg in the night—could see very little; camped about 1½ miles beyond with the division." George, in his July 17 letter, shows none of the thrill of a similar episode in the Gettysburg march: "We crossed the Potomac at Shepherdstown on the night of the 6th and marched through Sharpsburg and camped near there that night."

XV

WASHINGTON WOULD HAVE BEEN IN OUR POSSESSION

1 Company D's muster rolls include no return between February 29 and August 31, 1864; undoubtedly the usual bimonthly inspection was not completed at the end of June, while the headlong pursuit of the Federals was at its height. On August 31, a total of twenty-eight were present for duty, and a note says that seventy-one were on the company roll at the previous muster.

2 *II William Beavans*, entry of July 7, 1864, tells of forming line of battle, then: "Lt. Wills & myself went off after cherries; cut a great many very fine ones"; *I Cary Whitaker*, entry for same date, tells of George's expedition to the mountain and of Jack's effort to follow: "Jack remained out all night and I was very uneasy about him, thinking that in the darkness he might have fallen over a precipice and been killed. . . . after a time he returned had been lost three times, nearly day when he returned."

3 "Very hard marching as the Blankets are wet & heavy," says *II William Beavans*, entry of July 9, 1864. Billy carried his own camp equipment.

4 *I Cary Whitaker* and *II William Beavans*, entries of July 9–10, 1864, and George's July 17 letter all include spirited accounts of the Battle of Monocacy as seen and heard from the fringe.

5 Says *II William Beavans*, as early as July 8, 1864: "Moved on road to Washington City." Two days later, *I Cary Whitaker* says: ". . . marched in direction of Washington City," and, on the next day: "We began to believe that we were going in fact to attack Washington." Cary's indirect quotation of Early's words and his own is made direct by substitution of first person for third and present tense for past. Similar remarks by

Early to other units are mentioned in *III Lee's Lieutenants*, p. 565, citing the manuscript diary of Jed Hotchkiss, then on Early's staff.

6 As with many other first-hand accounts, *I Cary Whitaker* and *II William Beavans*, entries of July 11, 1864, and George's July 17 letter all mention the pause at Montgomery Blair's house. The fort seen from there was Fort Stevens.

7 Events of the afternoon and evening are from *I Cary Whitaker*, entry of July 11, 1864.

8 *I Cary Whitaker*, entry of July 11, 1864, describes movingly the Forty-third's advance and clash with Federals. *II William Beavans*, entry for same date, tells somewhat the same story, less circumstantially: "The regt on our left gave way which was followed by the whole line. They [the Federals] were driven back by some other troops. The 43rd was one."

9 Henry Kyd Douglas of Early's staff employed the phrase about being "scared as blue as hell's brimstone," but Early accepted it with a laugh. See Douglas, *I Rode with Stonewall*, p. 295.

10 Cary's first volume of daily journal concludes with the entry of July 12, 1864, and the account continues with July 13 in the second volume (hereafter cited as *II Cary Whitaker*), which, with *II William Beavans*, describes day-by-day incidents of the orderly return to the Potomac and across.

11 Owens had been wounded in the spring, and arrived just in time to take the brigade into action at Snicker's Ford. His record is that of an able and aggressive officer. He may not have completely recovered from his wound when he assumed brigade command.

12 Most of the details of the battle are from *II Cary Whitaker*, entry of July 18, 1864, the longest and most circumstantial in Cary's whole journal. Cary's dislike of Owens' cautiousness is restrained but manifest. Cary gives the number of casualties for the Forty-third, and George, to Lucy, July 23, 1864, gives names of the killed and seriously wounded in Company D. The Federal force was a division under Colonel Joseph Thoburn, which reported a loss of 422 (see *XXXVII OR*, pt. 1, p. 292). Early reported his casualties to Lee as "between 200 and 300" (*ibid.*, pt. 2, p. 597). The Federal colonel captured by Cary was Edward Murray, who commanded Thoburn's artillery.

13 *II Cary Whitaker*, entry of July 18, 1864, describes with concern and indignation his discovery of Billy and other wounded left without proper care.

14 The two parts of the entry of July 18, 1864, in *II William Beavans*, so strikingly different in handwriting and mood, have brought tears to the eyes of more than one modern reader.

XVI

NEVER YET DID I SEE FELLOWS RUN AS THEY DID

1 George Wills, to Lucy, July 23, 1864, says of Billy Beavans' wound and amputation: ". . . Wash and Jack were with him all the time, and they say he stood it remarkably well, was very cheerful, and at times entirely free from all pain." Billy's own feeble scrawl, in *II William Beavans*, entry for July 19, 1864, indicates great suffering. His nature was to minimize such things as best he could.

2 The last entry in *II William Beavans* is, if anything, more crudely written than the previous one. The agony of the amputation and the fatigue of the ambulance journey to Winchester would contribute to this.

3 Kate Shepherd, from all accounts, was an exceptionally beautiful young woman. A letter from her indicates that she was intelligent and educated as well. Her concern for the wounded Billy, perhaps colored with romantic feeling, is a legend among present-day Whitakers and Beavanses.

4 The entry for July 19, 1864, in *II Cary Whitaker* seems hastily written, but Cary's sympathy for Billy is manifest.

5 Details of the march to White Post, with news of Ramseur's defeat, are in *II Cary Whitaker*, entries for July 19–20, 1864. Ramseur expected to find only two Federal regiments near Winchester, and his confused retreat began when William Gaston Lewis' Brigade broke and ran. Report of the action is in *XXXVII OR*, pt. 2, pp. 326–27.

6 *II Cary Whitaker*, entry of July 21, 1864, quotes Boggan's tale of Grant's death, and George Wills, to Lucy, July 23, 1864, says he read the same report in "the Richmond papers of the 18th and 19th."

7 The Federals beaten by Early were commanded by George Crook. *Early*, pp. 399–400, describes the running fight. George Wills, to "Mother," July 27, 1864, exults over the victory. *II Cary Whitaker*, entry for July 24, 1864, tells of the Forty-third in action and agrees with George that "It was a complete route."

8 George's July 27 letter relates: "I went to Winchester the next day to see William, found him in good spirits, and doing very well he said he most went into ecstacies the day we took the town, was completely overcome with excitement. . . ." *II Cary Whitaker*, entry for July 24, 1864, quotes Jack Whitaker: "The excitement of taking the town had almost been too much for [Billy]. . . ."

9 *II Cary Whitaker*, entry for July 27, 1864, notes the ordering of George to picket duty. George had leisure to write a fairly long letter home.

10 To Lucy, August 1, 1864, George says the election was held "last Thursday," and remarks of the overwhelming vote for Vance: ". . . so you see the *soldiers* are not fools yet, I mean all of them are not, tho I must

say some of them are right ignorant. . . ." He mentions the nine Holden votes in the Forty-third. *II Cary Whitaker,* entry for July 28, 1864: "6 of these Holden votes were from H and 3 from C— There were several men in the Regiment who did not vote who no doubt wished to vote for Holden but had not the courage to brave public spirit and do so mean an act." Company H was Walter Boggan's old command from Anson County, and C came from Wilson County. North Carolina's mountain regions, where Unionist sentiment was reckonable from the war's beginning, gave no companies to the Forty-third.

11 Wash's farewell talk with his master is movingly described in a letter from Wash to Richard Wills, October 30, 1864. George's home message is quoted directly by W. H. Wills to Richard Wills, October 1, 1864, and in an article by John Paris, chaplain of the Fifty-fourth North Carolina, in the *Watchman and Harbinger,* Greensboro, N.C., November 11, 1864. All of these items are with *Wills Papers.*

12 Jack Whitaker's letter, written while Wash was waiting on July 29, 1864, is in possession of Mrs. Stanley Whitaker. The symptoms it lists—disordered bowels, fever, and a chill—were not considered baleful in the 1860's, but today doctors would think they indicated infection.

13 George's August 1 letter says of the stay opposite Williamsport: "The Commissaries went over in town and got a little molasses for the troops, & of course something extra for the A[ssistant] Ad[jutan]t G[enera]ls." *II Cary Whitaker,* entry for July 29, 1864, is not so coy: "Doles Brigade was in town acting Provost Guard, understand they took on a good deal of whisky. . . ."

14 *II Cary Whitaker,* entry of July 30, 1864, is the only evidence anywhere that the temperate Cary ever specifically yearned for a drink of liquor. George's August 1 letter says that Billy is "doing badly" and expresses hopes of seeing him soon.

15 George's August 1 request for a new homemade uniform is what his family might expect. He always preferred clothing, even military clothing, of family manufacture. Apparently Mrs. Wills, the big girls, and the neighbors were skillful seamstresses.

XVII

UPON THE VERGE OF TIME I STAND

1 Kate Shepherd wrote to Mr. and Mrs. John Beavans, Sr., on August 19, 1864, of her last interview with the dying Billy. It is a restrained and ladylike letter, yet cannot but reveal Miss Kate's deep-stirred emotional feeling. She quotes Billy's words directly. George Wills, to Lucy, August 18, 1864, quotes Cary Whitaker as saying that Miss Kate had repeated the last speech of Billy: "Tell [my parents] I have but one regret, in leaving this world, and that is, leaving them behind." Miss Kate's first-

hand quotation seems more like the speech of a dying man. Her letter, and others expressing condolence to the Beavans family, are in possession of Mrs. Stanley Whitaker.

2 Jack Whitaker's letter to John Beavans, Sr., August 2, 1864, is written on half a leaf torn from a ledger. Affectingly he describes the death of Billy, adding: "What things he had with him I will send home in a few days by George [Cary Whitaker's servant]. I will also send some of his hair and beard." He says that Billy was buried in Samuel Jones' private graveyard, but Kate Shepherd's August 19 letter says that Billy's body is in the Shepherd plot at Winchester Cemetery. It is still there, according to research by the indefatigable Miss Kate Riddick of Enfield.

3 Cary Whitaker did not write to Mr. Beavans until August 12, 1864. *II Cary Whitaker,* entries for August 2–12, 1864, show that Cary was busy with regimental reports, then marching to the Potomac and back. He managed the letter at last, while his troops were in line of battle awaiting enemy attack.

4 Details of the crossing into Maryland as the Forty-first accomplished it are in *II Cary Whitaker,* entries for August 4–7, 1864. Cary enjoyed both the food and the feminine company at the hospitable Dunkard home, and George Wills, to "Pa," August 8, 1864, mentions this entertainment for his uncle, then tells his own recipe for beef soup. "I love it as well as I did the asparagus soup at home," he elaborates. "I gave a good many, officers & men, directions how to make it, all, I believe, laughed at me, but then upon trying it found it good and now, I believe, it is the most fashionable dish in camp. . . ." But George still refused to eat mutton.

5 *II Cary Whitaker,* entry for August 7, 1864, records Jack Whitaker's return to duty, as does George's August 8 letter. Jack went to convalescent camp after Billy's death, and then spent several days guarding prisoners before rejoining Company D.

6 ". . . some excellent music," says *II Cary Whitaker,* entry for August 10, 1864, of the serenade for Grimes. *Grimes,* p. 58, calls the music "delightful."

7 As early as August 9, 1864, the Confederates knew the composition of the enemy's force and that Sheridan commanded it. See *Early,* p. 406, and *XLIII OR,* pt. 1, p. 995.

XVIII

I AM TIRED OF THIS FIGHTING

1 Sheridan's strength in the field is stated in *XLIII OR,* pt. 1, pp. 60–61. The figures as to active troops do not include various garrisons and detached units. *Early,* p. 412, says his force could muster 8500 infantry, 2900 cavalry, and three battalions of artillery.

2 Both Grant and Sheridan overestimated Early's numbers—see *XLIII OR,*

pt. 1, pp. 18–20, 43. Early computed Sheridan's effective force with fair accuracy (*Early*, p. 418), but was less than realistic when he decided that Sheridan himself lacked energy and courage.

3 *Early*, pp. 406–7, describes the retirement to Fisher's Hill and his position there. *II Cary Whitaker*, entry for August 13, 1864, visualizes it: ". . . line of battle upon a beautiful ridge—the line somewhat circular fronting a hollow the descent from which is very steep . . ." George Wills, to Mary, August 13, 1864, says: ". . . think it is rather doubtful about their fighting us here as we have a very formidable position."

4 *II Cary Whitaker*, entry for August 14, 1864, mentions Chaplain Thompson's three services. After the third, some noise of skirmishing was heard by Cary in front of the army's position.

5 *Early*, pp. 407–8, and *Grimes*, p. 59, briefly describe the army's approach to Winchester and the fight of August 17. *II Cary Whitaker*, entry for August 17, 1864, says Rodes' Division was not heavily engaged, but tells of watching the defeat of the Federals. George, to Lucy, August 18, 1864, wastes only a few words on the action.

6 ". . . quite a pretty young lady," says *II Cary Whitaker*, entry for August 18, 1864, of Miss Kate Shepherd, and continues: "Went back to see her for the purpose of thanking her for her kindness to Billy. I was very much pleased with her." His later call, he adds, was made "hoping to find out something about the last hours of my friend," but plainly he hoped for conversation more personal, perhaps more romantic.

7 George's August 18 letter quotes Cary as saying that Kate Shepherd intended to write to Billy's father. Her letter to Mr. and Mrs. Beavans is dated the following day.

8 *Early*, pp. 408–9, says of the fight in which Cary was wounded: ". . . very heavy skirmishing ensued and was continued until night, but I waited for General Anderson to arrive before making a general attack." *Grimes*, p. 60, in a letter to his wife on August 21, 1864, says: "I have had today a great many killed and wounded, we being in advance, but have not had all my command engaged." Apparently the affair was just short of a serious battle. *II Cary Whitaker*, entry for August 21, 1864, is clear and circumstantial about the Forty-third's part in the fight, and notes Cary's sensations on suffering a wound. This second and last of his journals comes to an end on August 25, as he reached a hospital at Mount Jackson.

9 George's letter of August 24, 1864, again speaks of Grant's rumored move to the Valley. Flagging battle spirit in the army apparently was discussed by Cary sometime before his wound. George quotes Cary as saying: ". . . if we had put our army at the beginning of the war under regular Army discipline this war would have ended ere this."

10 "They were more fleet-footed than us," George's letter to "Mother," August 28, 1864, says of the Federals retiring across the Potomac. He thinks his comrades took "50 or 100 prisoners." *Early*, p. 409, mourns the failure to cut off a large proportion of the retreating enemy. *Grimes*,

p. 61, tells of a two-hour chase, and the fainting of his fagged men.
George's reference to "secesh ladies" is the only passage in his home
letters that suggests flirtation on his part. Cary or Billy would have
rhapsodized over such fair entertainers.

11 George enjoyed Lucy's letters, as he tells her several times; and to Mary,
September 9, 1864, he admits writing "a few more [letters] to Lucy than
anyone else as she writes more to me." Ed may have read George's postscript at home, as he had been on sick leave at about that time. Nowhere else does George suggest anything so close to despondency as in
this revelation to Ed. Without vanity and self-assertion, nevertheless,
George maintained stout morale in all other home letters.

XIX

TELL MOTHER, IF I FALL

1 George tells Lucy, September 1, 1864, that he was making out company
payrolls in anticipation of the paymasters' visit. On September 8, 1864,
to Mary: "[The men] consequently are flushed with money, and are
rather at a loss to know what to do with it." George's payment of debts
is told in a letter from Wash to Richard Wills, October 30, 1864, with
Wills Papers.

2 The September 9 letter says: "Adj. Lacy has again returned to the Reg.
is messing with us for the present, can only give him common fare now
tho. . . ." To "Pa," September 17, 1864, George praises Lacy's singing.

3 The September 17 letter says "[The Federals] carry off their wounded
as soon as they fall, if the Ambulance Corps can't take them off fast
enough, then some of them, with arms in their hands, do so. . . . Different from the Yankees, we wait until after the fight is over to do what
the Ambulance Corps is unable to perform."

4 It is impossible to establish the exact date of Johnny's return to duty.
George mentions him in the September 17 letter.

5 The nature of the charges against Boggan cannot be established. On
August 8, 1864, George writes to Mary: "I am out with the Maj. more
than ever, he was guilty to say the least of it, of a serious crime a few
days ago, will not tell you now." George's September 17 letter says: "The
commission[ed] off. of the Reg. or a part of us, have requested the Maj.
to resign, offering, if he does, to have the charges against him withdrawn.
He has replied that he would do so, as soon as we complied with our
offer. . . . Gen'l Grimes has applied [agreed?] and I hope we will get
clear of him soon."

6 Jack Whitaker, to W. H. Wills, September 20, 1864, with *Wills Papers*,
says: "I met Cousin Sim at the Hospital where he had gone a day or two
before the battle of [September 19]."

7 Wash's October 30 letter to Richard Wills has much to say of George's

behavior on the night of September 18 and the morning of September 19, 1864.

8 George's temporary command of Company B is mentioned in letters from Jack Whitaker and Johnny Beavans to W. H. Wills, with *Wills Papers*.

9 *III Lee's Lieutenants*, pp. 577–79, with a useful map, details the opening of the Third Battle of Winchester. *Early*, pp. 420–23, and John W. Gordon, *Reminiscences of the Civil War* (hereafter cited as *Gordon*), are first-hand accounts.

10 "I being unarmed & not able to use a gun, John B. sent me back," says Jack Whitaker's September 20 letter to W. H. Wills.

11 John Paris, in the *Watchman and Harbinger*, November 11, 1864, describes vigorously the retirement and new stand of Grimes' Brigade, with some information about George's part. Paris, born in 1809, was one of the oldest chaplains to serve with a Confederate regiment in the field, but bore a reputation for energy, courage, and service.

12 The story of George's death in action is from the letters of Jack and Johnny to W. H. Wills, and from Wash's October 30 letter. The sergeant who was first to reach his body may have been Smiley W. Hunter, who was on duty with Company B during September, 1864, and survived to surrender at Appomattox.

13 "Between 3 & 4 o'clock John came out wounded in the head," writes Jack to Mr. Wills. Paris calls Johnny's wound serious but not dangerous.

14 The final defeat at Winchester is described in *III Lee's Lieutenants*, pp. 579–80. *Gordon*, pp. 322–23, and *Early*, pp. 425–28, are specific, as is *Grimes*, pp. 65–68, in telling of the brigade which included the Forty-third. Various letters to W. H. Wills establish the escape from the hospital at Winchester of Sim, Johnny, and Jack.

XX

LET US NOT MOURN AS THOSE WHO HAVE NO HOPE

1 The story of how George's sweetheart fainted at news of his death is remembered by descendants of Lucy Wills Hunter, but Miss Lulu's full name escapes them.

2 W. H. Wills' note is attached to George's last letter with *Wills Papers*, and bears no date.

3 Bravely W. H. Wills wrote to his son Richard, October 1, 1864, that his concern for George's body was not great. After the war, however, he made extensive inquiries in search of it, but without success. See a letter from Mrs. Philip Williams of Winchester, Va., to W. H. Wills, January 27, 1866, with *Wills Papers*.

4 The letters from Jack Whitaker, John Paris, and John Beavans are all with *Wills Papers*, as are the September 29 and October 1 letters to Richard from W. H. Wills.

5 Wash left to rejoin George on September 28, 1864; see W. H. Wills' October 1 letter. The family probably heard of George's death the following day.

6 Wash's letter to Richard, with *Wills Papers*, is in the handwriting of W. H. Wills, who may have written it at Wash's dictation, or made a copy of Wash's original for his own keeping. Wash could write clearly, though his spelling and punctuation were faulty. Mr. Wills, if he copied a letter written by Wash, corrected such mistakes.

7 "John Beavans is wounded in the head & gotten home," says W. H. Wills' October 1 letter. The exact date of Sim's return to duty cannot be established. According to present-day memories of his recital of wartime adventures, he took part in the battle at Cedar Creek on October 19, 1864, and suffered an arm wound that troubled him slightly for years to come. Muster rolls of Company D carry him as "absent, wounded," on October 31, 1864.

8 *Early*, p. 435, mentions reinforcements. Shuffling of division commanders is in *XLIII OR*, pt. 1, p. 574.

9 Sheridan's exact words, in *XLIII OR*, pt. 1, p. 31, are: "The Valley, from Winchester up to Staunton, ninety-two miles, will have little in it for man or beast." Early was hampered in his movements by the barrenness of this once fruitful country.

10 Reasons for the attack are in *Early*, p. 452, continuing: "General Lee, in a letter received a day or two before had expressed an earnest desire that a victory be gained in the Valley if possible, and it could not be gained without fighting for it."

11 The plan of surprise at Cedar Creek was evidently Gordon's—see *Gordon*, pp. 335–36. *Early*, pp. 440–45, relishes the early success. *Grimes*, p. 74, says his troops "flanked the enemy in their position, whipping them badly, and driving them from their breastworks, capturing twenty-odd pieces of artillery, driving them several miles."

12 *Gordon*, p. 341, says Early declined to attack the VI Corps, saying: "No use in that; they will all go directly." Early in *XLIII OR*, pt. 1, p. 563, blames plundering for the fatal delay. *Gordon*, p. 368, admits that some soldiers plundered, but adds that they were mostly walking wounded.

13 *Grimes*, p. 75, furiously and candidly excoriates the men who almost won at Cedar Creek, then fled in panic: "It was almost impossible to check the flight, officers and men behaving shamefully . . . I don't mean my brigade but *all*." Casualties of Early's force, 1000 or more exclusive of prisoners, are in *XLIII OR*, pt. 1, p. 560.

14 Cary may have rejoined the Forty-third late in November. His letter to Mrs. W. H. Wills, December 5, 1864, with *Wills Papers*, speaks of having been with the command some days.

15 The descriptive roll of the Forty-third dates Boggan's resignation as of November 6, 1864.

16 *Grimes*, p. 85, mentions the snow on November 6—"very hard on barefooted and half-naked men." Cary's heartfelt sympathy for ill-clad sol-

diers in the Valley is told in a letter to his brother G. A. T. Whitaker, February 6, 1865, in possession of Miss Susie Whitaker of Strawberry Hill.

17 *Grimes*, pp. 87–88, dolefully describes bitter weather and unground corn as rations. Grimes writes bravely of the action of November 23, 1864, but says his men, "cold, hungry and broken-down," were at the point of collapse. As of December 6: "We are again disappointed in receiving no orders to prepare for winter quarters."

18 "Brother and John Beavans arrived in camp a day or two back," says Cary's December 5 letter to Mrs. Wills.

19 The Forty-third's sense of loss in the death of George is told to W. H. Wills in a letter from Chaplain Thompson, November 7, 1864, with *Wills Papers*.

20 Orders for the recall of Gordon's and Pegram's divisions to Petersburg are in *XLIII OR*, pt. 2, p. 911. Those for the recall of Grimes, *ibid*. *Grimes*, p. 89, records receipt of his orders and arrival on December 15.

21 The camp of the division on Swift Creek is described in *III N.C. Regts.*, p. 15. *Grimes*, p. 90, says the men "are located about three miles from Petersburg."

22 "Camp Rodes," Cary dates several home letters from the Swift Creek bivouac. To Mrs. Wills, March 22, 1865, with *Wills Papers*, he mentions Jack Whitaker's service as clerk. Jack's wounded arm continued to hamper him to the end of the war and beyond.

XXI

WE CAN STILL WEATHER THIS STORM

1 Christmas in the Petersburg trenches, by various accounts, is described in *III Lee's Lieutenants*, pp. 620–21. Increases of desertion are summed up in *ibid.*, pp. 622–25.

2 Strength of the Second Corps, as of December 31, 1864, is in *XLII OR*, pt. 3, p. 1362.

3 Cary, in his February 6 letter to G. A. T. Whitaker, says his long court-martial assignment is nearly over.

4 *Grimes*, p. 96, tells of receiving his commission as major general and word directing him to report to General Gordon in case of battle, both on February 15, 1865.

5 February 24, 1865, is the date set in *Grimes*, p. 96, for the move to Sutherland's Station. *III N.C. Regts.*, p. 15, says the move was made February 15, to "Southerland's Depot." This is from Thomas Kenan's history of the Forty-third Regiment, and Kenan, who was a prisoner of war in February of 1865, wrote only from hearsay.

6 Cary's letters to Mrs. Wills of February 11 and 25, 1865, with *Wills Papers*, are written horizontally to fill the pages; then more is written vertically, making the whole hard to decipher.

7 *Gordon,* p. 376, describes the terrain around Sutherland's Station.

8 *Grimes,* pp. 97–98, describes the division's entry into the trenches, and of inspecting picket posts "at some points so close you could almost see the whites of the Yankees' eyes."

9 ". . . mud frequently more than shoe-deep and sometimes knee deep," says *III N.C. Regts.,* p. 15, of the plight of the Forty-third in the trenches. In *IV N.C. Regts.,* p. 516, William L. London writes for the brigade: "No one who has never tried the trenches can ever imagine what the brigade went through that Spring; up to their knees in mud and water; not half enough to eat; cold and wet. . . ."

10 The battle in which Ed Wills participated was Bentonville, where Johnston's twenty thousand fought Sherman, with three times as many, to a standstill for several days. "Those battles was the best things for our boys could have happened," writes Ed to "Mother," March 28, 1864. "I hardly ever hear an oath no more among our boys. Lieut. Purnell has altered more than any boy you ever saw he don't never swear reads his testament every day quit telling tales." The letter is with *Wills Papers.*

11 *III Lee's Lieutenants,* pp. 645–61, digests all reports and narratives of the attack on Fort Stedman and the rest of that day on the Petersburg front. *Grimes,* p. 98, quoting a letter to Mrs. Grimes: "Would to Heaven this carnage was over and I permitted to retire from such scenes and live a quiet and domestic life."

12 *Grimes,* pp. 104–7, describes the division's position on April 1, 1865, and the battle for Fort Mahone.

13 *Parker* includes the story of Cary Whitaker's wound while leading the Forty-third to retake Fort Mahone. Cary's sword was recovered, perhaps by his brother Sim, and is preserved today at Strawberry Hill.

14 The retreat of the Army of Northern Virginia from Richmond and Petersburg is described in *III Lee's Lieutenants,* pp. 684–88.

XXII

BLOW, GABRIEL, BLOW!

1 The retreat of the Army of Northern Virginia from Petersburg to Appomattox is described in vivid detail in *III Lee's Lieutenants,* pp. 686–725, citing almost every possible valid source.

2 Cary Whitaker, with other wounded, probably reached Danville by April 4, 1865. Gangrene was beginning in his bullet-torn hands.

3 *III Lee's Lieutenants,* p. 690, cites J. R. Stonebraker, *A Rebel of '61,* p. 95, for the cheering of Lee by the Second Corps.

4 Responsibility for the failure to supply the army at Amelia Court House has never been established. Perhaps the reduced staff was at fault.

5 *Grimes,* p. 110, in describing the rear-guard action, frets about "the wagon train and its most miserable management . . . the lagging wagon

train." *Gordon*, p. 423, calls protecting the retreat "an impossible task"; but the impossible was performed for days.

6 *Grimes*, p. 111, says ". . . I was so pressed that the space between the two wings of the enemy was not over two hundred yards, when I sought safety in retreat."

7 The food issued at Farmville was the closest approach to a full meal the army experienced during the entire march to Appomattox. See *III Lee's Lieutenants*, pp. 715–16.

8 After warning Lee back, the Fifty-fourth actually attempted an attack and was nearly wiped out. See *III N.C. Regts.*, pp. 283–84.

9 *Grimes*, pp. 112–13, tells of "charging the enemy and driving them well off from Mahone's works, recapturing the artillery taken by them and capturing a number of prisoners, and holding this position until sent for by General Lee, who complimented the troops of the division upon the charge made . . ."

10 "I concluded to halt and give my broken down men an opportunity to close up and rejoin us . . ." says *Grimes*, p. 114. "By dark my men were all quiet and asleep."

11 *Gordon*, pp. 436–37, describes the charge of April 9, but does not mention giving command to Grimes. *Grimes*, p. 115, tells the story, with direct quotation of Gordon, and includes, pp. 125–29, a letter from Gordon which states that "you offered to make the attack in front . . ." which seems to agree that Grimes actively led this dying attempt of the army.

12 *Grimes*, pp. 115–16, partially explains the order of battle, but does not mention a fourth unit, Gordon's old division under Brigadier General Clement A. Evans. Morris Schaff, *The Sunset of the Confederacy* (hereafter cited as *Schaff*), p. 210, places Evans at the extreme left, next to Grimes.

13 *Grimes*, pp. 115–18, describes the fight at the crossroads. A map in *Schaff*, between pp. 220–21, shows positions and movements of the troops. All that can be told of Sim Whitaker and Johnny Beavans is that they were in the action. No story survives of Jack Whitaker's part, if any.

14 *Grimes*, pp. 118–19, tells with feeling of events and emotions after the flag of truce went forward.

XXIII

VALOR AND DEVOTION COULD ACCOMPLISH NOTHING

1 *Grimes*, p. 119, says: "We then went beyond the creek at Appomattox Court House, stacked arms amid the bitter tears of bronzed veterans, regretting the necessity of capitulation." Walter A. Montgomery, in *V N.C. Regts.*, p. 262, describes the valley where the troops halted and the mood of Grimes' Division: ". . . a feeling of collapse, mental and physical, succeeded for some hours."

2 The return of Lee from accomplishing the surrender, with his words and those of the troops, are from David McRae, *The Americans at Home,* p. 178, citing a Confederate staff officer, Major Giles B. Cooke.

3 Some regiments were issued bread only, others meat only, when rations arrived from Grant. Undoubtedly bread was traded for meat. Soldiers of both armies often ate bacon raw; See W. W. Blackford, *War Years with Jeb Stuart,* p. 287, and reminiscences of many other veterans.

4 Montgomery, in *V N.C. Regts.,* p. 262, tells how the army's spirits rose after eating.

5 The twelve old Bethels still with the army, listed in *I N.C. Regts.,* p. 122, are often and erroneously described as serving together in the same regiment at Appomattox.

6 Rolls of the Forty-third, company by company, as present at the final parade and surrender of arms, are in *V N.C. Regts.,* pp. 497–98.

7 Joshua L. Chamberlain, *The Passing of the Armies,* pp. 257–61, describes the surrender of the Army of Northern Virginia as seen by the Federal troops detailed to receive it. Another sympathetic memory by a Federal is in *Schaff,* p. 298.

8 Says Montgomery, in *V N.C. Regts.,* p. 264: "We . . . came to a halt and faced to the left; the guns were then stacked and the flags laid on the stacks. . . . Not a word was spoken; we did not even look into each other's faces."

9 *Gordon,* pp. 449–50, tells of addressing the Second Corps. *V N.C. Regts.,* p. 264, quotes Gordon directly.

10 Several versions of Lee's farewell address are in print. The present quotation is from *IV B.&L.,* p. 747.

11 *Grimes,* p. 120, quotes the soldier's offer to "make three crops and then try them again." Grimes' reply is from *I N.C. Regts.,* p. 279.

12 Apparently Johnny Beavans often told his children and friends of how he thought of his sweetheart as he started home from Appomattox. The story is remembered today in Enfield.

BIBLIOGRAPHY

The chief sources for this work were the writings of the men whose story it is. These came to hand from various generous helpers. The home letters of George Wills, with a number of other writings concerning his life and death in the Confederate Army, are in the Southern Historical Collection at the University of North Carolina, as are the war diaries of Billy Beavans and Cary Whitaker. Other items by and about these three, as well as about Sim Whitaker and Johnny Beavans, were graciously lent by Mrs. Stanley Whitaker of Centerville Plantation and by Miss Susie Whitaker of Strawberry Hill Plantation.

Some works that have been of special or frequent use in following the story of George Wills, Sim and Cary Whitaker, and Billy and Johnny Beavans are here listed. Numerous others, less important, are cited in the Notes.

ALLEN, W. C. *History of Halifax County.* Boston, 1918.

    A fair county history, with some interesting notice of the coming of the Civil War.

Beavans, William. A two-volume diary of William Beavans' war service, which is in the Southern Historical Collection at the University of North Carolina. Referred to as *William Beavans.*

CLARK, WALTER L. (ed.). *History of the Several Regiments and Battalions from North Carolina in the Great War, 1861–65.* 5 vols. Raleigh, N.C., 1901.

    The various unit histories are written by actual officers and men who served with them, and vary in accuracy and readability.

COWPER, PULASKI (ed.). *Extracts of Letters of Maj. Gen. Bryan Grimes to his Wife.* Raleigh, 1883.

Grimes commanded the brigade in which the Whitaker-Wills-Beavans group served, and what he saw they saw.

EARLY, JUBAL A. *Autobiographical Sketch and Narrative of the War Between the States.* Philadelphia, 1912.

Especially useful here for a vivid account of the 1864 campaign to Washington's defenses and the subsequent fighting in the Shenandoah Valley.

FREEMAN, DOUGLAS SOUTHALL. *Lee's Lieutenants.* 3 vols. New York, 1942–44.

Indispensable for an understanding of the Army of Northern Virginia.

GILHAM, WILLIAM. *Manual of Instruction for Volunteers and Militia of the United States.* Philadelphia, 1861.

Bible of drill and organization for volunteers at the beginning of the war.

GORDON, JOHN B. *Reminiscences of the Civil War.* New York, 1904.

Helpful information with regard to how the fighting went in the Valley in 1864 and around Petersburg until April of 1865.

JOHNSON, R. V., and BUEL, C. C. (eds.). *Battles and Leaders of the Civil War.* 4 vols. New York, 1881–84.

High points from first to last, told from both sides, with partisan but often vivid spirit.

LEON, LOUIS. *Diary of a Tar Heel Confederate Soldier.* Charlotte, N. C., 1913.

Leon served in the Bethel Regiment in 1861, and later in the Fifty-third North Carolina Regiment, Daniel's Brigade, until his capture in 1864. He saw clearly and wrote well.

MOORE, JOHN W. *Roster of North Carolina Troops in the War Between the States.* Raleigh, 1882.

Apparently compiled from first muster rolls of the various regiments and battalions; occasionally inaccurate but helpful in establishing promotions and transfers.

PARKER, FRANCIS MARION. *History of the Enfield Blues.*

This comes to hand as a clipping from a newspaper, date and place uncertain, lent by Miss Susan Whitaker of Goldsboro, N.C. Parker was second lieutenant of the Blues, writes in vivid detail of the company's adventures before and during the fight at Big Bethel, and notices with admiration the record and character of Cary Whitaker.

RIDDICK, KATIE. "The Enfield Blues," in *Prize Essays Presented by the*

North Carolina United Daughters of the Confederacy. Wilmington, N.C., 1938.

Miss Riddick, granddaughter of a sergeant of the Blues and a lifelong student of the history of her native Enfield, has gathered all possible information about the company's organization, mobilization, and early military adventures.

SCHAFF, MORRIS. *The Sunset of the Confederacy.* Boston, 1912.

This Union officer writes with sympathetic understanding of the Appomattox campaign, noticing the last charge of the Confederates under Grimes.

SLOAN, JOHN A. *North Carolina in the War Between the States.* Washington, 1883.

How North Carolina left the Union and entered the Confederacy and the war. With appendixes helpful in clarifying records in the Bethel Regiment and the Enfield Blues.

Southern Historical Society Papers. 49 vols. Richmond, 1876–1944.

Helpful throughout, especially with a gathering of primary sources on the Bethel Regiment.

War of the Rebellion: Official Records of the Union and Confederate Armies. 128 vols. Washington, 1880–1901.

Invaluable here, as in all efforts to speak sensibly of the Civil War.

Whitaker, Cary. A two-volume diary of Cary Whitaker's war service in 1864, which is in the Southern Historical Collection at the University of North Carolina. Referred to as *Cary Whitaker.*

Whitaker, John Simmons. A penciled biographical note, a Cary Whitaker memorial, in the possession of Miss Susie Whitaker of Strawberry Hill. Referred to as *Cary Whitaker Memorial.*

Wills Papers. Family papers of the Reverend Mr. W. H. Wills, in the Southern Historical Collection at the University of North Carolina.

INDEX

Abraham's Creek, Va., 213
Addington, Lizzie, 76
Alabama, 16, 108, 232
Albemarle (ironclad ram), 153
Aldie, Md., 115
Amelia Court House, Va., 235, 237
Anderson, Lieut. Gen., 238-39
Anson County, N.C., 83
Anson Guards, 83
Antietam River, 98, 116, 168-69
Appomattox Court House, Va., battle of, 240-46, 250
Appomattox River, 224, 229, 235, 238-39, 241, 247
Archer, Lieut. Col. F. H., 232-33
Arkansas, 80
Army of Northern Virginia, 110-11, 118, 126, 134, 140, 169, 225, 227, 237, 245-46, 252; First Corps, 110, 115, 198, 207, 236; Second Corps, 109-10, 112, 114-18, 120, 132, 137, 139, 143, 145-46, 149, 155-59, 164, 226, 230, 236-41, 251-52; Third Corps, 110, 115, 121, 146, 236; strength, 102, 111, 123, 159, 163, 169, 196, 209, 220, 227, 241
Army of the Potomac, 98, 115, 210
Arrington, Pvt. Jo, 54
Arrington, Samuel, 269
Artillery: Confederate, 50-53, 93,

122, 126, 159; Union, 121-22, 126, 128-30
Asheville, N.C., 39, 71
Ashly, Va., 115
Atlanta, Ga., 197, 203
Atlanta (gunboat), 116
Aulsbrook, Marcus, 269

Baker, John W., 68
Baker, Lieut. Thomas A., 81, 122-123, 131-33, 142
Ball, William, 177
Baltimore, Md., 184
Baltimore and Ohio Railroad, 184
Baltimore Turnpike, 120
Baptists, 20, 28, 67
Beards, 27, 48-49, 80, 84
Beavans, Absolum, 80
Beavans, John, 19, 25, 66, 186, 192-193
Beavans, Sgt. Johnny, 16, 26, 29, 34-35, 38, 42, 55, 69, 71-72, 74-77, 79, 88, 90, 96, 101, 109-10, 142, 146-47, 152, 155, 157, 204, 207, 210-11, 213-14, 220, 223, 225, 230, 232, 237, 242-43, 246, 250, 253-55; *cited*, 218
Beavans, Maggie, 82, 85-86, 88-89, 95, 144, 151
Beavans, Mrs. Peggy Whitaker, 259

Beavans, Walter, 258
Beavans, Lieut. William (Billy), 16-23, 26, 29, 35, 38, 41-42, 49-52, 55, 63, 71-82, 84, 90, 92, 96, 101, 153, 156, 158, 162, 164-67, 169-71, 173-177; commissioned lieutenant, 84-85, 88; brigade ordnance officer, 104, 110, 112-14, 116, 119, 121, 128, 130, 132-33, 135; on furlough, 151; loses leg, 177-88; dies, 189-192, 204-5, 256; *cited,* 17, 21, 36, 44, 59-60, 74-79, 82, 88, 118, 121, 126, 138-39, 167, 175-76, 178, 180, 190-91
Bell, Capt. David B., 26-27, 29, 38, 43, 69
Bentonville, battle of, 300
Berryville, Va., 113-14, 180, 209
Bertie County, N.C., 64, 120
Big Bethel Church, Va., action at, 49-50, 52, 56, 63, 67-72, 88-89
Blair, Montgomery P., home of, 171-73
Bloody Angle, battle of, 154
Blue Ridge Mountains, 113, 115, 143
Boggan, Maj. Walter, 83, 87-88, 112, 156, 159, 181-82, 201, 208, 222
"Bombardment of Fort Sumter" (song), 76
Bonny Blue Flag," "The (song), 119
Botetourt Springs, Va., 163
Bowman's Ford, Va., 221
Boyd, James, 283
Bragg, Gen. Braxton, 115
Branch, John R., 76-77
Brandy Station, Va., 112
Braxton, Lieut. Col. Carter, 209
Breckenridge, Gen. John C., 161, 170, 182, 209, 211, 213, 220
Brewer, Dr. William T., 133, 150, 160
Bridgers, Capt. John L., 28, 70
Brinkleyville, N.C., 16, 19, 24, 40, 63-64, 66-67, 72, 74-75, 77, 80, 91, 96, 102, 147, 153, 185, 198, 202, 216, 219
Bristoe Station, battle of, 146
Britt, Pvt. B. F., 61
Broadfoot, Charlie, 81, 98

Brown, John, 26, 166
Brownburg, Va., 164
Buhman, Private, 56
Bull Run. *See* Manassas, battles of
Buncombe Rifles, 36, 39, 51, 71
Bunker Hill, Va., 183, 188, 194, 202-203, 206-7
Burke Rifles, 36, 39, 72
Burkeville, Va., 235
Burkittsville, Md., 170
Burnside, Gen. Ambrose E., 108, 181
Butler, Gen. B. F., 45

Cambridge University, Saint Jude's College, 25
Camp Ellis, Raleigh, 22-23, 26, 29-40, 56, 81, 83
Camp Fayetteville, Cocklestown, 68, 70
Camp Holmes, N.C., 89
Camp Lee, Va., 108
Camp Mangum, N.C., 79-85
Camp Rodes, Va., 225, 227
Cape Girardeau, Mo., 73
Carlisle, Pa., 118-20
Carlisle, W. R., 131
Carolina Railroad, 19-20
Casualties: Confederate, 56, 93, 106, 114, 123, 131-32, 154-56, 170, 173, 177-78, 181, 184, 214-15, 232-33; Union, 56, 156, 170, 184, 222
Cavalry, Confederate, 93, 102, 110-115, 126
Cedar Creek, Va., 196, 221
Cemetery Ridge, Gettysburg, 126-128, 131, 153
Centerville Plantation, N.C., 16, 72, 76, 151-52, 186, 192
Chambersburg, Pa., 117
Chancellorsville, Va., battle of, 106, 124, 181
Chapel Hill, N.C., 27
Charlestown, Va., 166, 174-75, 201
Charlotte, N.C., 28, 38, 71
Charlotte Grays, 28, 30, 38-39, 46, 51, 56, 72, 250
Charlottesville, Va., 160-61
Chattanooga, Tenn., 116
Cherry, George, 154
Cherry, John, 61

Chickamauga River, battle of, 145
Chowan, N.C., 64
City Point, Va., 97
Clark, Governor, 73
Clarksburg, Md., 171
Cobb, Capt. Wiley J., 201, 208, 210, 234
Cochran, John, 132
Cockade Cadets, 41
Cocklestown, Va., 67
Cohen, Sgt. Jonas, 28-29
Coker, John, 269
Cold Harbor, Va., 154, 159
Columbus Guards, 31
Cook, Maj. Giles B., 302
Corbitt, Lieut. C. B., 69-71
Core Creek, engagement at, 279
Corinth, Miss., 86, 90
Cornwallis, Gen. Charles, 43, 46
Coulling, Dr., 67
Cowand, Col. D. G., 222, 228, 233, 284
Cowand, Joe John, 96, 132, 232, 238; cited, 120
Cowand, Winifred, 120, 277
Cox, Col. W. R., 232, 238, 244
Cramp colic, 35, 37
Crampton's Gap, Md., 170
Crater, battle of, 194, 232
Craven County, N.C., 39
Culpeper Court House, Va., 112, 115, 145
Culp's Hill, Gettysburg, 128, 130-31
Cumberland County, N.C., 48, 81
Cumberland Valley, 116

"Dancies," 96
Daniel, Brig. Gen. Junius, 83, 87, 91, 96-100, 102, 108-10, 112, 118-119, 121-29, 131-33, 135, 137-38, 145, 148, 151, 154, 156, 228
Danville, Va., 235, 237, 255
Darksville, Va., 135, 137, 206
Davidson College, N.C., 32-33
Davis, Jefferson, 119, 236
Dawson Cross Roads, N.C., 60
Della, Miss, 74, 76
Desertions, 104, 106-7, 143-44, 226, 230
Devil's Den, Gettysburg, 127
"Dixie" (song), 119

Doles, General, 108, 121
Douglas, Henry Kyd, 291
Drewry's Bluff, 92-94, 98, 154
Drill, infantry, 29-32, 46, 89, 95
Duplin Rifles, 30, 83
Duryea, Abram, 56

Early, Gen. Jubal, 143, 159, 161, 163-65, 170-74, 181-82, 185, 187, 194-96, 198-201, 206, 208-9, 213-214, 220-24, 226
Edenburg, Va., 166
Edge, Joseph, 107
Edge, Marshall, 107
Edgecombe County, N.C., 16
Edgecombe Guards, 28, 36, 39, 53, 55-56, 70, 88
Eggerson, Mrs., 190-91
Elba Female Academy, Brinkley-ville, 19, 21, 38, 107-8, 216
Ellis, Gov. John W., 22, 63, 257
Enfield, N.C., 15, 19, 26, 29, 38, 40, 60, 74-77, 79-80, 88, 142, 203, 220, 255
Enfield Blues, 15-17, 19, 22, 26-30, 33, 36-39, 41-43, 46-48, 61, 64-66, 69-72, 81; at Big Bethel, 50-58
Etheridge, Pvt. James, 81, 90
Evans, Gen. Clement A., 102, 242, 301
Ewell, Lieut. Gen. Richard Stoddard, 109-10, 112-16, 119, 126, 134, 137, 143, 146, 155, 236, 238-39
Exchange Hotel, Richmond, Va., 72

Fairfield, Pa., 132
Fannie, Miss, 26, 35, 38, 64, 69, 85-86, 88, 107-8, 144, 198; cited, 95
Farmville, Va., 239
Fayetteville, N.C., 39, 68
Fayetteville Independent Light Infantry, 39-40, 48, 52-54, 56, 72, 81, 250
Fayetteville Observer, cited, 48-49
Fisher's Hill, Va., 196, 198, 214, 220
Five Forks, Va., 233
Flint Hills, Va., 113
Florida, 15-16
Fort Fisher, N.C., 225
Fort Hatteras, 67, 69
Fort Henry, 78

Fort Johnston, N.C., 91
Fort Macon, N.C., 28, 36, 86
Fort Mahone, Va., 234
Fort Royal, Va., 113
Fort Stedman, Va., 230-32, 234
Franklin, Tenn., battle of, 225
Frederick, Md., 170, 175
Fredericksburg, Va., 108, 112, 181

Galloway, Captain, 124
Gammons, J. R., 131
Garnett, General, 105
George (servant), 179
Georgia, 16, 108, 160
Gettysburg, Pa., battle of, 120-31
Godwin, Gen. A. C., 215
Goldsboro, N.C., 18, 20, 33, 80, 82, 100-102, 107
Goode's Bridge, Va., 235
Gordon, Gen. John B., 159, 161, 170, 209-11, 213, 221, 224, 226-28, 230-31, 238, 241-44, 251-52
Graham, Dr. D. M., 250
Grant, Gen. Ulysses S., 115, 153, 155-57, 164-65, 181, 196, 207, 209, 221-22, 224, 229-31, 234, 241
Granville Grays, 31, 37
Gray, Sgt. William T., 82
Greencastle, Pa., 116-17
Greensboro, N.C., 255
Gregg, General, 131
Grier, Sergeant, 137
Grimes, Gen. Bryan, 156, 159, 162, 167, 172, 176, 194, 200, 208, 211, 214, 222-24, 228-29, 232-35, 237-46, 250-51, 253
Gunter, Laura, 26, 35, 74-75, 79, 96, 142, 253-55

Hagerstown, Md., 116, 133, 136, 203
Hale, Maj. E. J., 250
Halifax County, N.C., 15, 18, 24, 26, 27, 40, 64, 73, 83, 151
Halifax Light Infantry, 28, 37, 77
Halifax Mounted Rifles, 77
Hall, Dr., 49
Hamilton, N.C., 16, 17
Hamilton's Crossing, Va., 281
Hammill, John, 58, 64, 154, 269
Hammond, Capt. W. M., 136

Hampton, Gen. Wade, 160
Hampton, Va., 44-45, 47-48, 51, 65
Hampton Roads, 80
Harding, Chaplain, 158
Harpers Ferry, W. Va., 26, 166-68, 170, 175, 200
Hatteras Inlet, 67
Hazel River, 145
Heidlesburg, Pa., 120
Hickory Road, Va., 235
Hill, Gen. A. P., 110, 115, 120, 126, 132, 156, 236
Hill, Maj. Gen. Daniel Harvey, 29, 32-33, 37, 39-40, 42, 45-48, 50-53, 55-56, 58, 63, 65, 67, 102; cited, 56, 103-4
Hill, Jonathan, 131
Hillsboro, N.C., 29
Hines, Dr. Peter, 39, 66
Hobson, Edwin W., 232
Hoke, Adj. Gen. John F., 33
Hoke, Maj. Robert F., 67
Hoke, Capt. W. J., 36, 52
Holden, W. W., 185
Holly Gap, Pa., 120
Holmes, Major General, 92-95
Hood, Gen. John B., 184, 225
Hooker, Gen. Joe, 107, 181
Hopkins, Capt. J. A., 282
Hornet's Nest Rifles, 28, 30, 36-37, 39, 43, 45, 70-71
Hotchkiss, Jed, 291
Howard's Grove, Va., 41
Hudson, Pvt. James, 37-38, 56
Hunter, Gen. David, 158, 160-65
Hunter, Dick, 71, 75
Hunter, Mrs. Lucy Wills, 24, 33, 38, 68, 82, 84, 92, 99, 104, 107-8, 119, 137, 141, 144, 151-53, 160, 182, 192, 197, 203, 258
Huske, Capt. Wright, 48, 53
Hyattstown, Md., 171

Inflation, wartime, 95-97, 151, 166
Iverson, General, 108, 121-24, 128

Jackson, Gen. Stonewall, 90, 98, 107, 109, 115, 163
Jacocks, Capt. Jesse C., 64
James River, 41, 93, 224

Jefferson, Thomas, 168
Jeffersonton, Va., 145
Jews, 28
Johnson, Bushrod, 229
Johnson, Gen. Edward, 116, 128, 143
Johnston, Gen. Joe, 65, 160, 165-66, 230, 234, 240, 255
Jones, Col. Richter, 279
Jones, Samuel, 192

Kelley's Ford, Va., 146, 148
Kenan, Lieut. Col. Thomas, 30, 83, 87, 89-90, 92, 101, 128-33, 156, 282
Kentucky, 67
Kernstown, Va., 182
Kershaw, General, 220-22
Kinston, N.C., 102, 104-6, 151-53
Kyle, Lieut. W. E., 250

Lacy, Sgt. Drury, 87
Lacy, Adj. John, 206, 212-13
La Fayette Light Infantry, 36, 39-40, 50, 72
Lane, Lieut. Col. James H., 37, 51, 67, 250
Lee, Col. Charles C., 37-38, 40, 50, 62, 67-68, 70
Lee, Maj. Gen. Custis, 238
Lee, Fitzhugh, 198, 215, 241-42
Lee, Gen. Robert E., 73, 92, 98, 106, 109-10, 112, 115, 118-19, 124, 126-127, 133-34, 136, 140, 143, 164-66, 173, 181, 196-97, 209, 224, 226-28, 232-35, 237-40, 242, 244, 247-48; cited, 134-35, 248, 252-53
Leon, Pvt. Louis, 46-47, 51, 96, 106, 113, 129, 132, 144, 148; cited, 100, 106, 116-17, 127, 133, 135
Letcher, Gov. John, 163
Leventhorpe, Col. Collett, 273
Lewis, Eli, 177
Lewis, Lieut. Col. William Gaston, 88, 108, 130-32, 134, 137, 153, 155, 266, 282; cited, 97, 115 117, 131, 137
Lexington, Va., 163
Liberty, Va., 161
Liberty Mills, Va., 145

Lincoln, Abraham, 40, 165
Lincolnton, N.C., 36
Little Bethel Church, Va., 50
Little Round Top, Gettysburg, 127
London, William L., cited, 300
Long Roll, 46-47, 60-61, 90, 148
Longstreet, Gen. James, 98, 110, 115, 120, 126-27, 132, 155, 228
Louisa Court House, Va., 160
Louisiana, 16, 57
Louisiana Zouaves, 57, 62-63
Lulu, Miss, 107, 109, 142, 144, 147, 150, 198, 204-5, 216
Lumberton Guards, 30
Lynchburg, Va., 158, 160-63, 165, 240-42

Macon, Priscilla, 78-79
Madison Court House, Va., 139
Magruder, Maj. Gen. John Bankhead, 45, 53-54, 62, 71
Mahone, Gen. William, 240
Malvern Hill, Va., 94
Manassas, battles of, 65, 67, 98, 146
Manning, G. A., 131
Marshall, Capt. J. K., 64
Martin, Col. William, 273
Martinsburg, Va., 114, 139, 165, 183, 185, 187, 202-3, 209, 214
Maryland, 115, 173, 194
Maryland Heights, Md., 167
Massachusetts, 56
McCausland, John, 170
McCay, J. A., 250
McClellan, Gen. George B., 73, 86, 90, 92-95, 98, 181, 203
McIlwaine, Mr., 96-97
McIver, Private, 56
McKinney, Col. Robert M., 64
Mechanicsville, battle of, 92
Mechanicsville Pike, 154
Mecklenburg County, N.C., 210
Methodists, 19, 22, 24, 27-28, 39, 99, 212
Mexican War, 32, 53
Middlebrook, Va., 164
Middleton, Pa., 116, 120
Middletown, Va., 181, 221
Milroy, Maj. Gen. Robert H., 113
Mine Run, Va., 149
Mississippi, 15, 67

Missouri, 73, 80
Monitor (ironclad), 80
Monocacy River, 170
Monterey Gap, Pa., 133, 139
Montgomery, Walter A., *cited*, 301
Monticello, N.C., 151
Morgan, Gen. John Hunt, 80, 140, 203
Morton's Ford, Va., 143, 148
Mount Jackson, Va., 166
Murray, Col. Edward, 291
Muskets, 31, 53-54, 89, 112, 129, 138, 242
"My Maryland" (song), 76

Nash, E. A., 232-33
Nashville, Tenn., 80, 225
Negroes: impressed labor, 97
Neosho, Mo., 73
Neuse River, 103
New Bern, N.C., 80, 89, 102, 104
New Market, Va., 165, 221-23
Newport, Va., 164
New York Journal of Health, 49
New York Zouaves, 56, 63
North Carolina, 15-16, 22, 30, 33, 40, 63, 68, 70-71, 100-101, 185
North Carolina Military Institute, Charlotte, 30, 33, 37
North Carolina Volunteer Regiments: Eleventh, 83, 100, 142, 250-51; Fifth, 64; Fiftieth, 92, 108; Fifty-second, 250; Fifty-third, 92, 96, 104-5, 122, 129, 132; First, 36-45, 48, 52, 57, 62, 64, 68, 70; Forty-fifth, 87, 92-93, 122, 124-25, 173, 176, 242, 244; Forty-fourth, 250; Forty-third, 83-84, 87, 89-96, 99-108, 110, 112-13, 115, 118, 120-125, 127-29, 131-34, 136, 138, 140-144, 146, 149, 151-56, 159-62, 166-169, 171-73, 176-77, 180-84, 187-188, 194-95, 198, 200, 208, 210-213, 222, 229-30, 234-35, 246, 250-251; Nineteenth, 70-71; Second Battalion, 108, 122, 124-25; Third Cavalry, 77; Thirtieth, 70; Thirty-second, 92, 96, 118-19, 122-23, 125, 132; Thirty-seventh, 250; Thirty-third, 88, 250; Twelfth, 77; Twentieth, 124; Twenty-eighth, 70; Twenty-fourth, 77; Twenty-sixth, 185
North Hampton (steamer), 71

Ohio, Seventh Regiment, 144
Old Point Comfort, Va., 80
O'Neal, General, 108, 121
Opequon Creek, 207, 209, 211
Orange Court House, Va., 140-41
Orange Light Infantry, 29-30, 36, 39, 72
Outlaw, Capt. E. R., 251
Owens, Col. William, 96, 176-77, 180

Page, Rev. Jesse, 19-24, 29, 34, 38, 54-55, 63-64, 66
Page, Martha Eliza Wills, 19, 24
Pamlico River, 106
Papertown, Pa., 120
Paris, Chaplain John, 211-12, 293; *cited*, 218
Parker, Col. Francis Marion, 27, 30-31, 42, 52-54, 69-70, 258
Parks, Andrew, 177
Paschal, Dr. Herbert, 260
Pay rates, Confederate army, 65, 85, 90, 97
Peach Orchard, Gettysburg, 127
Peagram, Gen. John, 220-21, 224
Pea Ridge, Ark., 80
Pender, Mittie, 267, 277-78, 280-82, 284-86
Pennsylvania, 115-18
Petersburg, Pa., 120, 225
Petersburg, Va., 41, 72, 91-93, 95-96, 100, 164, 166, 194, 203, 207, 209, 220, 224, 229-30, 232-34
Pettigrew, General, 102, 105
Pickett, Maj. Gen. George E., 131, 153, 233, 236
Pittman, Pvt. Flavius Cicero, 28, 54
Pittman, Pvt. Oliver, 28, 54-55
Plymouth, Va., 152-53
Pope, Gen. John, 98, 165, 181
Poquoson River, 67
Portsmouth, Va., 19
Poteat, Adj. J. M., 39, 68
Potomac River, 115, 118, 133, 135-137, 166-68, 174, 185-86, 194, 201
Presbyterians, 33

Prisoners: Confederate, 124, 131, 181, 231-33, 238, 240; Union, 51, 57, 65, 112, 114, 123, 145-46, 162-163, 165, 183-84, 198, 234
Purnell, Lieutenant, 300

Quinine, 91

Raleigh, N.C., 16, 19, 22, 34, 40, 49, 63, 70, 73, 79-80, 82-83, 85
Raleigh *News*, 38
Raleigh *Standard, cited*, 63-64
Ramseur, Gen. Stephen Dodson, 108, 122, 159, 161, 170, 181, 183, 209-11, 220-21
Randalsburg Rifles, 36, 39
Rapidan River, 112, 143-46, 148-49
Rappahannock River, 113, 145-46, 148
Rations, 35, 50-51, 61-62, 64, 67, 69, 90-91, 95, 97-98, 101, 105-6, 162, 223, 237, 239, 248
Rebel yell, 133, 171, 237, 242
Red Bud Creek, Va., 213
Richmond, Va., 40-42, 44, 49, 56, 60, 63, 71, 90, 92, 107, 165, 172, 181, 184, 196, 220, 222, 224, 226, 234-35
Richmond *Examiner*, 165
Riddick, Katie, 257, 267, 294
Rifles, 54
Roanoke Island, 78
Roberson River, 145
Robertson, Beverly, 102
Robinson, Adj. John H., 250
Rockville, Md., 171, 174
Rodes, Maj. Gen. Robert E., 108-10, 113-16, 119-21, 124, 132, 134, 142-143, 149, 159, 161-63, 167, 170, 173, 177, 181, 183, 187-88, 200, 202-3, 206, 208-11, 213, 215, 228
Rosecrans, W. S., 115

Sadler, Pvt. Julius, 43, 45, 56
St. James College, Md., 194
St. Joseph, Mo., 73
St. Louis, Mo., 73
Sanitation, camp, 66
Savannah, Ga., 225
Saylor's Creek, Va., 238, 241
Scheer, George, 264
Seddon, James A., 278

Seminary Ridge, Gettysburg, 125-27, 130
Seven Days battles, 94-95
Sharpsburg, Md., 98, 168
Shearman, Pvt. L., 27-28
Shenandoah River, 113, 166, 174, 203, 221
Shenandoah Valley, 90, 114, 139-40, 158, 183, 187, 196-98, 220, 223
Shepherd, Kate, 180, 189-90, 192, 198-99, 256
Shepherdsburg, Pa., 118
Shepherdstown, Va., 168, 202
Sheridan, Maj. Gen. Phil, 160, 195-196, 198, 200-201, 206-7, 209, 213-214, 220-23, 233, 243
Sherman, Gen. William Tecumseh, 160, 165, 184, 203, 225, 230, 234, 255
Shiloh, battle of, 86
Ship's Point Camp, 67
Sickness, 35, 37, 66, 70, 94, 96, 106, 146
Slaughter, Sgt. John, 82
Smith, W. N. H., 279
Smithfield, Va., 166
Smyrna Station, Ga., 166
Snicker's Ford, 180
Snicker's Gap, 174-75
South Carolina, 15
Southern Railroad, 224
Southern Stars, 36, 39-40, 52, 67, 72
South Mountain, Md., 170
South Mountain, Pa., 133
Southside Railroad, 229
Staunton, Va., 116, 136, 164, 201, 203, 220
Steadman, Maj. Charles M., 250
Stephenson's Depot, Va., 209
Steuart, Gen. George, 129
Strasburg, Va., 181, 221
Strawberry Hill Plantation, N.C., 16, 27, 74-76, 151, 255
Stuart, Jeb, 110-12, 115, 120, 126, 131, 143, 156
Suffolk, Va., 98
Sutherland's Station, Va., 229
Swift Creek, Va., 224-25, 227, 229

Taylor, Pvt. James B., 81, 90
Taylor, Walter B., 250

Tennessee, 78, 115, 184, 225
Texas, 16
Thoburn, Col. Joseph, 291
Thompson, Chaplain Eugene W., 99, 140, 178, 197-98
Thomasville Rifles, 30
Traveller (Gen. Lee's horse), 126, 237
Trent River, 103
Trimble, Brig. Gen. Isaac, 119
Troy, N. Y., 51
Turner (body servant), 38

Uniforms, Confederate, 33, 48-49, 57, 81, 111
Union army: strength, 196, 209-10, 224; VI Corps, 172-74, 210, 221, XIX Corps, 210
Union navy, 60, 67, 69, 78, 93, 97, 106
Union County, N.C., 210

Vance, Zebulon, 185
Vicksburg, Miss., 115, 139
Virginia, 34, 41, 45, 73, 77, 237
Virginia Home Cavalry, 41
Virginia Junior Reserves, 232
Virginia (ironclad), 80
Virginia Military Institute, 37, 163
Virginny Tangle-leg, 68

Waldo, Susan, 255, 272
Walker, Gen. James A., 242
Waring, Capt. Robert P., 274
Warran (Gen. Grimes' horse), 241
Warrenton, Va., 145-46
Warrenton Guards, 30, 37
Washington, D.C., 171-72, 175
Washington, N.C., 105-6
Washington College, Va., 32
Wassaw Sound, Ga., 116
Watson, Sgt. Curys B., cited, 276
Wayt, John Henry, 39
Weldon, N.C., 37, 72, 100, 153, 204, 224
Welles, John, 58
West Point, 32, 37, 83
Wharton, Gen. Gabriel, 221
Wheat Field, Gettysburg, 127
Wheeless, S. C., 131

Whitaker, Capt. Cary, 16, 27, 30, 41, 49, 52, 66, 69-70, 73, 78-81, 83, 85, 87, 89, 93-94, 96-97, 101-2, 104, 109, 116, 122, 125, 135-37, 142, 146, 151, 155-59, 161, 163, 166-71, 173-74, 176-78, 180-88, 194, 198-99, 212, 222-23, 225, 227-30, 232; wounded, 200-201, 203, 234-235; dies, 255; cited, 160, 164-65, 167, 180, 182, 187, 192-94, 196, 199, 227-30
Whitaker, Dr. Cary, 258
Whitaker, G. A. T., 227
Whitaker, Jack R., 88, 151-52, 155, 160, 164, 170, 174, 179-81, 183, 186, 189-92, 194, 197-98, 200, 211, 214, 225, 230, 246; cited, 193, 217
Whitaker, Capt. James, 28
Whitaker, Lieut. John Simmons ("Uncle Sim"), 16, 26-27, 29, 38, 42, 49, 55, 63, 65, 73-76, 81, 85, 88, 91, 94, 98-99, 101, 105, 109, 116, 136, 142, 152, 155, 158, 166, 169, 172, 201, 204, 206, 208, 214, 220, 222-23, 225, 230, 232, 255; commands Company D, 237, 242-243, 246, 250-51
Whitaker, Lawrence, 49
Whitaker, Capt. Montgomery T., 27, 29, 49, 69-70, 261
Whitaker, Adj. Spier, 29-30, 250
Whitaker, Mrs. Stanley, 258, 272-273, 275-76, 285, 293-94
Whitaker, Susie, 258, 299
Whitaker, Lieut. Theodore Lucien, 27, 57, 77, 154, 261
Whitaker, Waldo, 258
Whitaker, William (ancestor), 24-25
Whitaker, Sgt. William E., 60, 268-269
Whitaker, William H. ("Major"), 27, 42
Whitaker's Chapel Academy, 19, 25-26, 255
White, Amanda, 138
Whitehead, James A., 60-61, 63-64, 66; cited, 60-61, 64-65
Whitehead, Pvt. Jimmy, 55, 60, 81, 90, 148-50
Whitehead, Rev. Laurence, 60
Whitehead, Robert, 60-61

White Post, Va., 180
White's Ford, 174
Whitfield, Fannie, 257
Wilderness, battle of, 153-54
Williams, Capt. J. Marshall, 70, 250
Williams, Pvt. John, 81, 90
Williams, Mrs. Philip, 297
Williams, Capt. W. R., 153
Williamsburg, Md., 115-16
Williamsport, Md., 116, 133, 186
Wills, Agnes, 24
Wills, Mrs. Anna Maria Baker Whitaker, 20, 24-26, 64, 99, 197-198, 259
Wills, Cornelia, 24
Wills, Eddie, 24, 58, 134, 153, 158, 204, 219, 230, 255
Wills, Professor George S., 258-59
Wills, Sgt. George Whitaker, 16, 58, 108, 256; to Camp Ellis, 18-26, 29, 31-35, 38; to Richmond, 40-44; at Big Bethel, 49-52, 54-55; at Yorktown, 46-47, 60-67; at Camp Fayetteville, 68-69, 71-72; on furlough, 74-77, 79; re-enlists, 80-88; to Camp Holmes, 89-91; at Drewry's Bluff, 93-99; at Goldsboro, 100-102, 107; to Gettysburg, 112-14, 122, 125, 130, 133-137; commissioned lieutenant, 142, 145-50; on sick leave, 150-54; returns to duty, 156-57; to Lynchburg, 160-62; Maryland campaign, 169, 173-74, 177; Valley campaigns, 179-80, 183-84, 194, 201-210; killed in action, 212-16; letters cited, 33-34, 36-38, 40, 47-48, 57-58, 62-63, 65, 67-70, 82-87, 89-92, 94-100, 102, 104-5, 107, 109, 114, 116-17, 119, 134, 136-37, 140-142, 144, 152, 157-58, 160-62, 164-168, 175, 181-82, 184-85, 188, 192, 197-205, 207-8
Wills, Harriet, 24

Wills, Leah, 21, 102, 144
Wills, Mrs. Lou Norman, 151
Wills, Lucy. See Hunter, Mrs. Lucy Wills
Wills, Martha Eliza. See Page, Mrs. Martha Eliza Wills
Wills, Mary, 24, 58, 62, 76-77, 100, 153, 157, 175, 197
Wills, Mrs. Mary Whitaker, 229-30
Wills, Rev. Richard, 24-25, 99, 150-151, 153, 208, 218-19
Wills, Washington ("Wash"), 20-23, 25, 35, 38, 40, 46, 50, 58, 63-64, 66, 80, 82-84, 90-91, 97-99, 101-2, 105-6, 109, 117, 137, 141-42, 146-147, 150, 152-54, 156, 165, 177-79, 185-86, 189, 197, 201-2, 218-19, 255; cited, 219-20
Wills, Rev. William H., 20, 24, 66-67, 91, 96, 152, 201, 207, 216; cited, 66, 216, 218
Wilmington, N.C., 89, 91, 225
Wilmington and Weldon Railroad, 18-19
Winchester, Va., 113-14, 139, 166, 179-83, 186-87, 189, 192, 195-98, 201, 208-9, 211, 213-14, 216-17, 220-22
Winfrey, John, 177
Winter quarters, 99, 149, 223-24
Woodfin sisters, 39
Woodstock, Va., 166
Wortham, Capt. George, 31
Wyatt, Pvt. Henry Lawson, 56-57

"Yankee Retreat at Manassas" (song), 76
Yates, Chaplain Edwin A., 39, 45, 62, 211
York Hospital, Winchester, 179, 181, 183, 186, 189
York River, 44
Yorktown, Va., 43-46, 57-60, 63-67, 81, 86, 90, 100

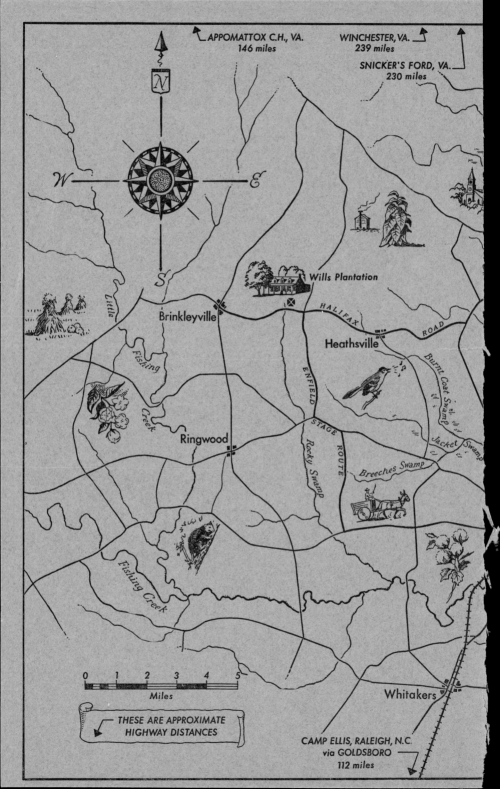

APPOMATTOX C.H., VA.
146 miles

WINCHESTER, VA.
239 miles

SNICKER'S FORD, VA.
230 miles

Wills Plantation

HALIFAX

ROAD

Brinkleyville

Heathsville

Little

Fishing

Creek

ENFIELD

STAGE

ROUTE

Burnt Coat Swamp

Jacket Swamp

Ringwood

Rocky Swamp

Breeches Swamp

Fishing Creek

0   1   2   3   4   5
Miles

THESE ARE APPROXIMATE
HIGHWAY DISTANCES

Whitakers

CAMP ELLIS, RALEIGH, N.C.
via GOLDSBORO
112 miles